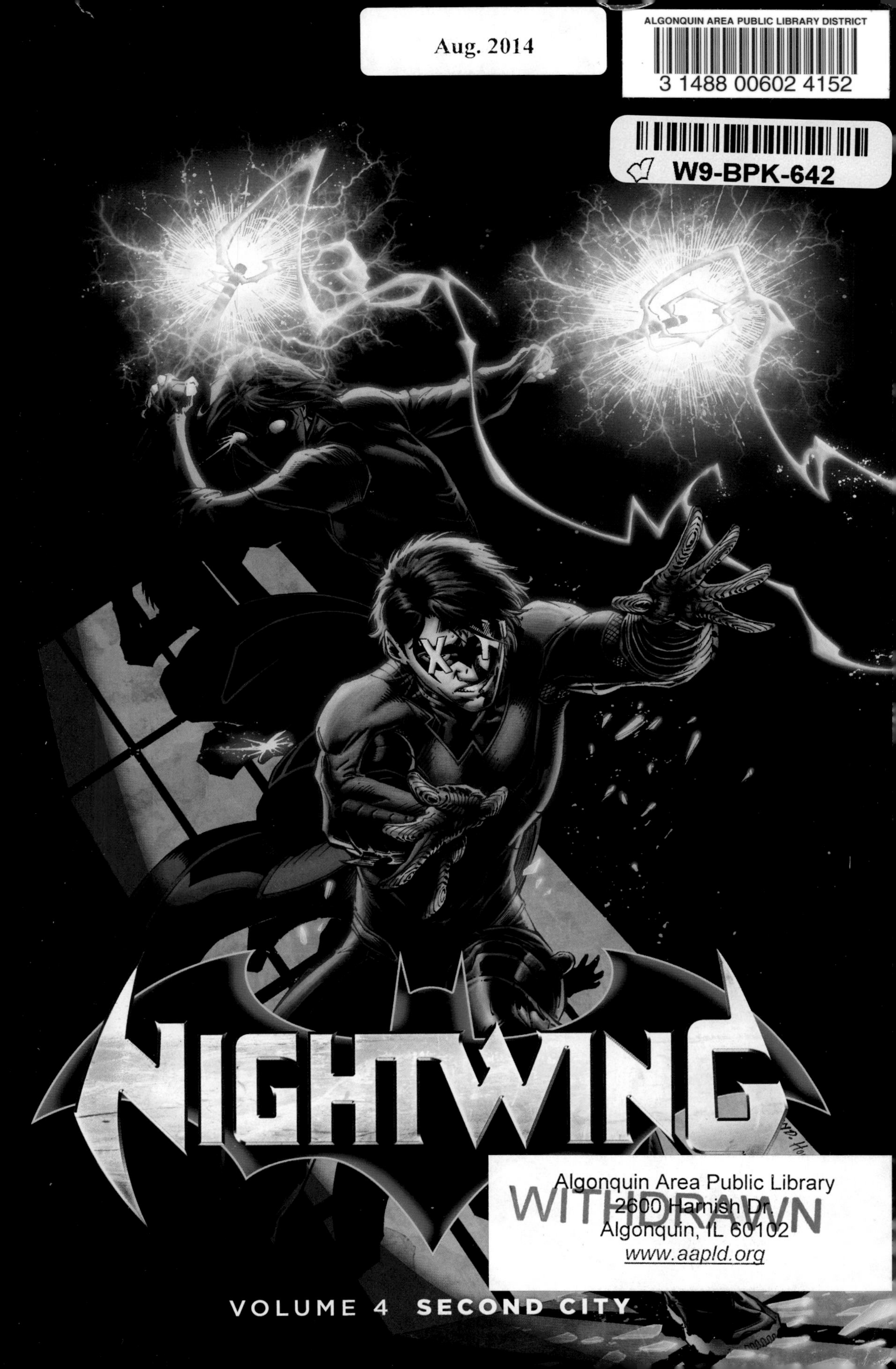
NIGHTWING
VOLUME 4 SECOND CITY

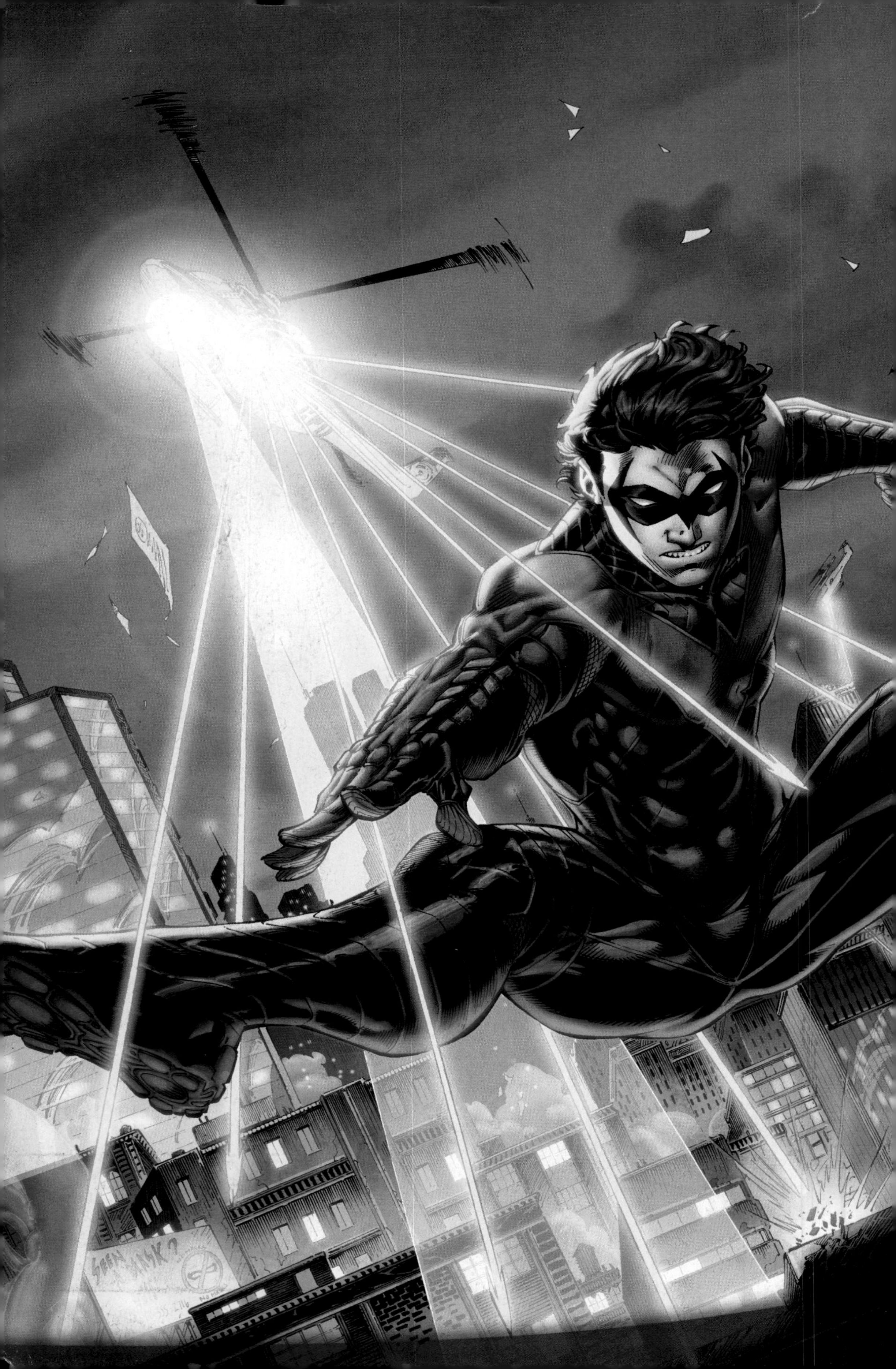

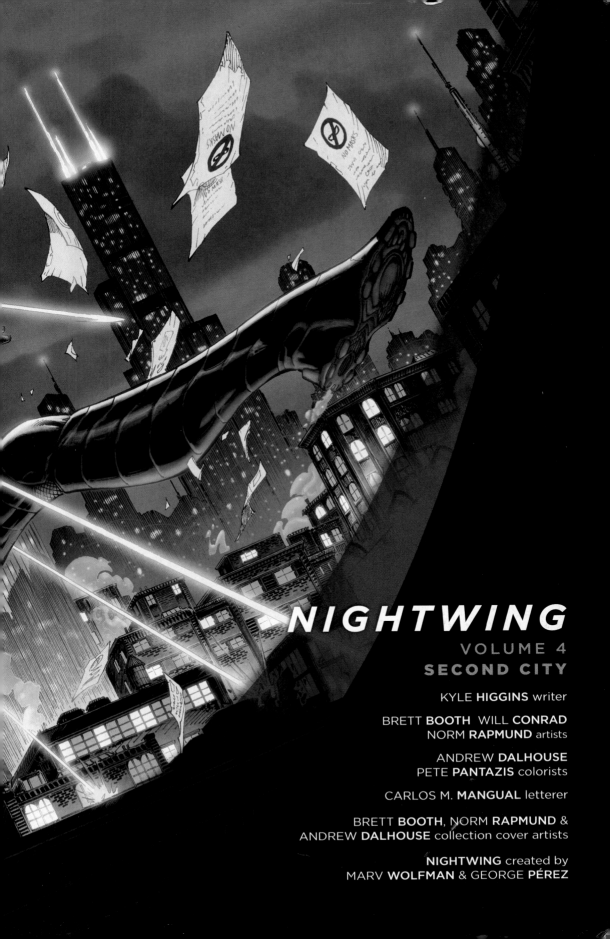

NIGHTWING

VOLUME 4
SECOND CITY

KYLE **HIGGINS** writer

BRETT **BOOTH** WILL **CONRAD**
NORM **RAPMUND** artists

ANDREW **DALHOUSE**
PETE **PANTAZIS** colorists

CARLOS M. **MANGUAL** letterer

BRETT **BOOTH**, NORM **RAPMUND** &
ANDREW **DALHOUSE** collection cover artists

NIGHTWING created by
MARV **WOLFMAN** & GEORGE **PÉREZ**

RACHEL GLUCKSTERN Editor – Original Series KATIE KUBERT Associate Editor – Original Series
DARREN SHAN Assistant Editor – Original Series ROWENA YOW Editor
ROBBIN BROSTERMAN Design Director – Books ROBBIE BIEDERMAN Publication Design

BOB HARRAS Senior VP – Editor-in-Chief, DC Comics

DIANE NELSON President DAN DIDIO and JIM LEE Co-Publishers
GEOFF JOHNS Chief Creative Officer
JOHN ROOD Executive VP – Sales, Marketing & Business Development
AMY GENKINS Senior VP – Business & Legal Affairs NAIRI GARDINER Senior VP – Finance
JEFF BOISON VP – Publishing Planning MARK CHIARELLO VP – Art Direction & Design
JOHN CUNNINGHAM VP – Marketing TERRI CUNNINGHAM VP – Editorial Administration
ALISON GILL Senior VP – Manufacturing & Operations HANK KANALZ Senior VP – Vertigo and Integrated Publishing
JAY KOGAN VP – Business & Legal Affairs, Publishing JACK MAHAN VP – Business Affairs, Talent
NICK NAPOLITANO VP – Manufacturing Administration SUE POHJA VP – Book Sales
COURTNEY SIMMONS Senior VP – Publicity BOB WAYNE Senior VP – Sales

NIGHTWING VOLUME 4: SECOND CITY

Published by DC Comics. Copyright © 2014 DC Comics. All Rights Reserved.

Originally published in single magazine form in NIGHTWING 19-24 © 2013 DC Comics. All Rights Reserved.
All characters, their distinctive likenesses and related elements featured in this publication are trademarks of DC Comics.
The stories, characters and incidents featured in this publication are entirely fictional.
DC Comics does not read or accept unsolicited ideas, stories or artwork.

DC Comics, 1700 Broadway, New York, NY 10019
A Warner Bros. Entertainment Company.
Printed by RR Donnelley, Salem, VA, USA. 6/6/14. First Printing.

ISBN: 978-1-4012-4630-3

SUSTAINABLE
FORESTRY
INITIATIVE

Certified Chain of Custody
20% Certified Forest Content,
80% Certified Sourcing
www.sfiprogram.org
SFI-01042
APPLIES TO TEXT STOCK ONLY

Library of Congress Cataloging-in-Publication Data is Available.

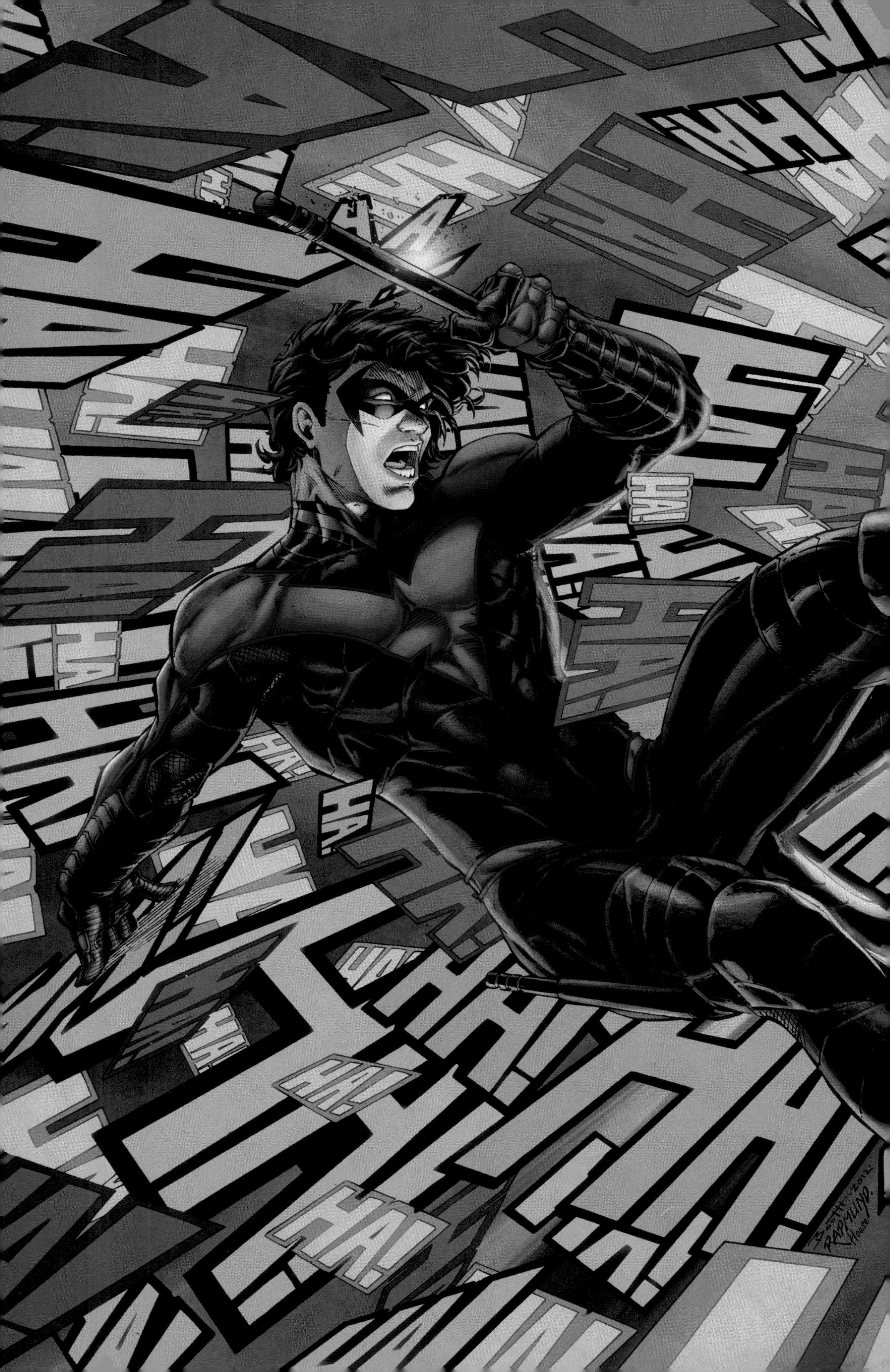
HA!
HA!
HA!
HA!
HA!
HA!
HA!
HA!
Booth 2012
Rapmund.
House

GGINS writer BRETT BOOTH penciller NORM RAPMUND inker cover art by BRETT BOOTH, NORM RAPMUND & ANDREW DALHOUS

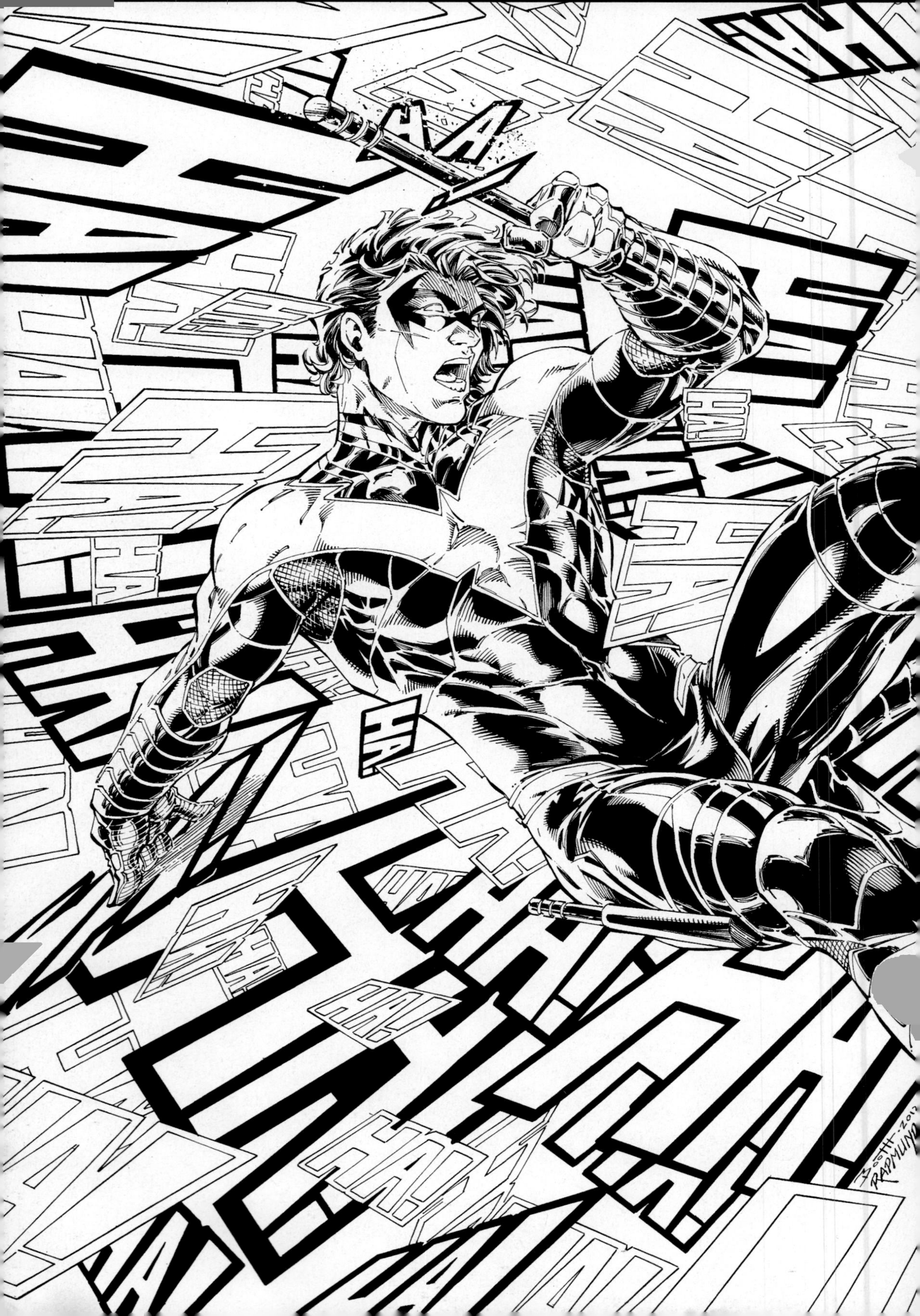
HA!
HA!
HA!
HA!
HA!
BOOTH · 2012
RAPMUND

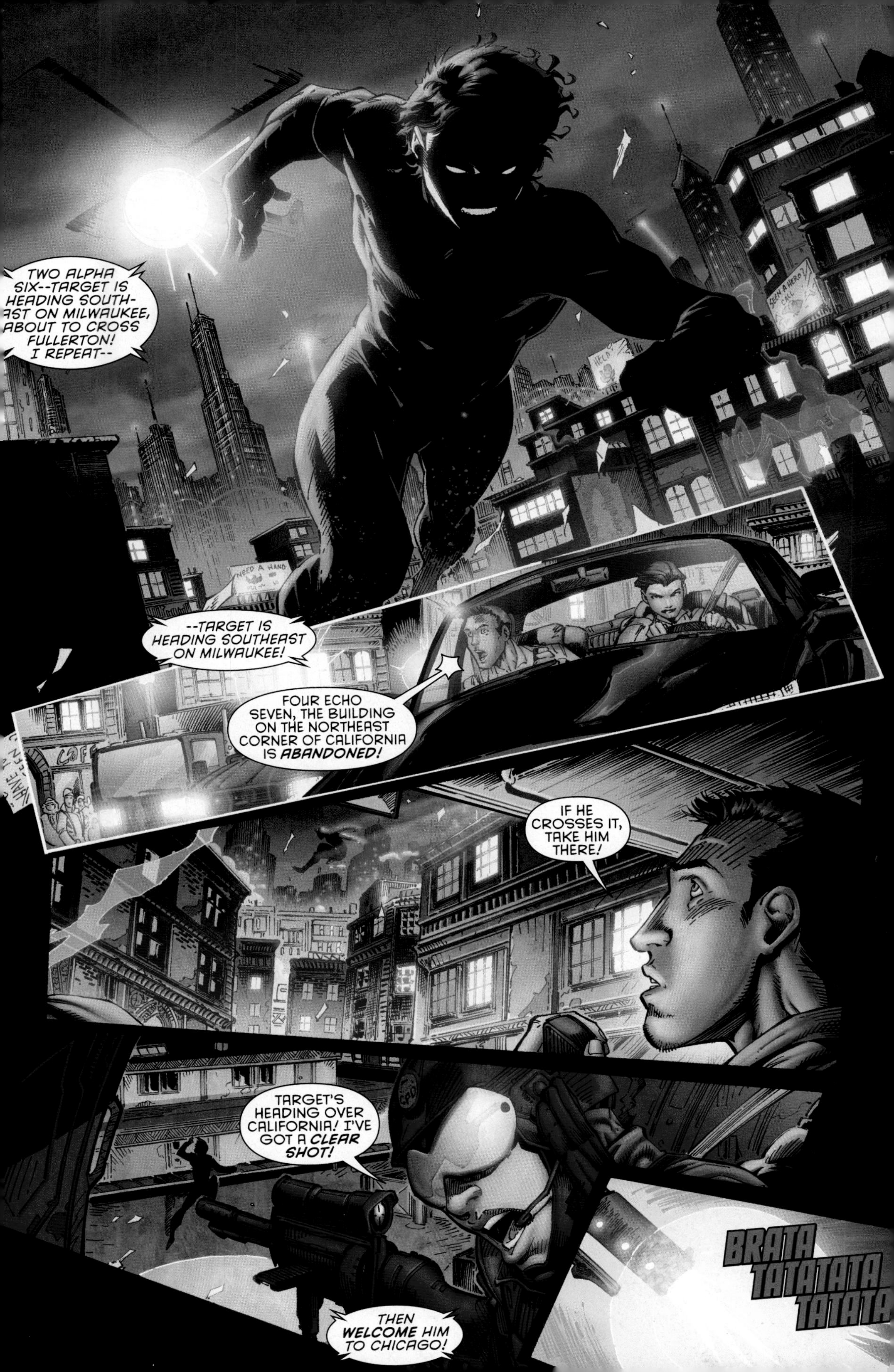
TWO ALPHA SIX--TARGET IS HEADING SOUTH-EAST ON MILWAUKEE, ABOUT TO CROSS FULLERTON! I REPEAT--
SEEN A HERO? CALL
HELP
NEED A HAND
--TARGET IS HEADING SOUTHEAST ON MILWAUKEE!
FOUR ECHO SEVEN, THE BUILDING ON THE NORTHEAST CORNER OF CALIFORNIA IS ABANDONED!
CAFE
IF HE CROSSES IT, TAKE HIM THERE!
TARGET'S HEADING OVER CALIFORNIA! I'VE GOT A CLEAR SHOT!
CPD
BRATA TATATATA TATATA
THEN WELCOME HIM TO CHICAGO!

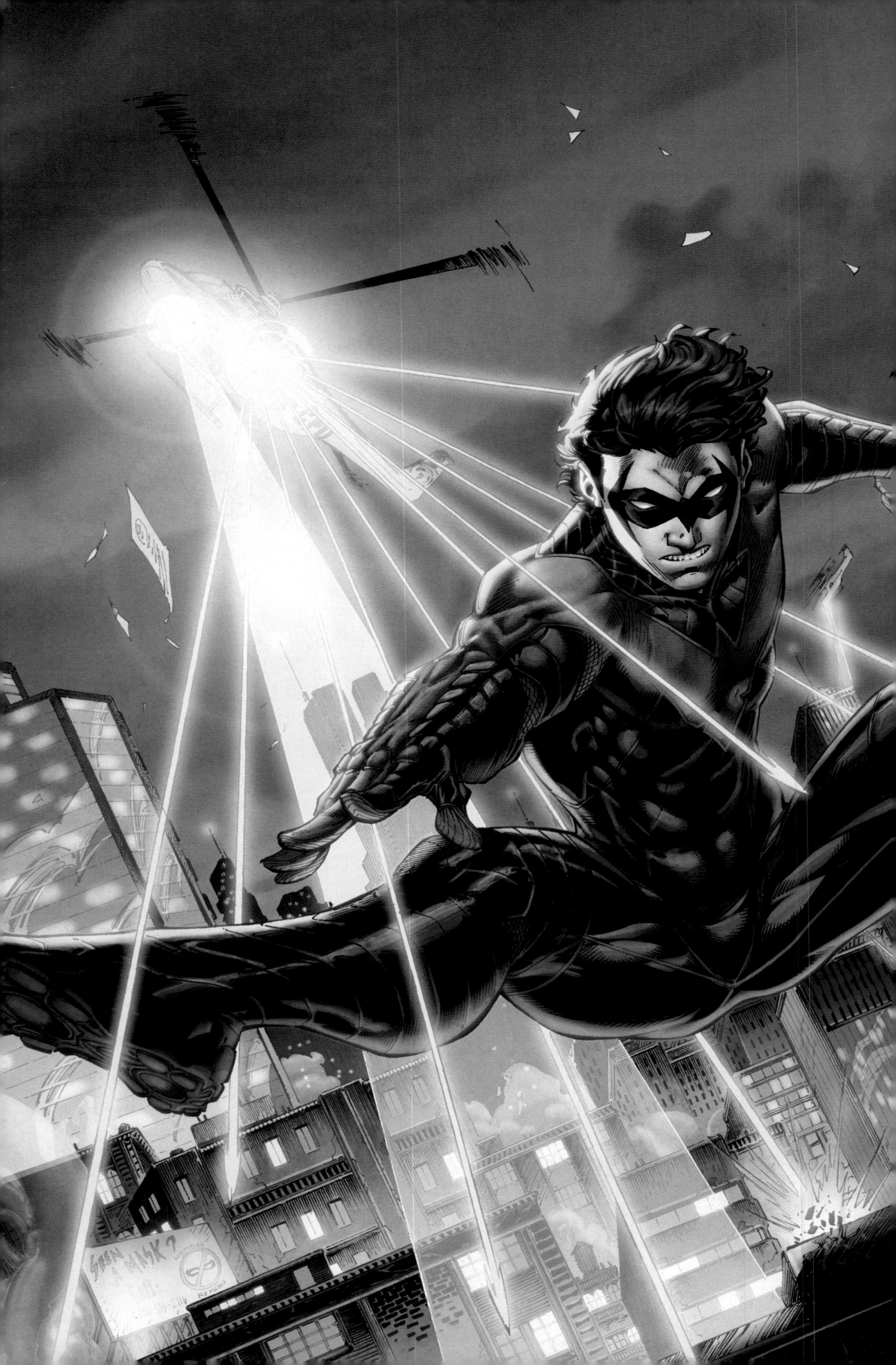
SEEN
MASK?
NO MASKS

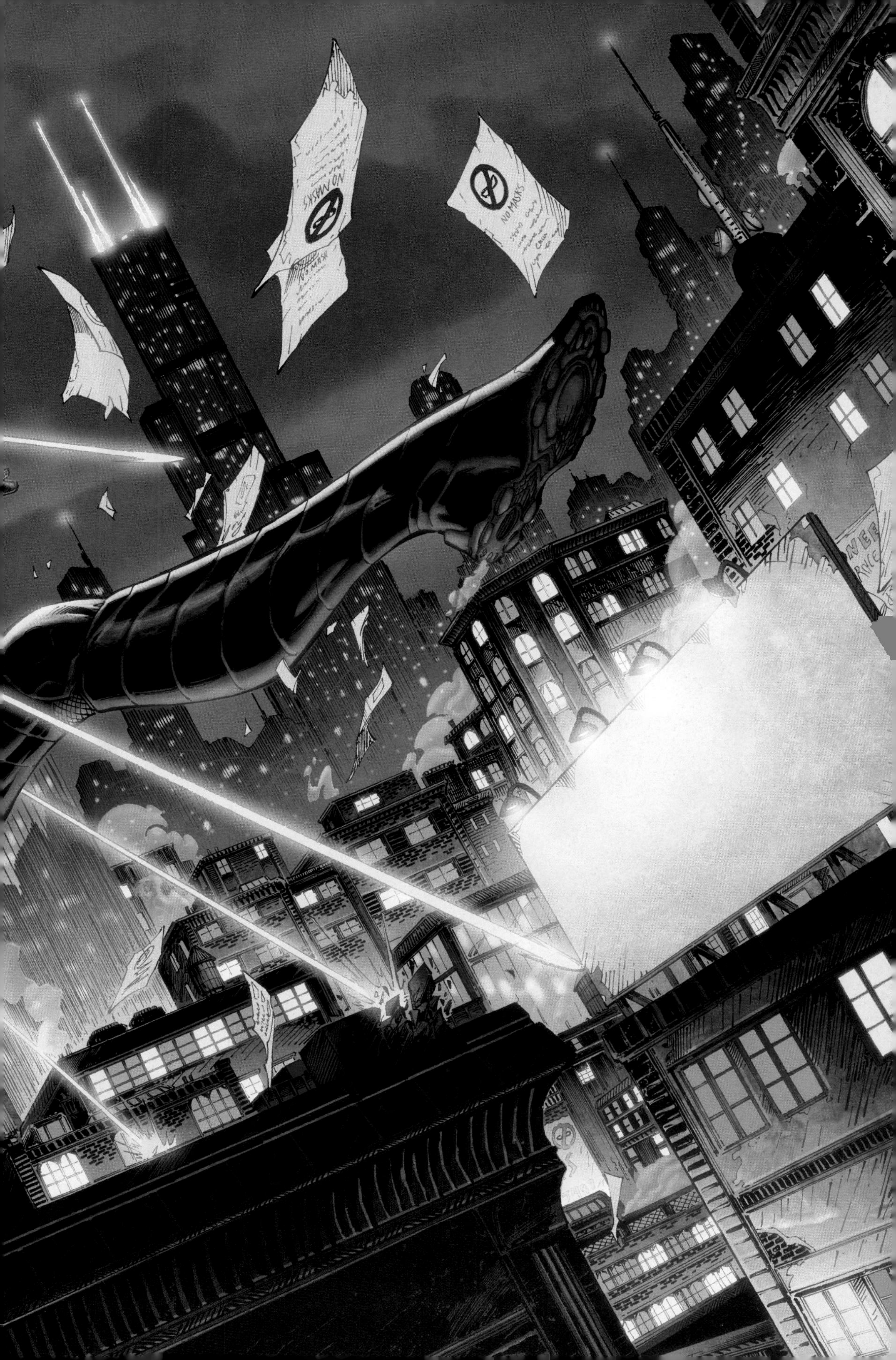
NO MASKS
NO MASKS

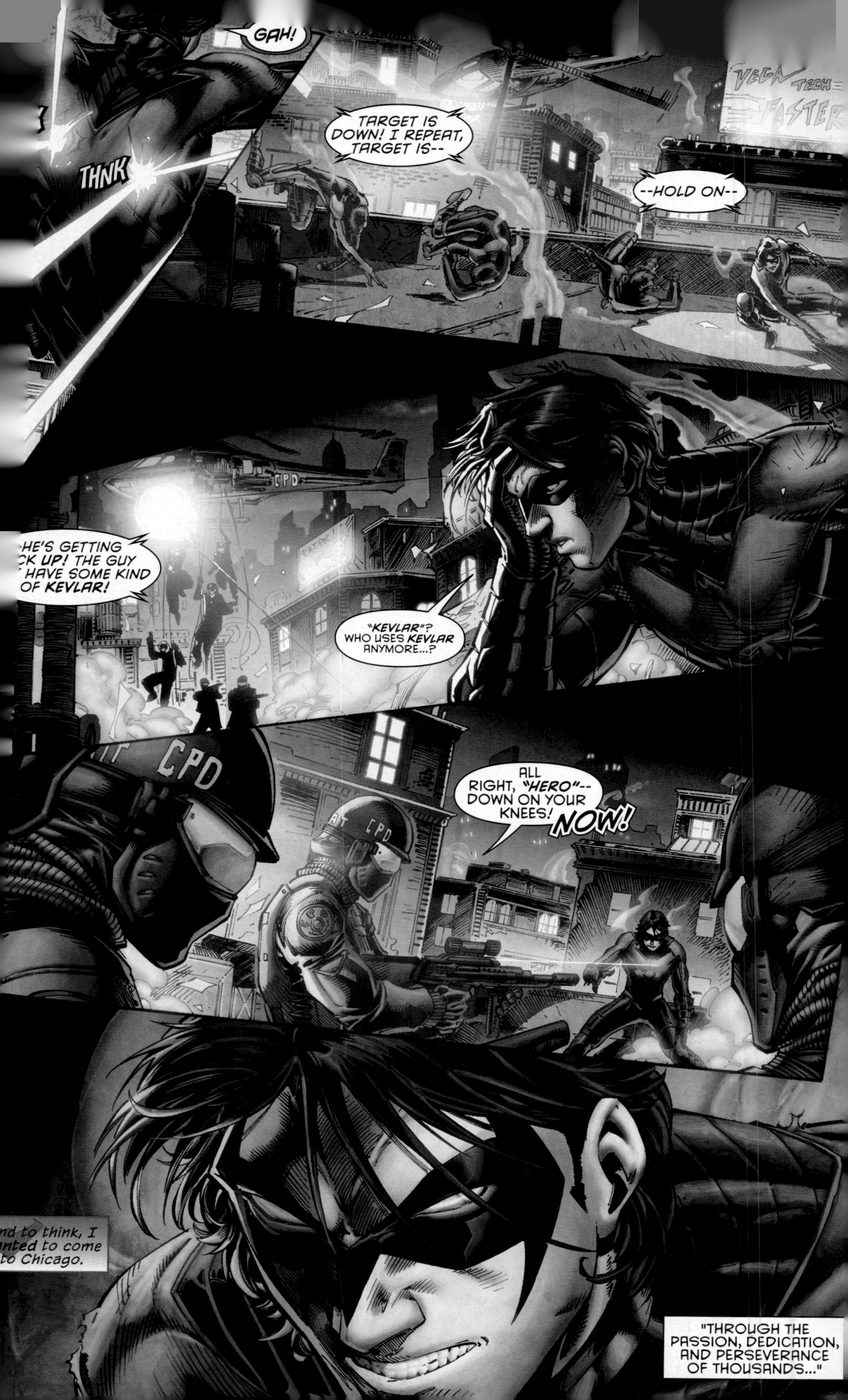
GAH!
THNK
TARGET IS DOWN! I REPEAT, TARGET IS--
--HOLD ON--
VEGA TECH FASTER
HE'S GETTING CK UP! THE GUY T HAVE SOME KIND OF KEVLAR!
"KEVLAR"? WHO USES KEVLAR ANYMORE...?
CPD
ALL RIGHT, "HERO"-- DOWN ON YOUR KNEES! NOW!
And to think, I anted to come to Chicago.
"THROUGH THE PASSION, DEDICATION, AND PERSEVERANCE OF THOUSANDS..."

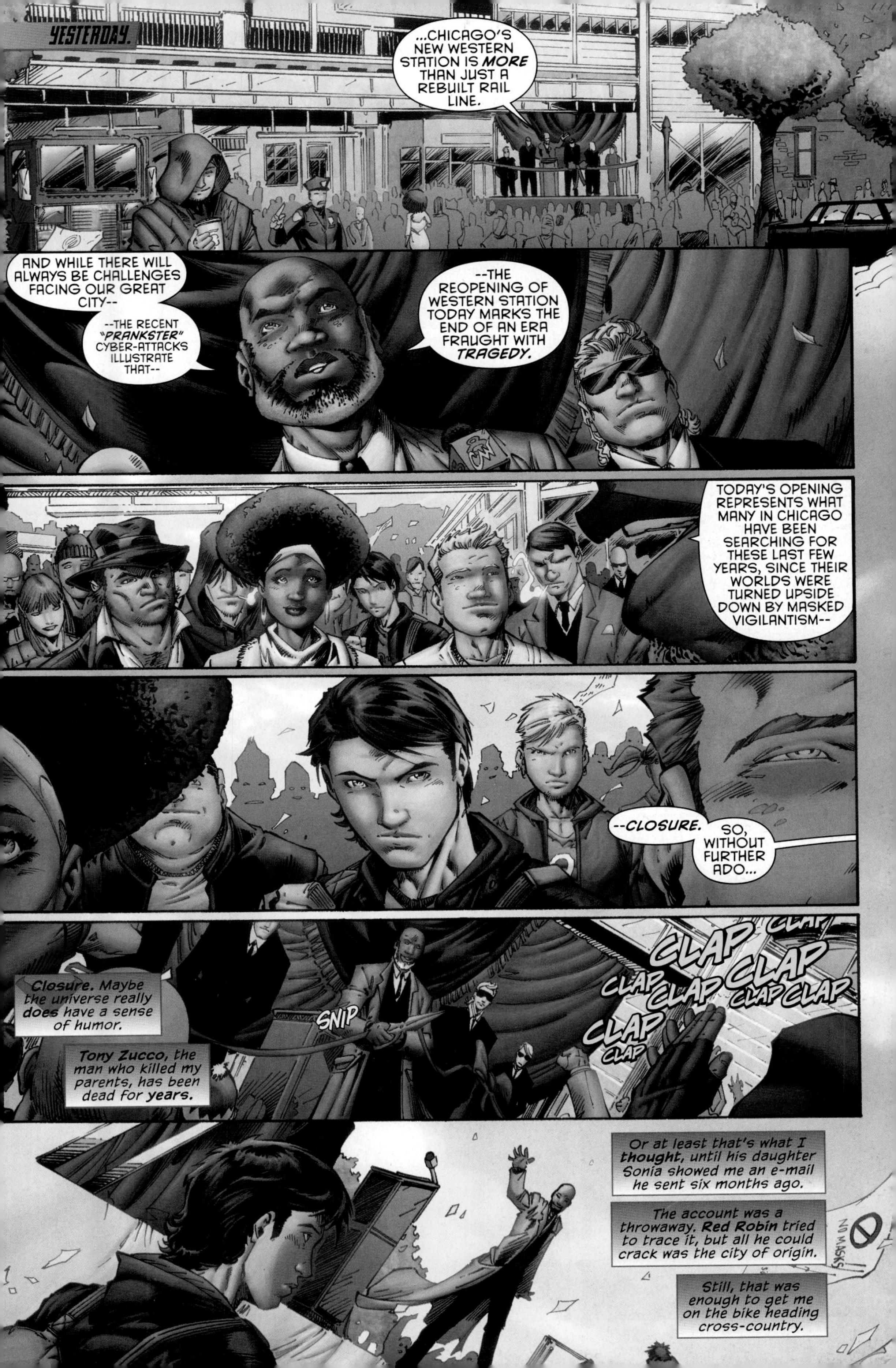
YESTERDAY.
...CHICAGO'S NEW WESTERN STATION IS MORE THAN JUST A REBUILT RAIL LINE.
AND WHILE THERE WILL ALWAYS BE CHALLENGES FACING OUR GREAT CITY--
--THE RECENT "PRANKSTER" CYBER-ATTACKS ILLUSTRATE THAT--
--THE REOPENING OF WESTERN STATION TODAY MARKS THE END OF AN ERA FRAUGHT WITH TRAGEDY.
TODAY'S OPENING REPRESENTS WHAT MANY IN CHICAGO HAVE BEEN SEARCHING FOR THESE LAST FEW YEARS, SINCE THEIR WORLDS WERE TURNED UPSIDE DOWN BY MASKED VIGILANTISM--
--CLOSURE.
SO, WITHOUT FURTHER ADO...
Closure. Maybe the universe really does have a sense of humor.
Tony Zucco, the man who killed my parents, has been dead for years.
SNIP
CLAP CLAP CLAP CLAP CLAP CLAP CLAP CLAP CLAP CLAP
Or at least that's what I thought, until his daughter Sonia showed me an e-mail he sent six months ago.
The account was a throwaway. Red Robin tried to trace it, but all he could crack was the city of origin.
Still, that was enough to get me on the bike heading cross-country.
NO MASKS

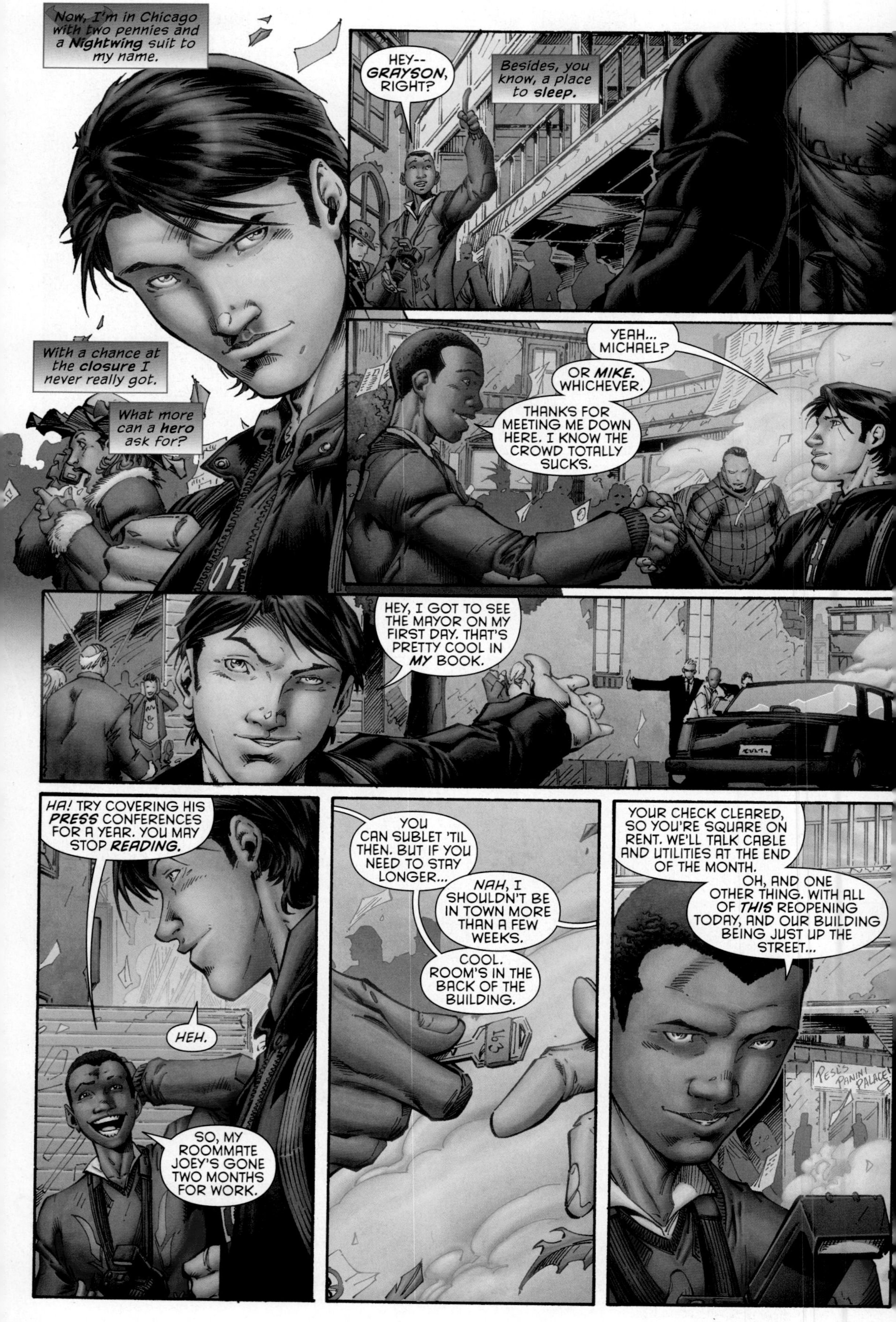

Now, I'm in Chicago with two pennies and a Nightwing suit to my name.
HEY-- GRAYSON, RIGHT?
Besides, you know, a place to sleep.
With a chance at the closure I never really got.
What more can a hero ask for?
YEAH... MICHAEL?
OR MIKE. WHICHEVER.
THANKS FOR MEETING ME DOWN HERE. I KNOW THE CROWD TOTALLY SUCKS.
HEY, I GOT TO SEE THE MAYOR ON MY FIRST DAY. THAT'S PRETTY COOL IN MY BOOK.
HA! TRY COVERING HIS PRESS CONFERENCES FOR A YEAR. YOU MAY STOP READING.
HEH.
SO, MY ROOMMATE JOEY'S GONE TWO MONTHS FOR WORK.
YOU CAN SUBLET 'TIL THEN. BUT IF YOU NEED TO STAY LONGER...
NAH, I SHOULDN'T BE IN TOWN MORE THAN A FEW WEEKS.
COOL. ROOM'S IN THE BACK OF THE BUILDING.
YOUR CHECK CLEARED, SO YOU'RE SQUARE ON RENT. WE'LL TALK CABLE AND UTILITIES AT THE END OF THE MONTH.
OH, AND ONE OTHER THING. WITH ALL OF THIS REOPENING TODAY, AND OUR BUILDING BEING JUST UP THE STREET...
PESI'S PANINI PALACE

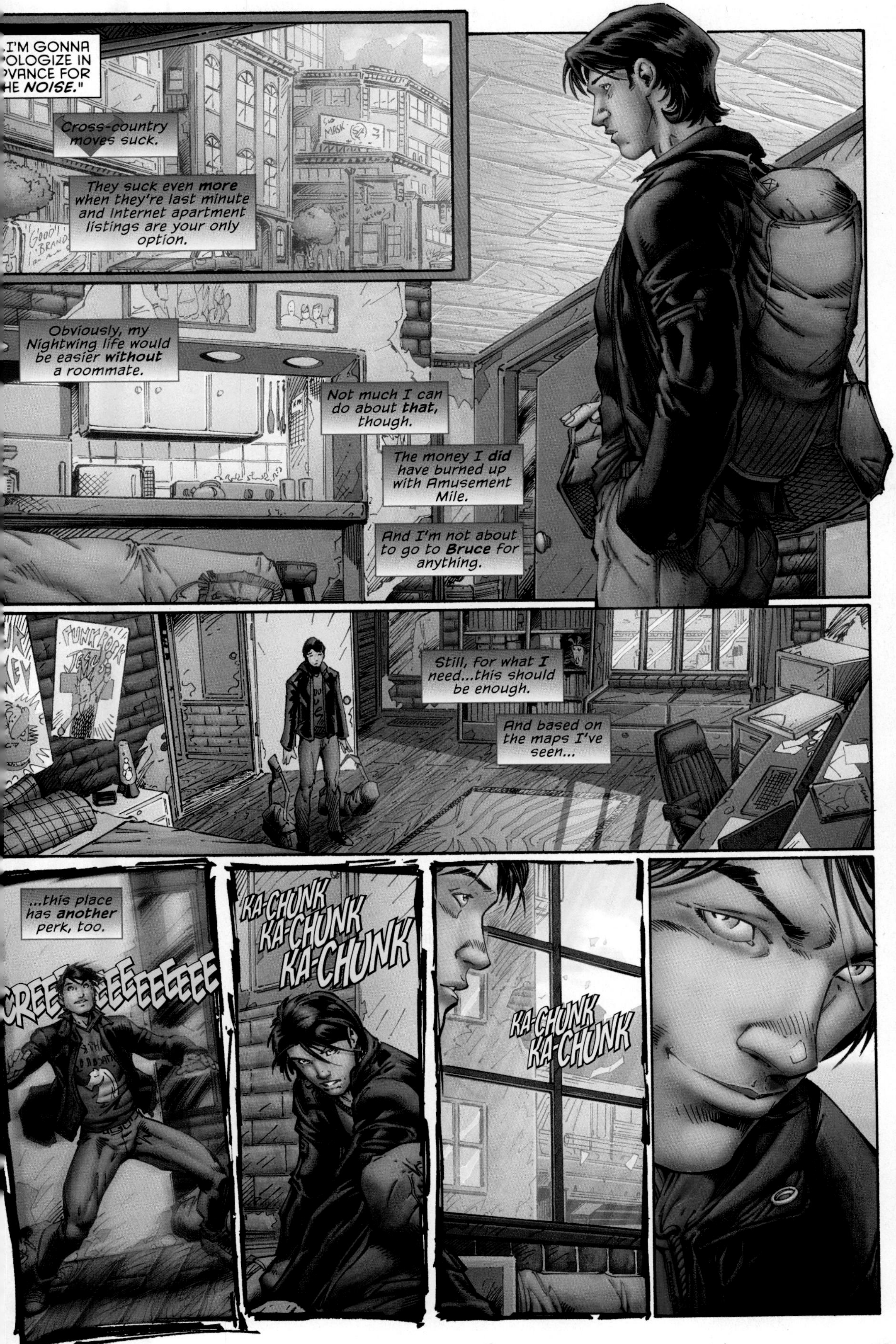

...I'M GONNA ...POLOGIZE IN ...DVANCE FOR ...HE NOISE."
Cross-country moves suck.
They suck even more when they're last minute and internet apartment listings are your only option.
Obviously, my Nightwing life would be easier without a roommate.
Not much I can do about that, though.
The money I did have burned up with Amusement Mile.
And I'm not about to go to Bruce for anything.
Still, for what I need...this should be enough.
And based on the maps I've seen...
...this place has another perk, too.
CREEEEEEEEEEEE
KA-CHUNK KA-CHUNK KA-CHUNK
KA-CHUNK KA-CHUNK

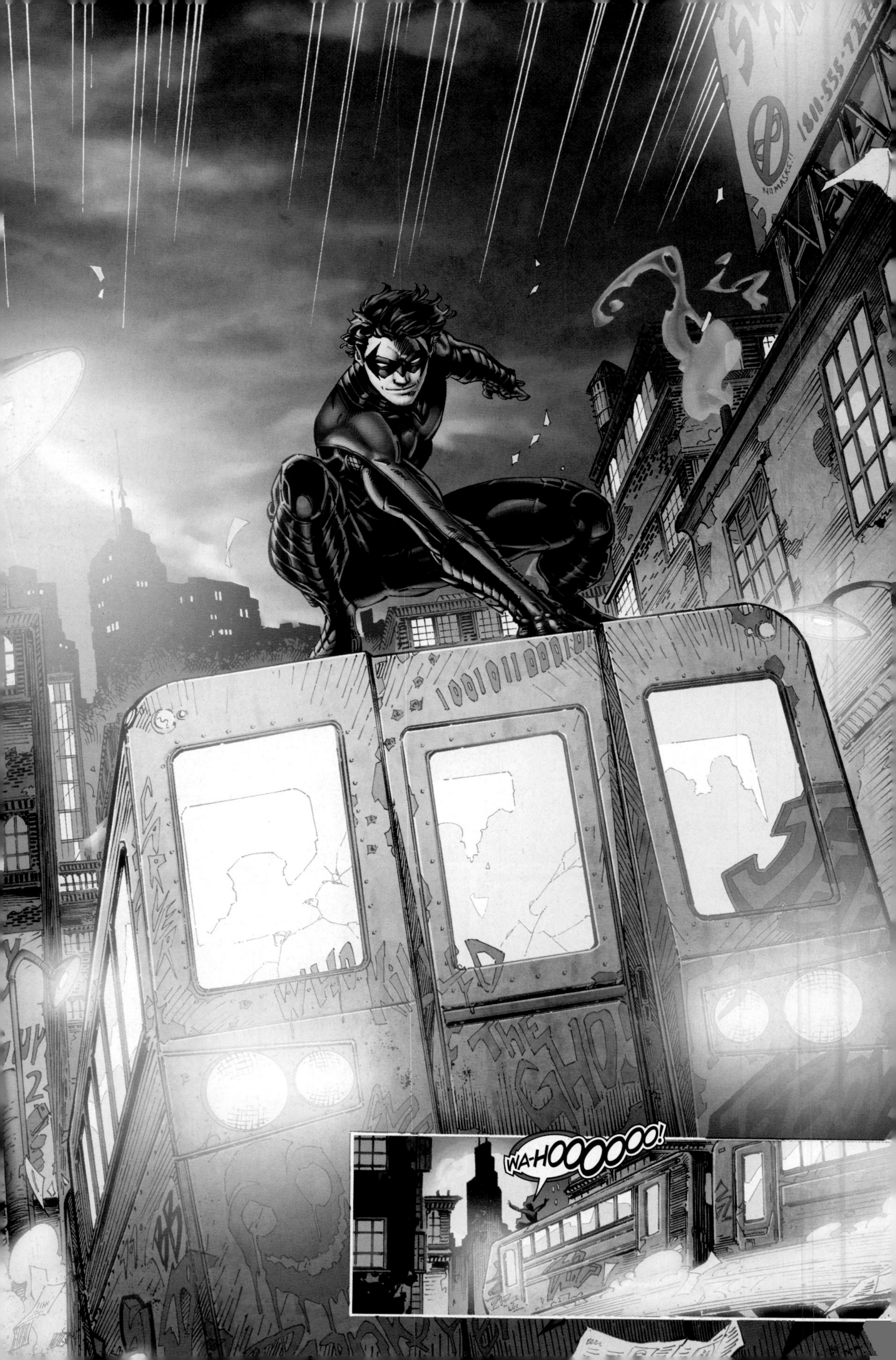
WA-HOOOOOOO!

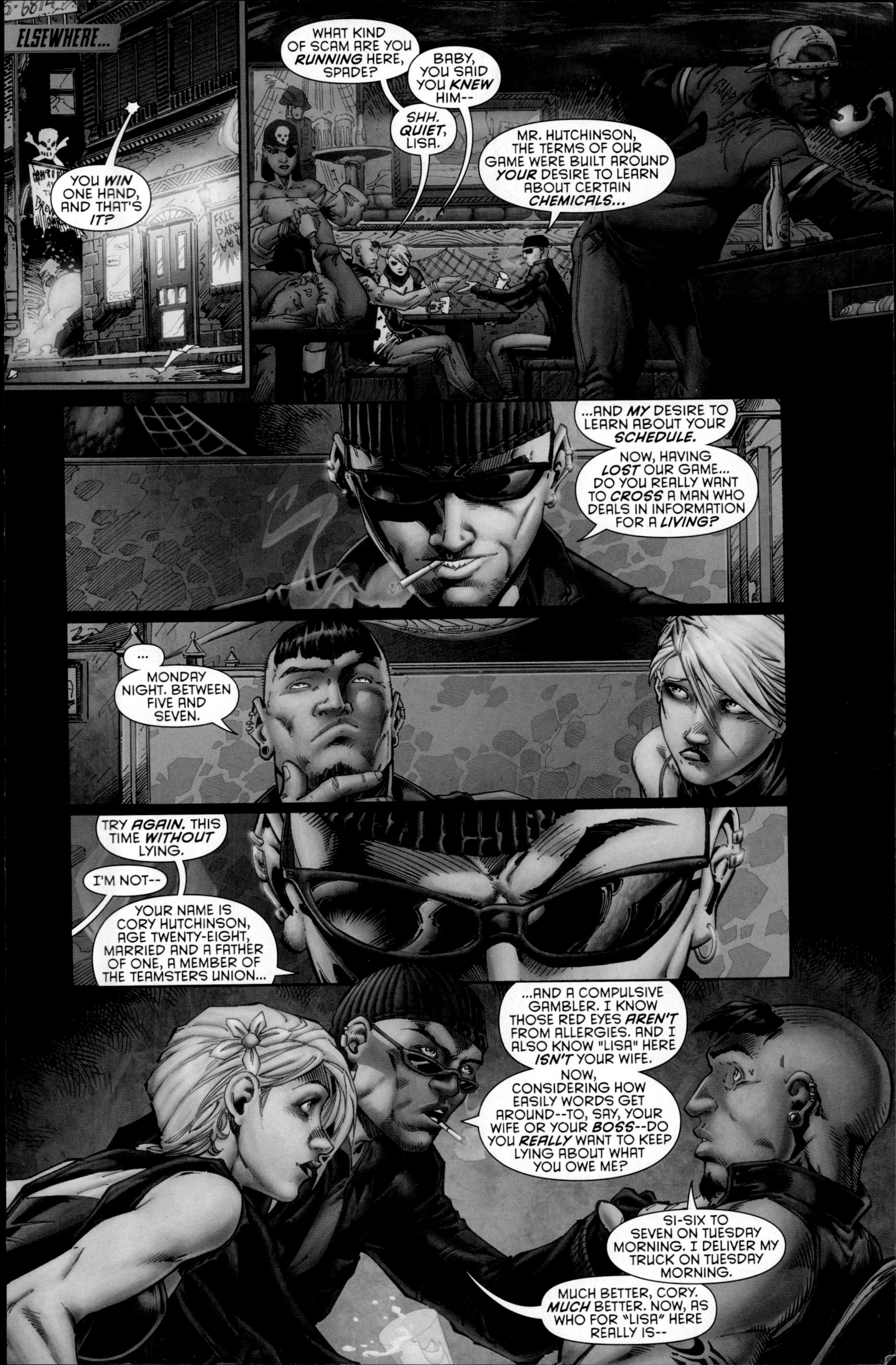
ELSEWHERE...
YOU WIN ONE HAND, AND THAT'S IT?
WHAT KIND OF SCAM ARE YOU RUNNING HERE, SPADE?
BABY, YOU SAID YOU KNEW HIM--
SHH. QUIET, LISA.
MR. HUTCHINSON, THE TERMS OF OUR GAME WERE BUILT AROUND YOUR DESIRE TO LEARN ABOUT CERTAIN CHEMICALS...
...AND MY DESIRE TO LEARN ABOUT YOUR SCHEDULE.
NOW, HAVING LOST OUR GAME... DO YOU REALLY WANT TO CROSS A MAN WHO DEALS IN INFORMATION FOR A LIVING?
... MONDAY NIGHT. BETWEEN FIVE AND SEVEN.
TRY AGAIN. THIS TIME WITHOUT LYING.
I'M NOT--
YOUR NAME IS CORY HUTCHINSON, AGE TWENTY-EIGHT, MARRIED AND A FATHER OF ONE, A MEMBER OF THE TEAMSTERS UNION...
...AND A COMPULSIVE GAMBLER. I KNOW THOSE RED EYES AREN'T FROM ALLERGIES. AND I ALSO KNOW "LISA" HERE ISN'T YOUR WIFE.
NOW, CONSIDERING HOW EASILY WORDS GET AROUND--TO, SAY, YOUR WIFE OR YOUR BOSS--DO YOU REALLY WANT TO KEEP LYING ABOUT WHAT YOU OWE ME?
SI-SIX TO SEVEN ON TUESDAY MORNING. I DELIVER MY TRUCK ON TUESDAY MORNING.
MUCH BETTER, CORY. MUCH BETTER. NOW, AS WHO FOR "LISA" HERE REALLY IS--

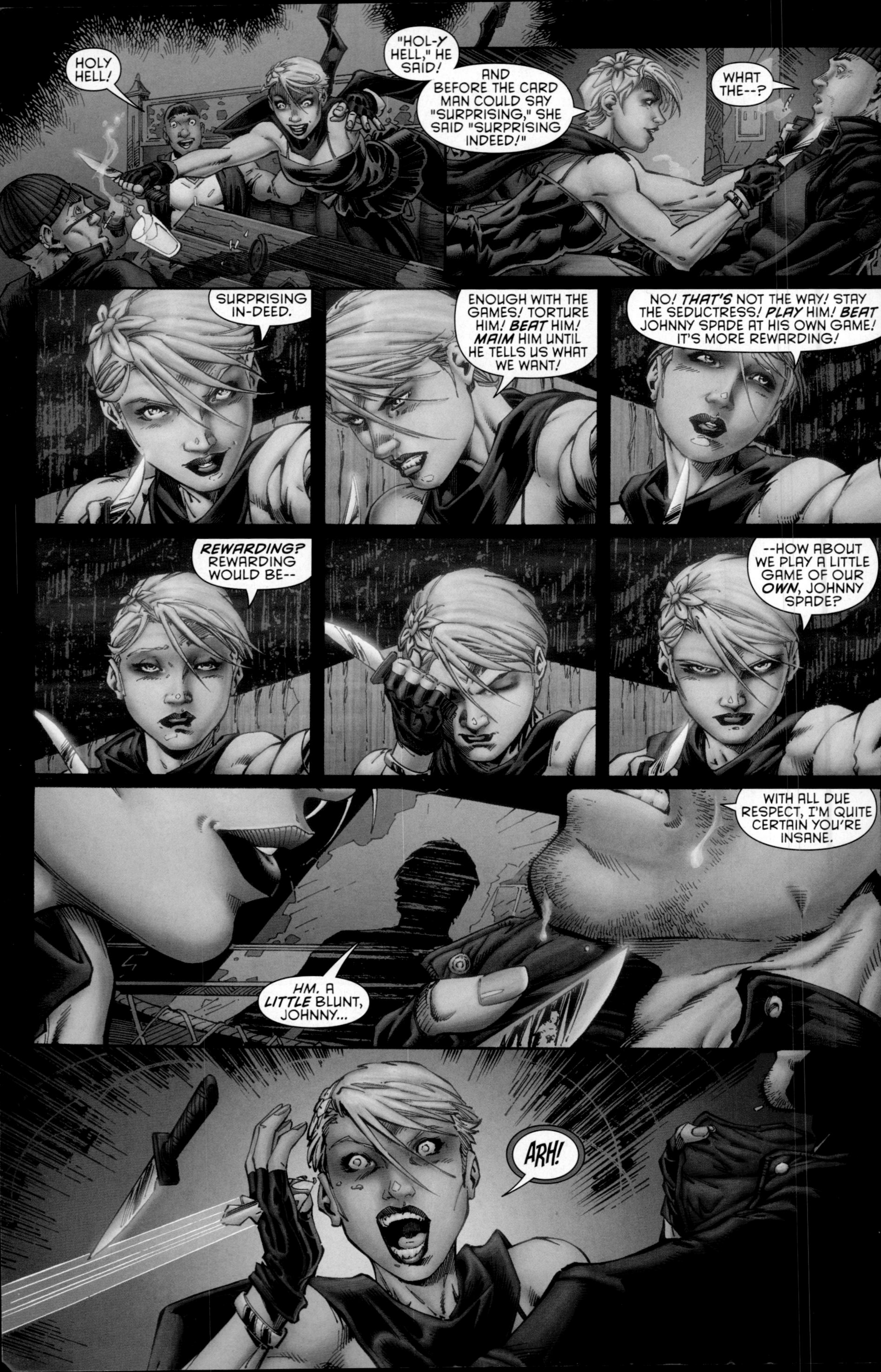
HOLY HELL!
"HOL-Y HELL," HE SAID!
AND BEFORE THE CARD MAN COULD SAY "SURPRISING," SHE SAID "SURPRISING INDEED!"
WHAT THE--?
SURPRISING IN-DEED.
ENOUGH WITH THE GAMES! TORTURE HIM! BEAT HIM! MAIM HIM UNTIL HE TELLS US WHAT WE WANT!
NO! THAT'S NOT THE WAY! STAY THE SEDUCTRESS! PLAY HIM! BEAT JOHNNY SPADE AT HIS OWN GAME! IT'S MORE REWARDING!
REWARDING? REWARDING WOULD BE--
--HOW ABOUT WE PLAY A LITTLE GAME OF OUR OWN, JOHNNY SPADE?
WITH ALL DUE RESPECT, I'M QUITE CERTAIN YOU'RE INSANE.
HM. A LITTLE BLUNT, JOHNNY...
ARH!

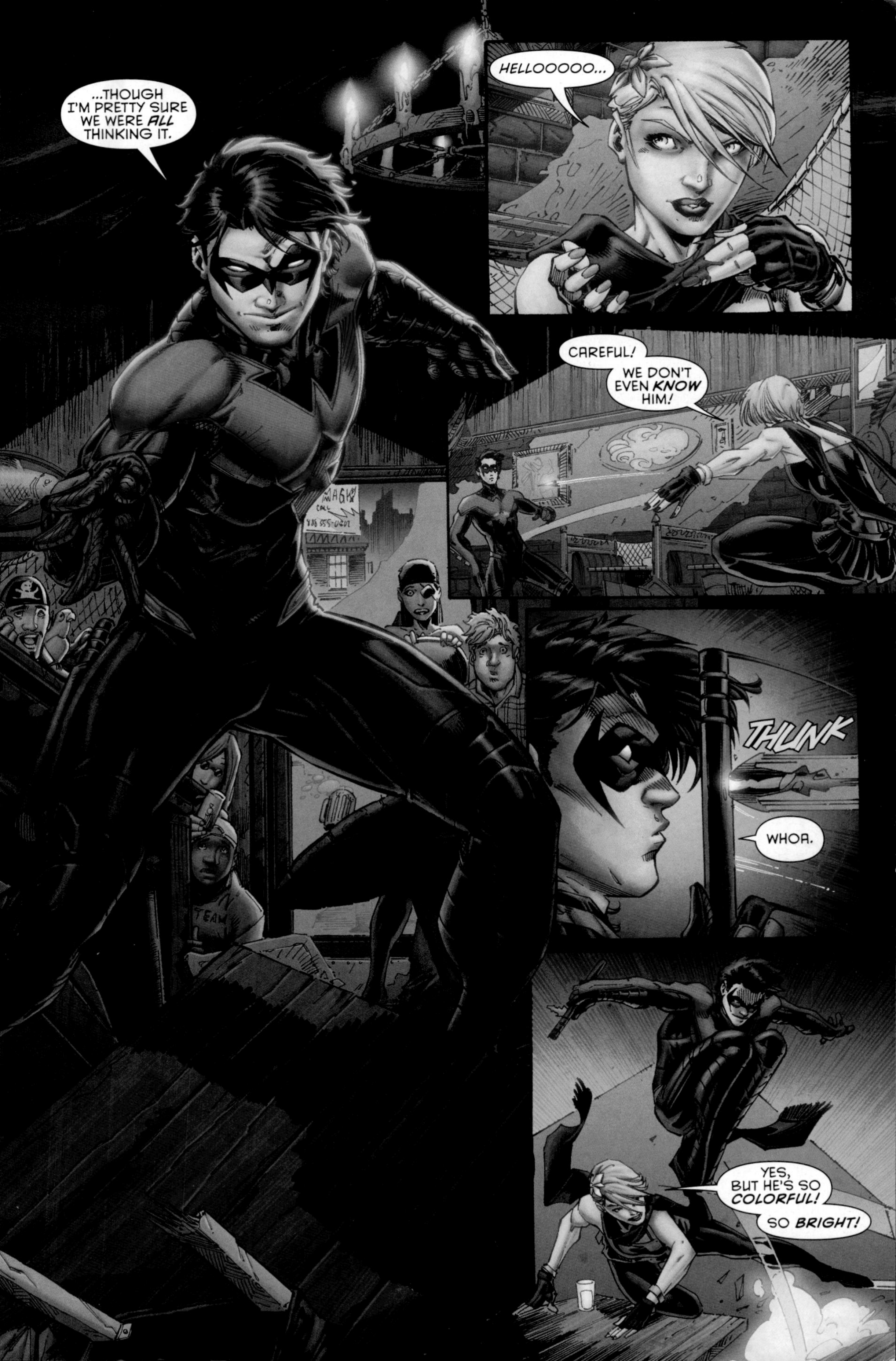

...THOUGH I'M PRETTY SURE WE WERE *ALL* THINKING IT.
HELLOOOOO...
CAREFUL!
WE DON'T EVEN *KNOW* HIM!
THUNK
WHOA.
YES, BUT HE'S SO *COLORFUL!*
SO *BRIGHT!*

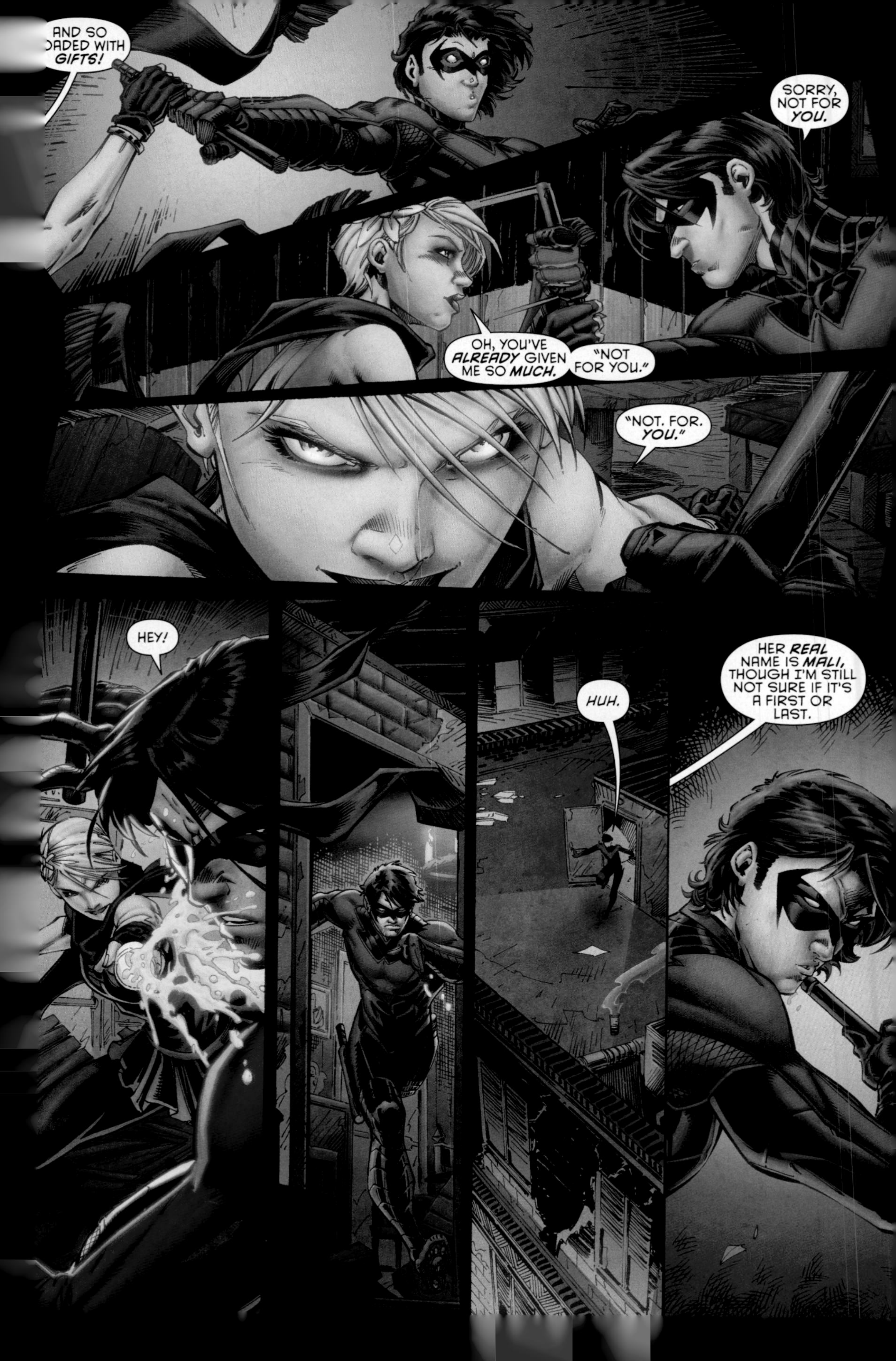
AND SO
OADED WITH
GIFTS!
SORRY, NOT FOR YOU.
OH, YOU'VE ALREADY GIVEN ME SO MUCH.
"NOT FOR YOU."
"NOT. FOR. YOU."
HEY!
HUH.
HER REAL NAME IS MALI, THOUGH I'M STILL NOT SURE IF IT'S A FIRST OR LAST.

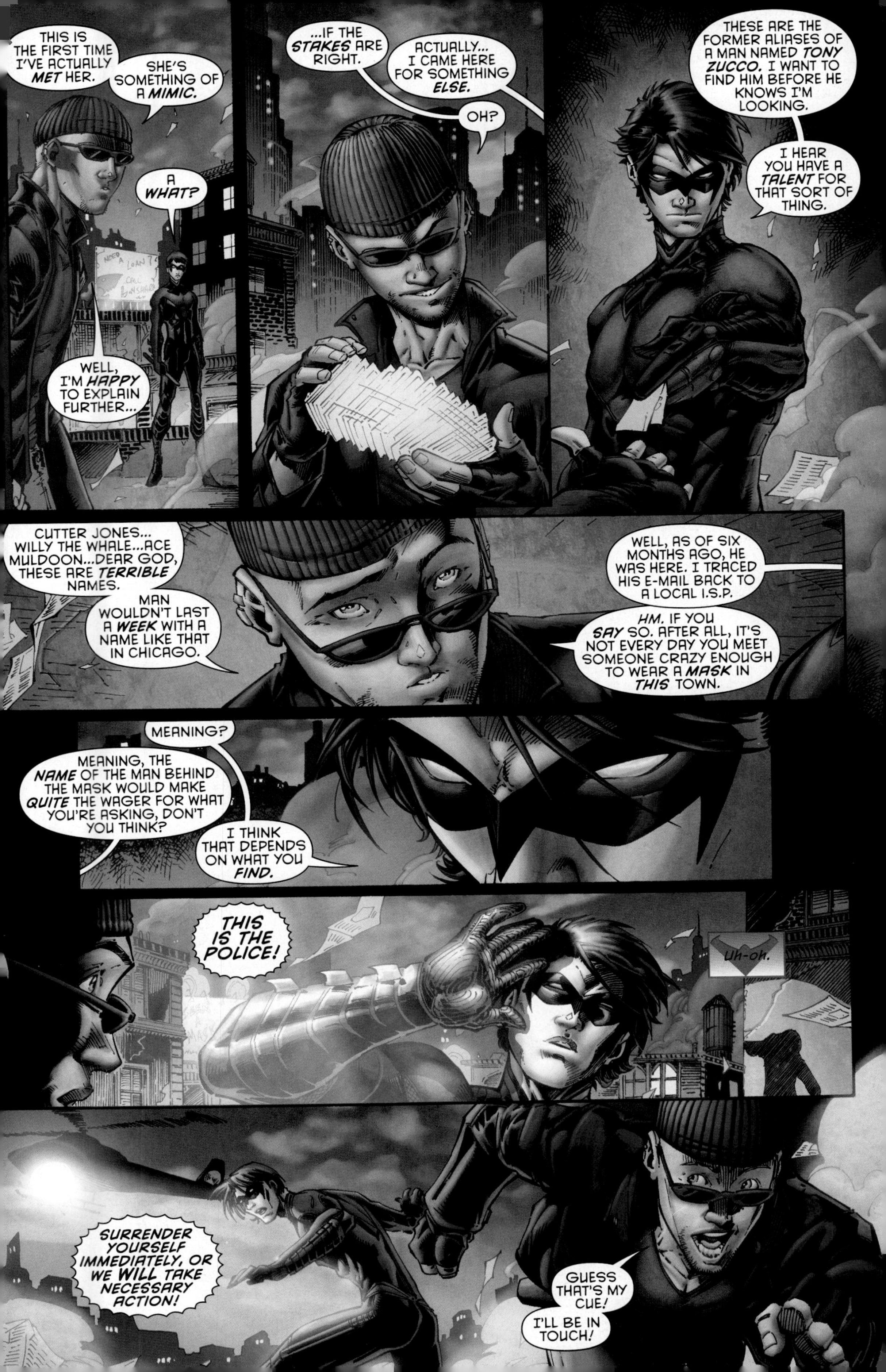
THIS IS THE FIRST TIME I'VE ACTUALLY MET HER.
SHE'S SOMETHING OF A MIMIC.
A WHAT?
WELL, I'M HAPPY TO EXPLAIN FURTHER...
...IF THE STAKES ARE RIGHT.
ACTUALLY... I CAME HERE FOR SOMETHING ELSE.
OH?
THESE ARE THE FORMER ALIASES OF A MAN NAMED TONY ZUCCO. I WANT TO FIND HIM BEFORE HE KNOWS I'M LOOKING.
I HEAR YOU HAVE A TALENT FOR THAT SORT OF THING.
CUTTER JONES... WILLY THE WHALE...ACE MULDOON...DEAR GOD, THESE ARE TERRIBLE NAMES.
MAN WOULDN'T LAST A WEEK WITH A NAME LIKE THAT IN CHICAGO.
WELL, AS OF SIX MONTHS AGO, HE WAS HERE. I TRACED HIS E-MAIL BACK TO A LOCAL I.S.P.
HM. IF YOU SAY SO. AFTER ALL, IT'S NOT EVERY DAY YOU MEET SOMEONE CRAZY ENOUGH TO WEAR A MASK IN THIS TOWN.
MEANING?
MEANING, THE NAME OF THE MAN BEHIND THE MASK WOULD MAKE QUITE THE WAGER FOR WHAT YOU'RE ASKING, DON'T YOU THINK?
I THINK THAT DEPENDS ON WHAT YOU FIND.
THIS IS THE POLICE!
Uh-oh.
SURRENDER YOURSELF IMMEDIATELY, OR WE WILL TAKE NECESSARY ACTION!
GUESS THAT'S MY CUE!
I'LL BE IN TOUCH!

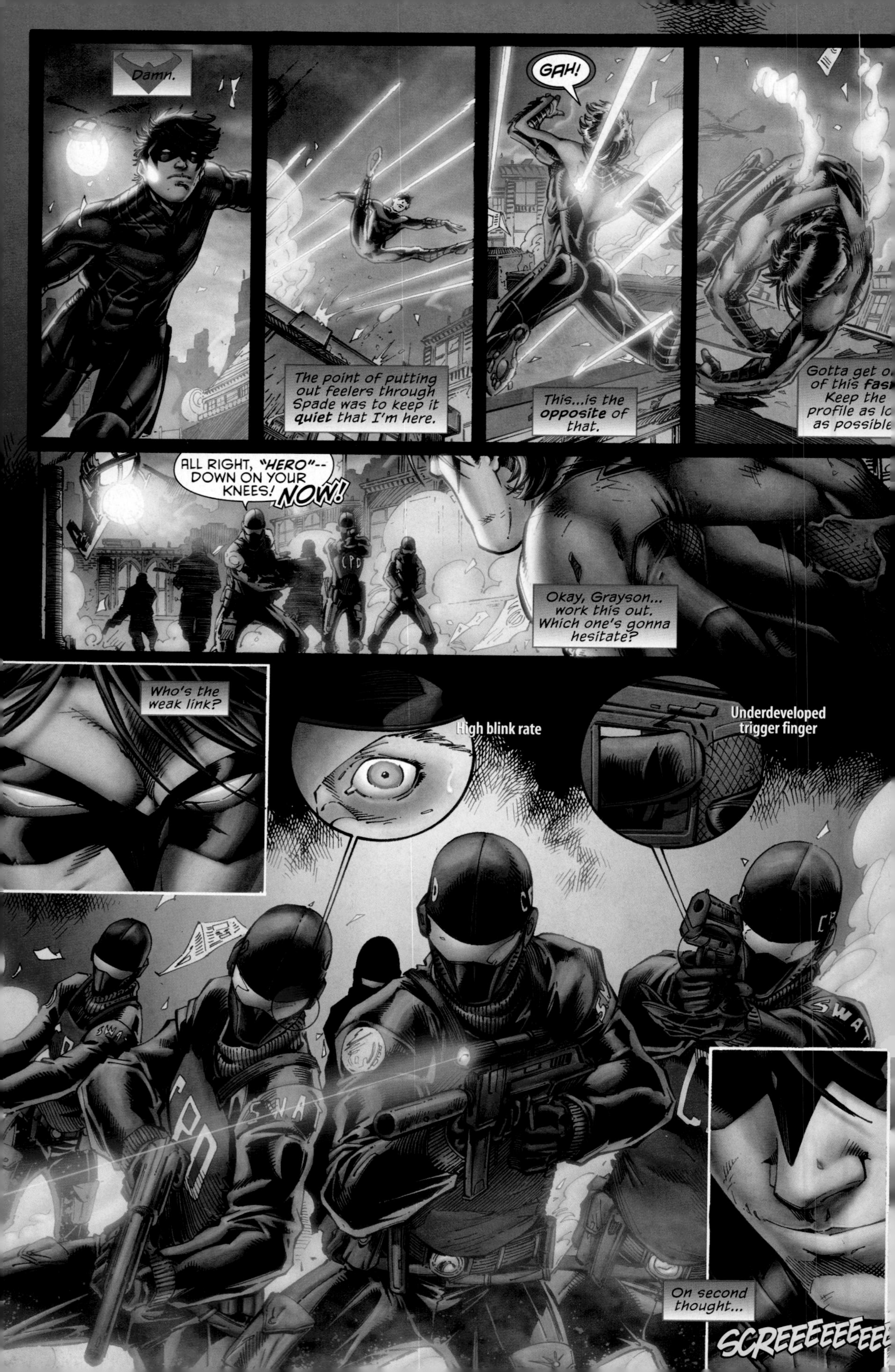
Damn.
The point of putting out feelers through Spade was to keep it quiet that I'm here.
GAH!
This...is the opposite of that.
Gotta get o
of this fas
Keep the
profile as lo
as possible
ALL RIGHT, "HERO"-- DOWN ON YOUR KNEES! NOW!
Okay, Grayson... work this out. Which one's gonna hesitate?
Who's the weak link?
High blink rate
Underdeveloped trigger finger
On second thought...
SCREEEEEEEEE

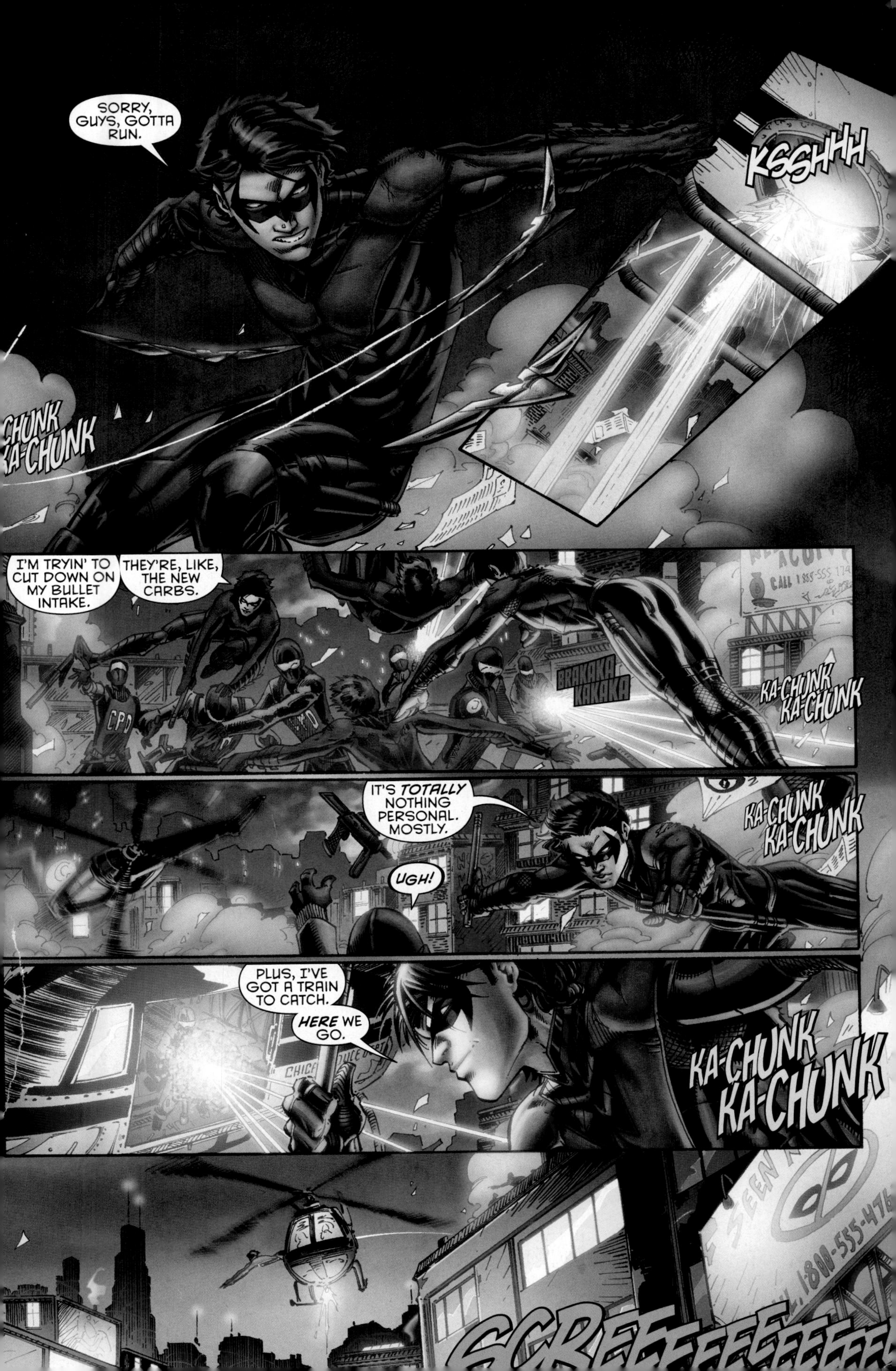

SORRY, GUYS, GOTTA RUN.
KSSHHH
CHUNK KA-CHUNK
I'M TRYIN' TO CUT DOWN ON MY BULLET INTAKE.
THEY'RE, LIKE, THE NEW CARBS.
BRAKAKA KAKAKA
KA-CHUNK KA-CHUNK
IT'S *TOTALLY* NOTHING PERSONAL. MOSTLY.
UGH!
KA-CHUNK KA-CHUNK
PLUS, I'VE GOT A TRAIN TO CATCH.
HERE WE GO.
KA-CHUNK KA-CHUNK
SCREEEEEEEEEE

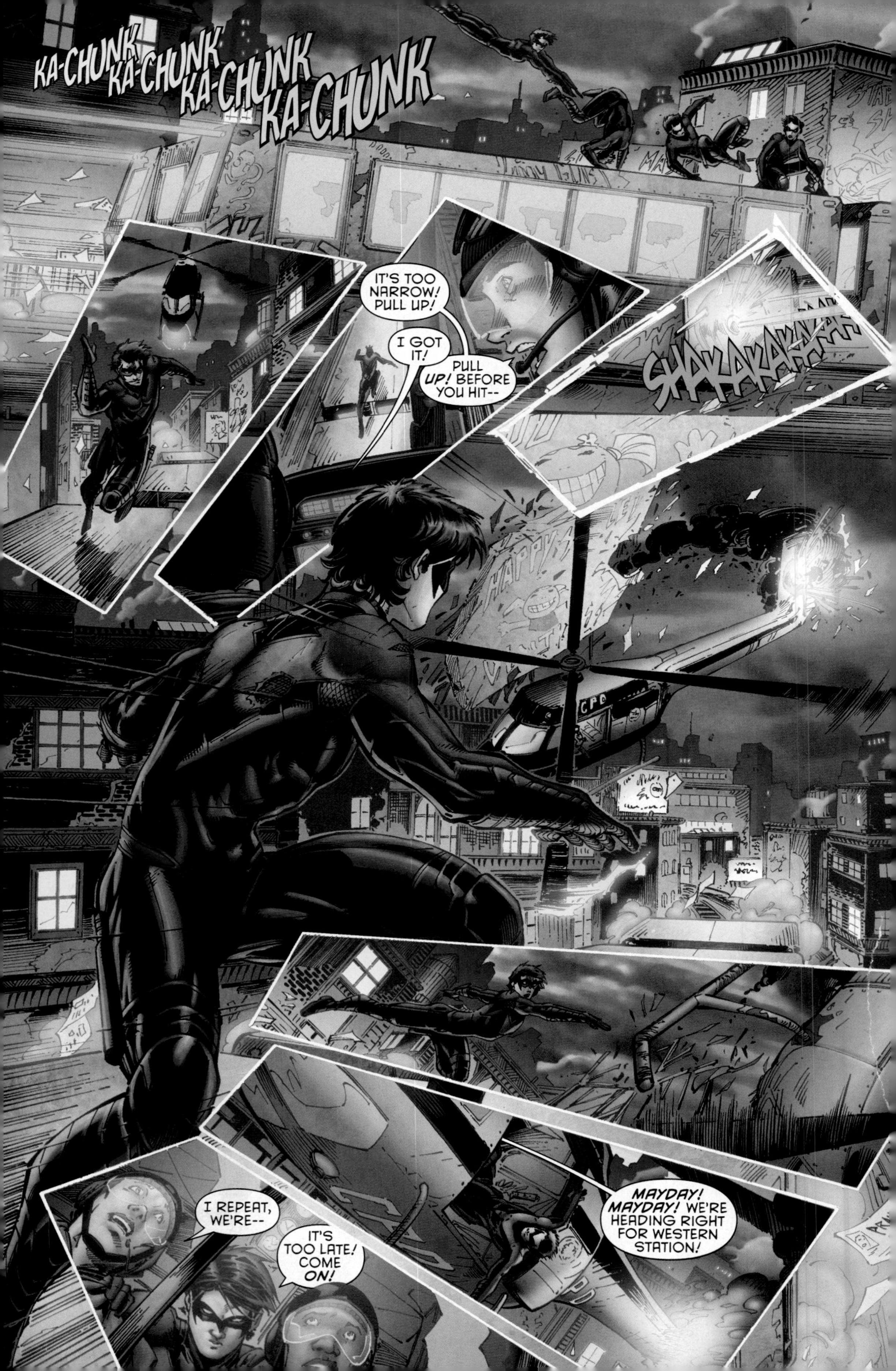
KA-CHUNK
KA-CHUNK
KA-CHUNK
KA-CHUNK
IT'S TOO NARROW! PULL UP!
I GOT IT!
PULL UP! BEFORE YOU HIT--
SHAKAKAKAKAK
I REPEAT, WE'RE--
IT'S TOO LATE! COME ON!
MAYDAY! MAYDAY! WE'RE HEADING RIGHT FOR WESTERN STATION!

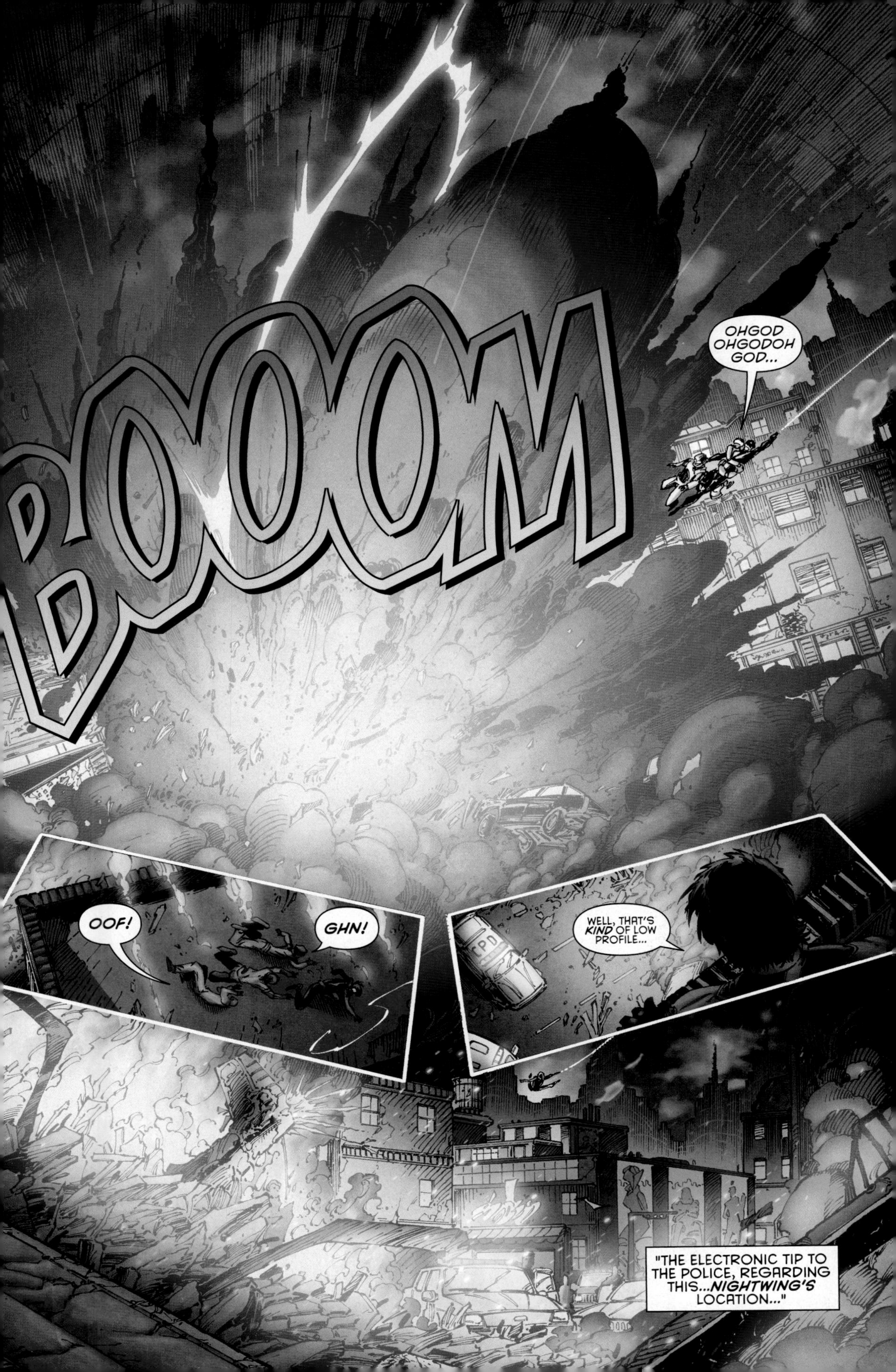
BOOOM
OHGOD OHGODOH GOD...
OOF!
GHN!
WELL, THAT'S KIND OF LOW PROFILE...
"THE ELECTRONIC TIP TO THE POLICE, REGARDING THIS...NIGHTWING'S LOCATION..."

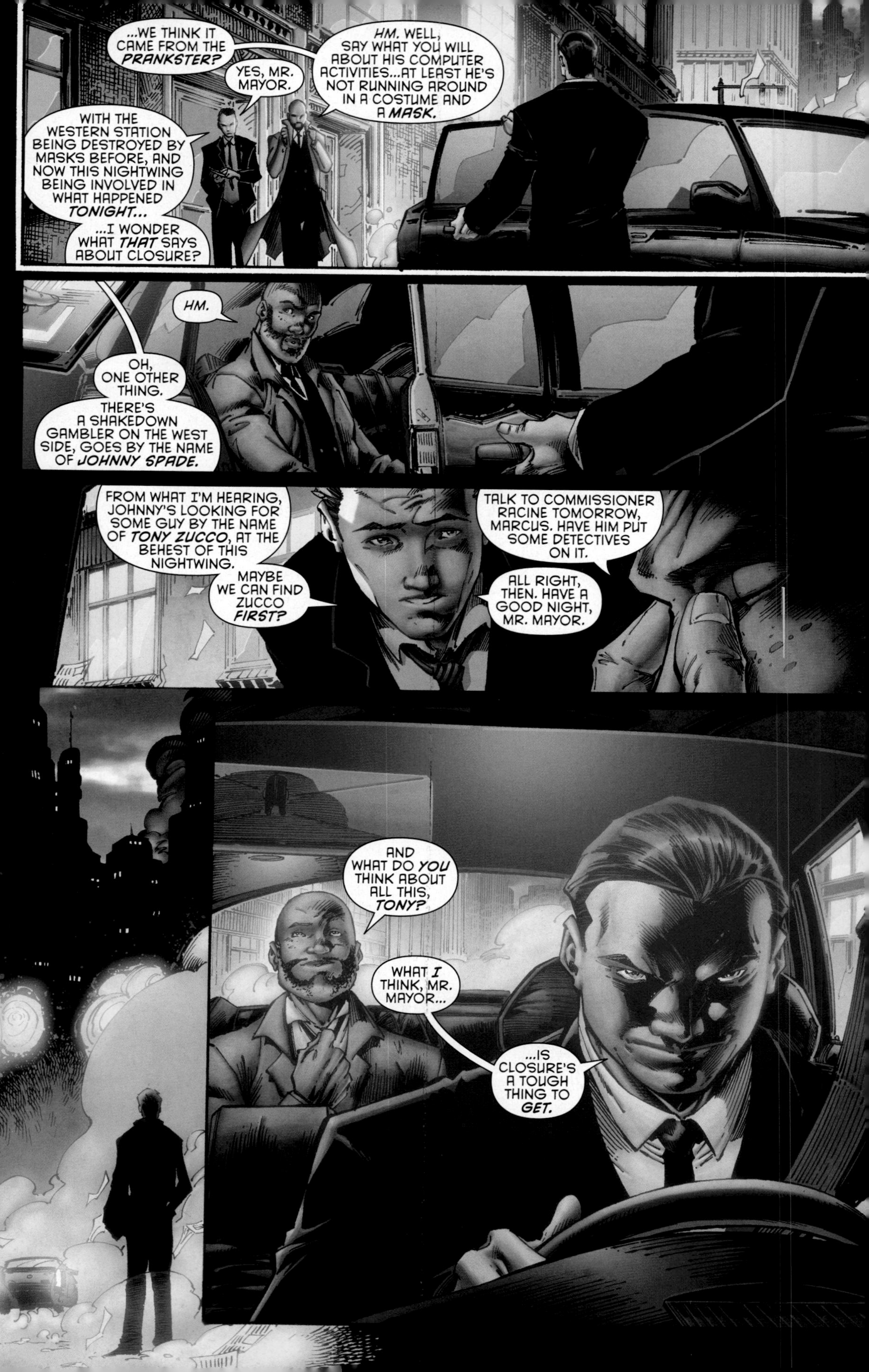
...WE THINK IT CAME FROM THE PRANKSTER?
YES, MR. MAYOR.
HM. WELL, SAY WHAT YOU WILL ABOUT HIS COMPUTER ACTIVITIES...AT LEAST HE'S NOT RUNNING AROUND IN A COSTUME AND A MASK.
WITH THE WESTERN STATION BEING DESTROYED BY MASKS BEFORE, AND NOW THIS NIGHTWING BEING INVOLVED IN WHAT HAPPENED TONIGHT...
...I WONDER WHAT THAT SAYS ABOUT CLOSURE?
HM.
OH, ONE OTHER THING.
THERE'S A SHAKEDOWN GAMBLER ON THE WEST SIDE, GOES BY THE NAME OF JOHNNY SPADE.
FROM WHAT I'M HEARING, JOHNNY'S LOOKING FOR SOME GUY BY THE NAME OF TONY ZUCCO, AT THE BEHEST OF THIS NIGHTWING.
MAYBE WE CAN FIND ZUCCO FIRST?
TALK TO COMMISSIONER RACINE TOMORROW, MARCUS. HAVE HIM PUT SOME DETECTIVES ON IT.
ALL RIGHT, THEN. HAVE A GOOD NIGHT, MR. MAYOR.
AND WHAT DO YOU THINK ABOUT ALL THIS, TONY?
WHAT I THINK, MR. MAYOR...
...IS CLOSURE'S A TOUGH THING TO GET.

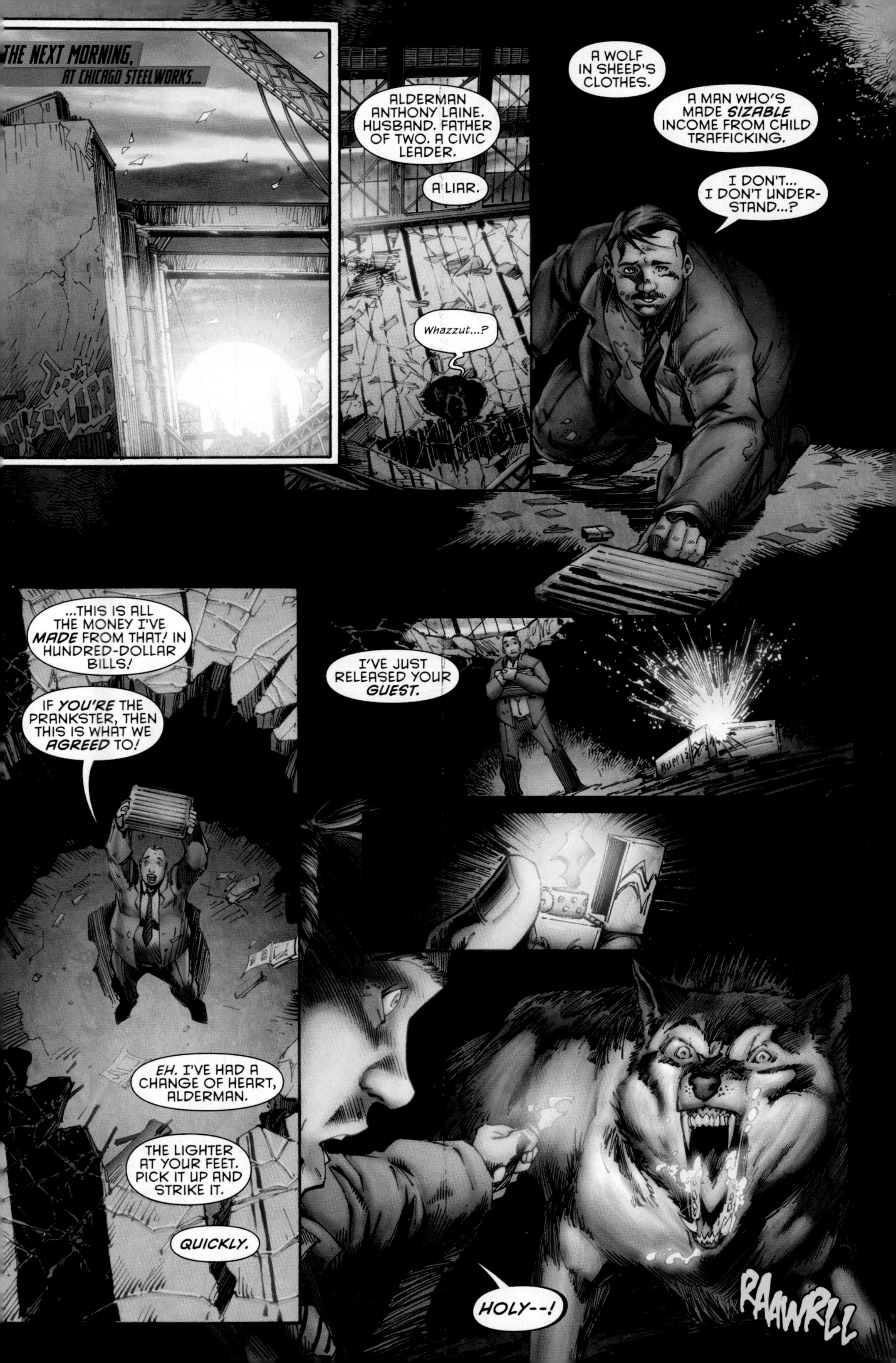
THE NEXT MORNING,
AT CHICAGO STEELWORKS...
ALDERMAN ANTHONY LAINE. HUSBAND. FATHER OF TWO. A CIVIC LEADER.
A LIAR.
Whazzut...?
A WOLF IN SHEEP'S CLOTHES.
A MAN WHO'S MADE SIZABLE INCOME FROM CHILD TRAFFICKING.
I DON'T... I DON'T UNDERSTAND...?
...THIS IS ALL THE MONEY I'VE MADE FROM THAT! IN HUNDRED-DOLLAR BILLS!
IF YOU'RE THE PRANKSTER, THEN THIS IS WHAT WE AGREED TO!
EH. I'VE HAD A CHANGE OF HEART, ALDERMAN.
THE LIGHTER AT YOUR FEET. PICK IT UP AND STRIKE IT.
QUICKLY.
I'VE JUST RELEASED YOUR GUEST.
HOLY--!
RAAWRLL

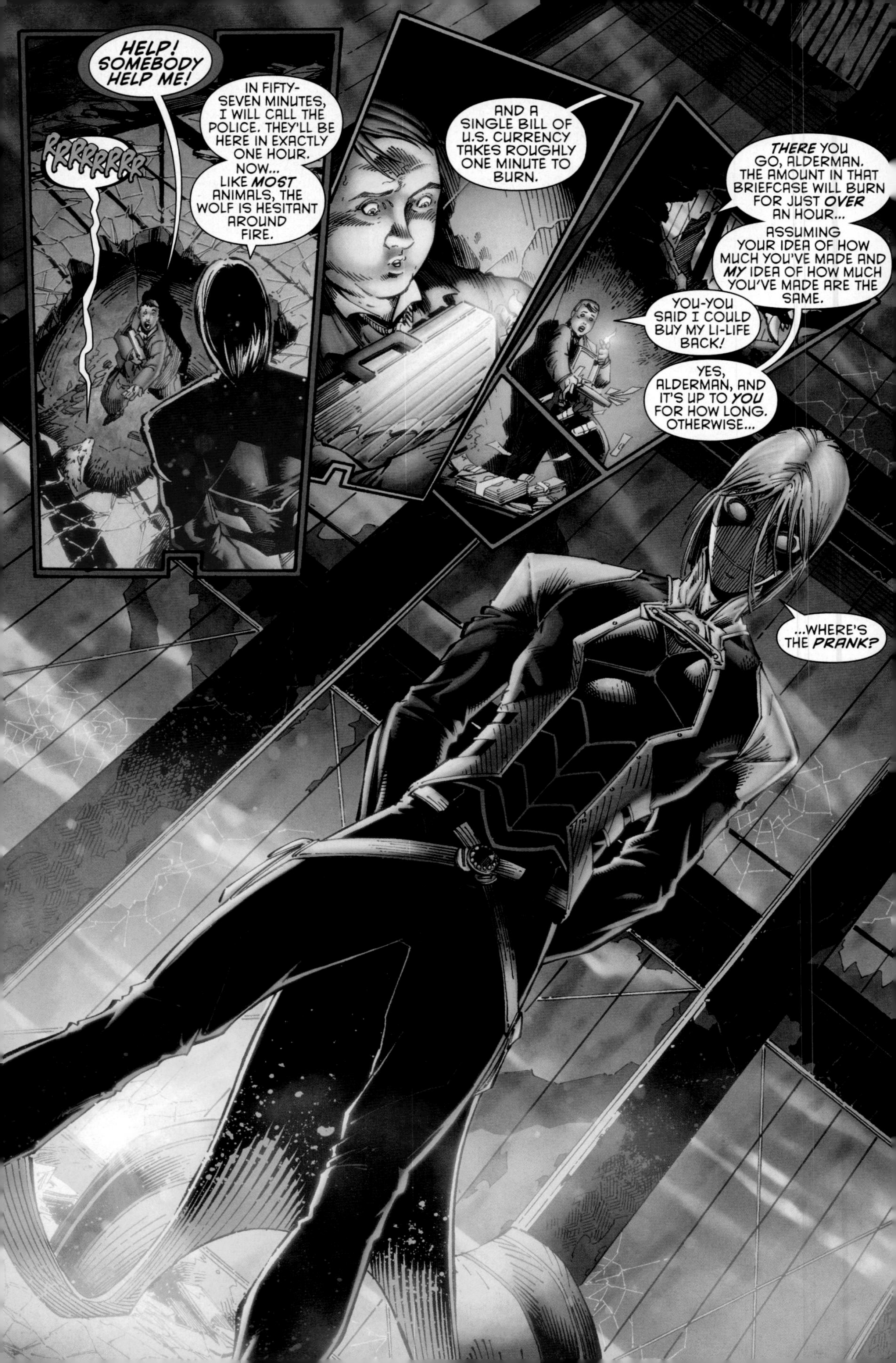
HELP! SOMEBODY HELP ME!
RRRRRRRR
IN FIFTY-SEVEN MINUTES, I WILL CALL THE POLICE. THEY'LL BE HERE IN EXACTLY ONE HOUR.
NOW... LIKE MOST ANIMALS, THE WOLF IS HESITANT AROUND FIRE.
AND A SINGLE BILL OF U.S. CURRENCY TAKES ROUGHLY ONE MINUTE TO BURN.
THERE YOU GO, ALDERMAN. THE AMOUNT IN THAT BRIEFCASE WILL BURN FOR JUST OVER AN HOUR...
ASSUMING YOUR IDEA OF HOW MUCH YOU'VE MADE AND MY IDEA OF HOW MUCH YOU'VE MADE ARE THE SAME.
YOU-YOU SAID I COULD BUY MY LI-LIFE BACK!
YES, ALDERMAN, AND IT'S UP TO YOU FOR HOW LONG. OTHERWISE...
...WHERE'S THE PRANK?

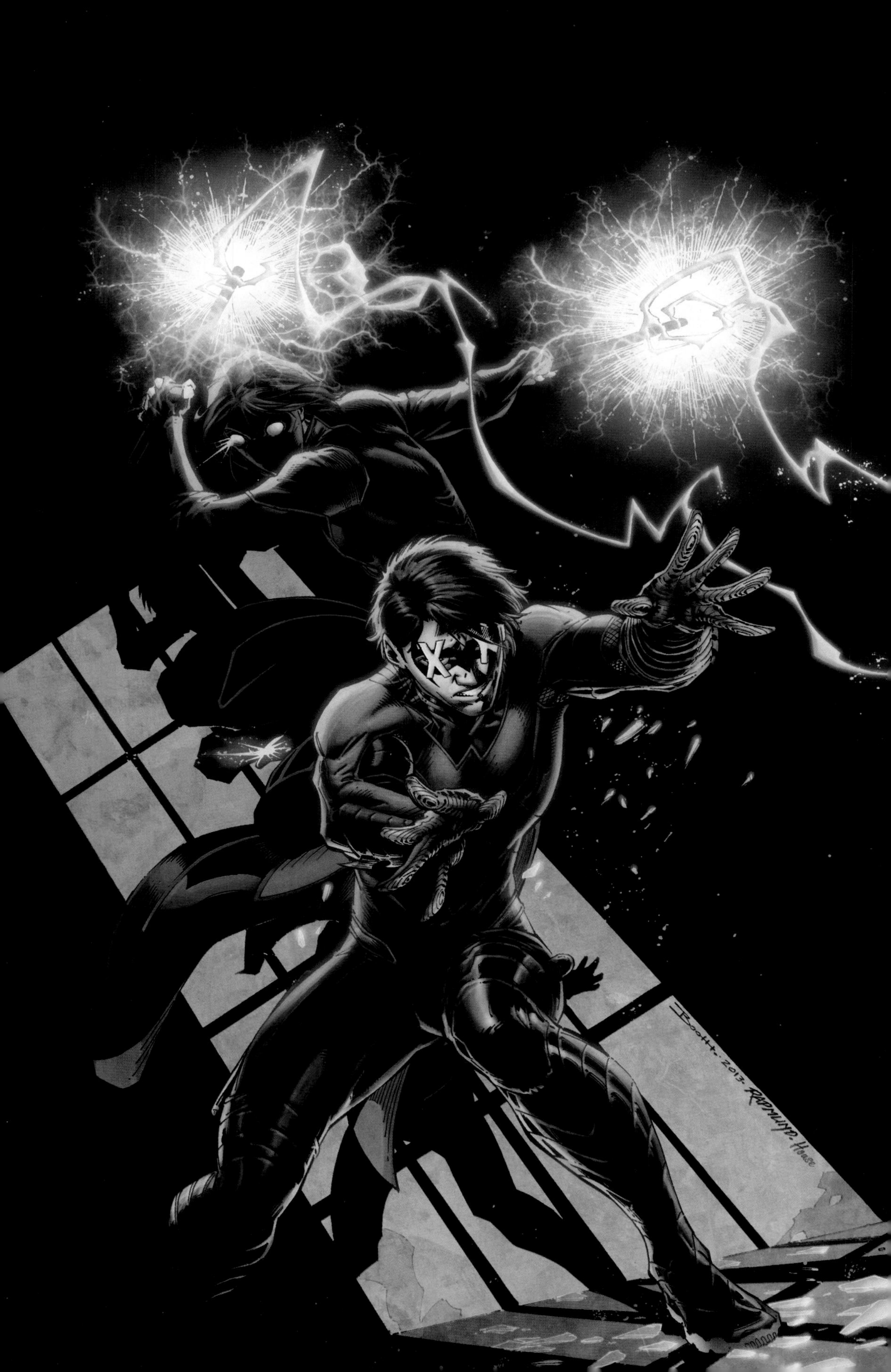

FLYING BLIND

KYLE HIGGINS writer **BRETT BOOTH** penciller **NORM RAPMUND** inker cover art by **BRETT BOOTH, NORM RAPMUND & ANDREW DALHOUSE**

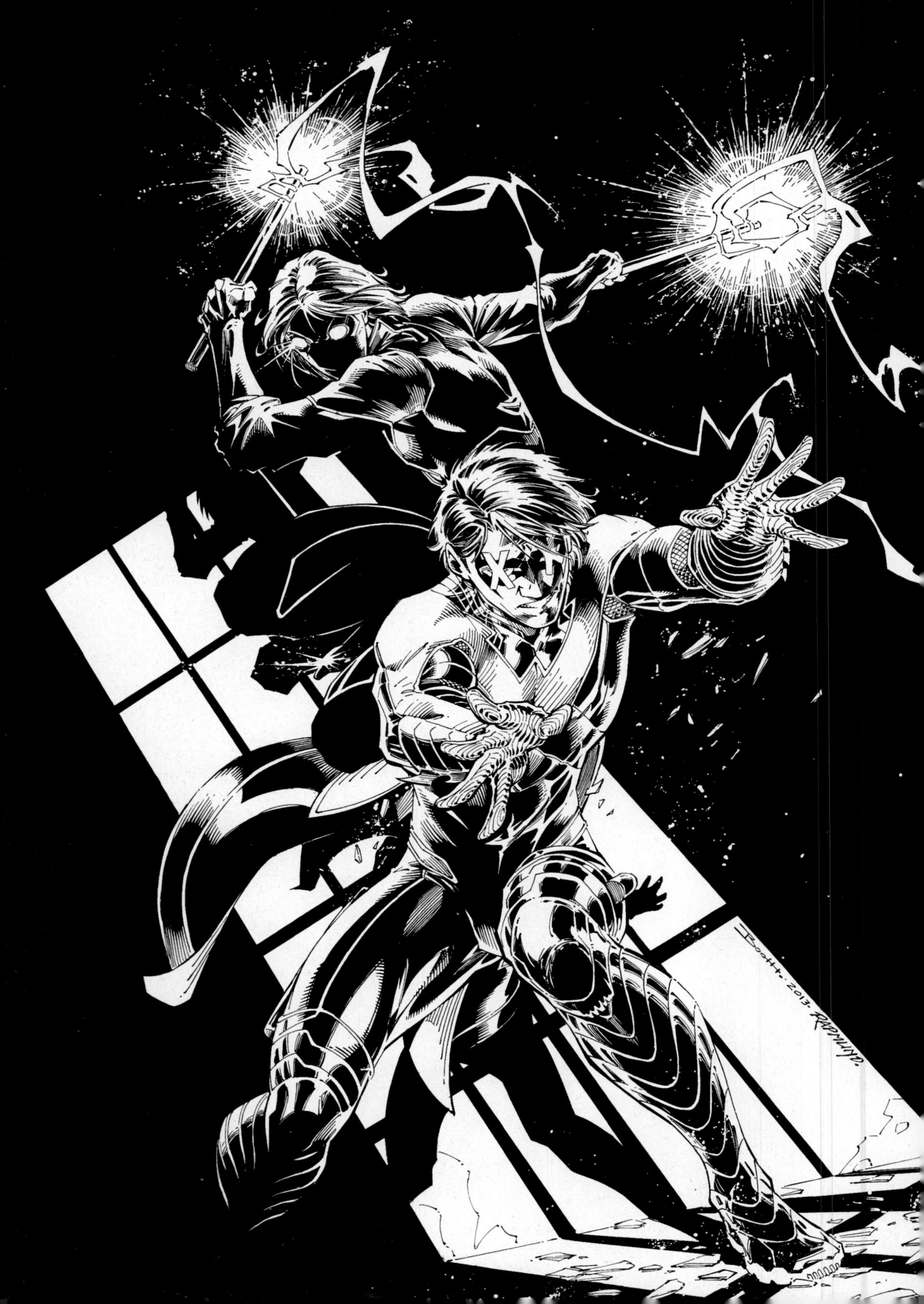

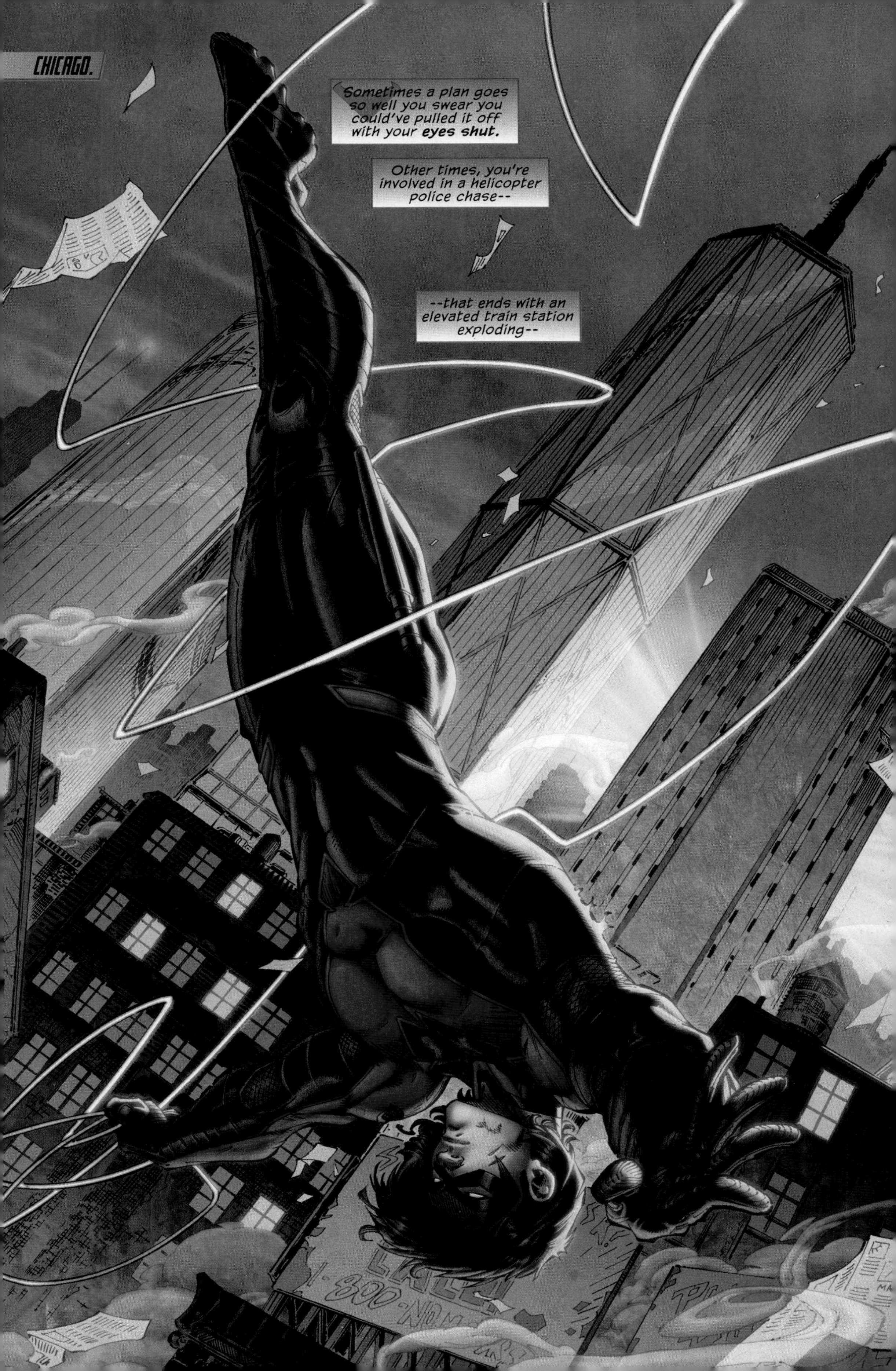
CHICAGO.
Sometimes a plan goes so well you swear you could've pulled it off with your **eyes shut.**
Other times, you're involved in a helicopter police chase--
--that ends with an elevated train station exploding--

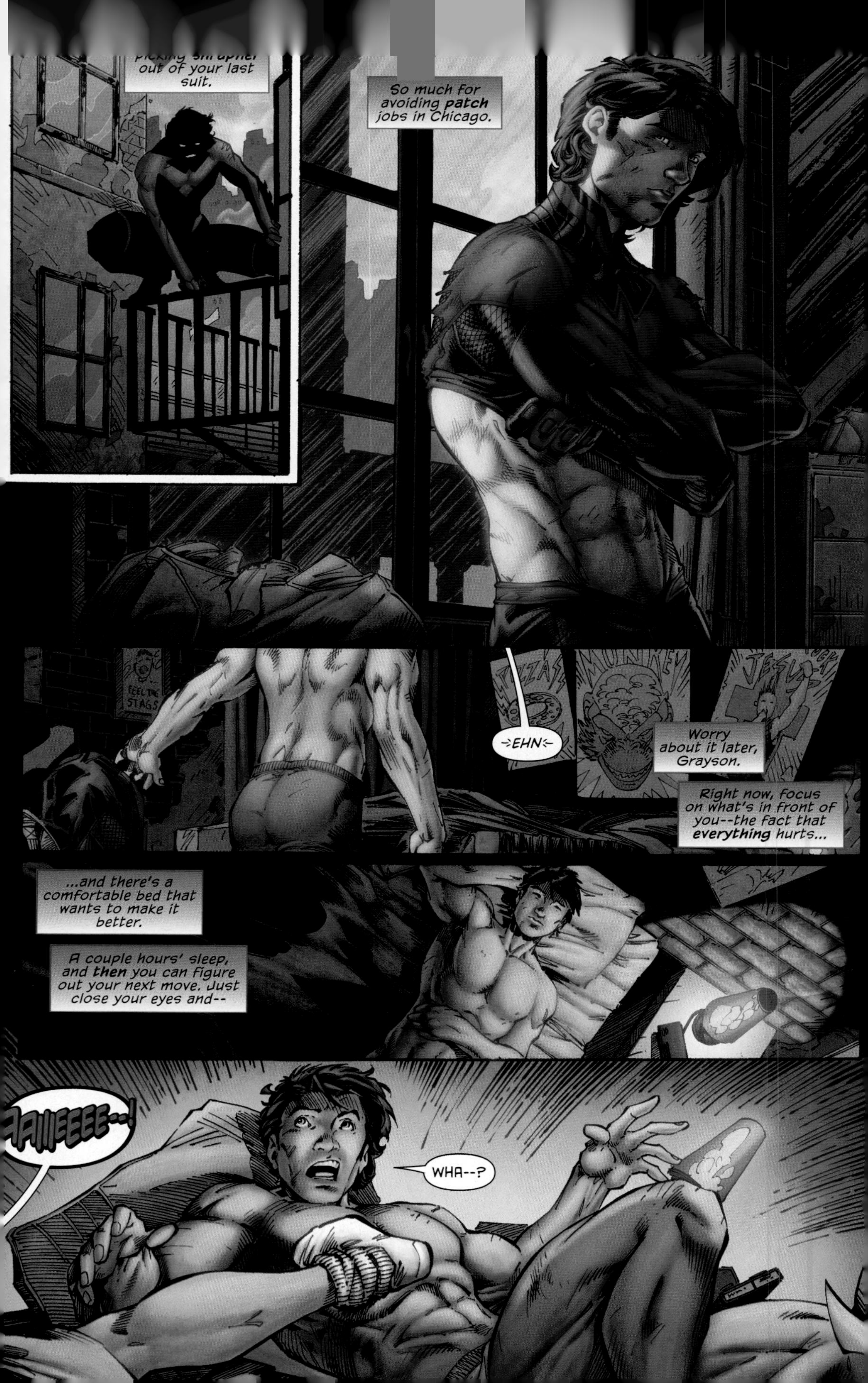

out of your last suit.
So much for avoiding **patch** jobs in Chicago.
FEEL THE STAGS
-EHN-
Worry about it later, Grayson.
Right now, focus on what's in front of you--the fact that **everything** hurts...
...and there's a comfortable bed that wants to make it better.
A couple hours' sleep, and **then** you can figure out your next move. Just close your eyes and--
AAIIIEEEE--!
WHA--?

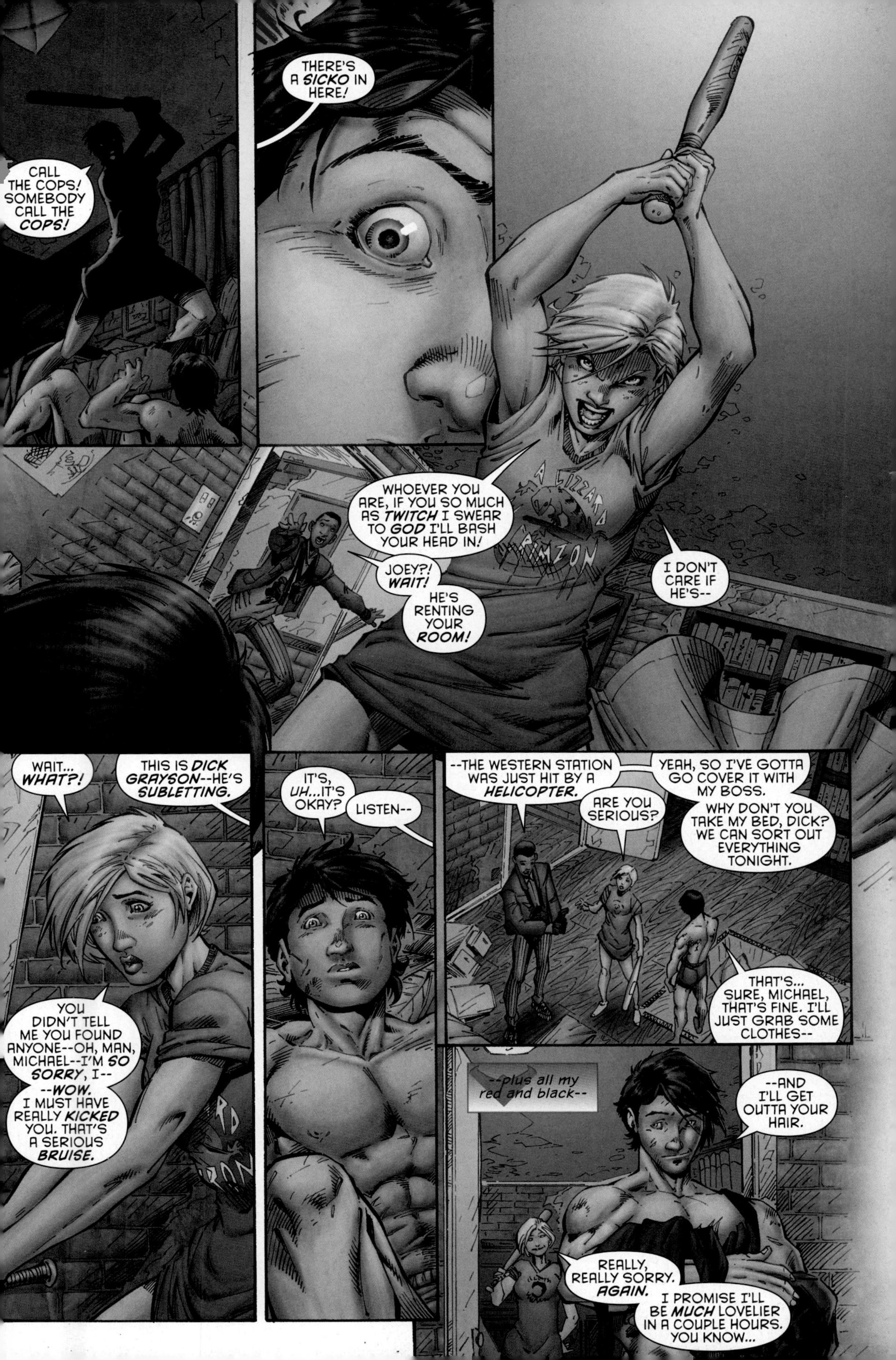
CALL THE COPS! SOMEBODY CALL THE COPS!
THERE'S A SICKO IN HERE!
WHOEVER YOU ARE, IF YOU SO MUCH AS TWITCH I SWEAR TO GOD I'LL BASH YOUR HEAD IN!
JOEY?! WAIT!
HE'S RENTING YOUR ROOM!
I DON'T CARE IF HE'S--
WAIT... WHAT?!
THIS IS DICK GRAYSON--HE'S SUBLETTING.
YOU DIDN'T TELL ME YOU FOUND ANYONE--OH, MAN, MICHAEL--I'M SO SORRY, I--
--WOW. I MUST HAVE REALLY KICKED YOU. THAT'S A SERIOUS BRUISE.
IT'S, UH...IT'S OKAY?
LISTEN--
--THE WESTERN STATION WAS JUST HIT BY A HELICOPTER.
ARE YOU SERIOUS?
YEAH, SO I'VE GOTTA GO COVER IT WITH MY BOSS.
WHY DON'T YOU TAKE MY BED, DICK? WE CAN SORT OUT EVERYTHING TONIGHT.
THAT'S... SURE, MICHAEL, THAT'S FINE. I'LL JUST GRAB SOME CLOTHES--
--plus all my red and black--
--AND I'LL GET OUTTA YOUR HAIR.
REALLY, REALLY SORRY. AGAIN.
I PROMISE I'LL BE MUCH LOVELIER IN A COUPLE HOURS. YOU KNOW...

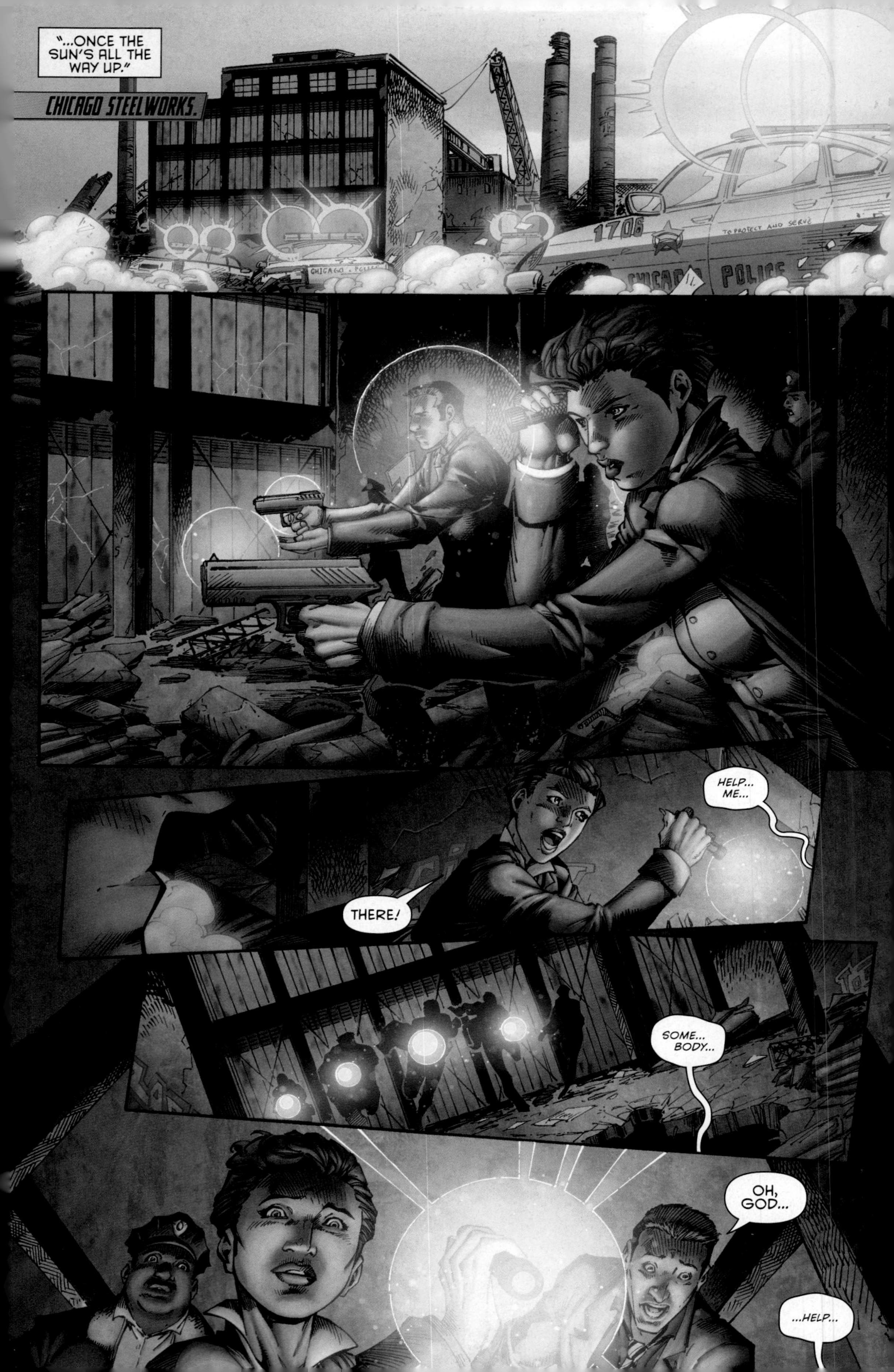
"...ONCE THE SUN'S ALL THE WAY UP."
CHICAGO STEELWORKS.
1706
TO PROTECT AND SERVE
CHICAGO POLICE
HELP... ME...
THERE!
SOME... BODY...
OH, GOD...
...HELP...

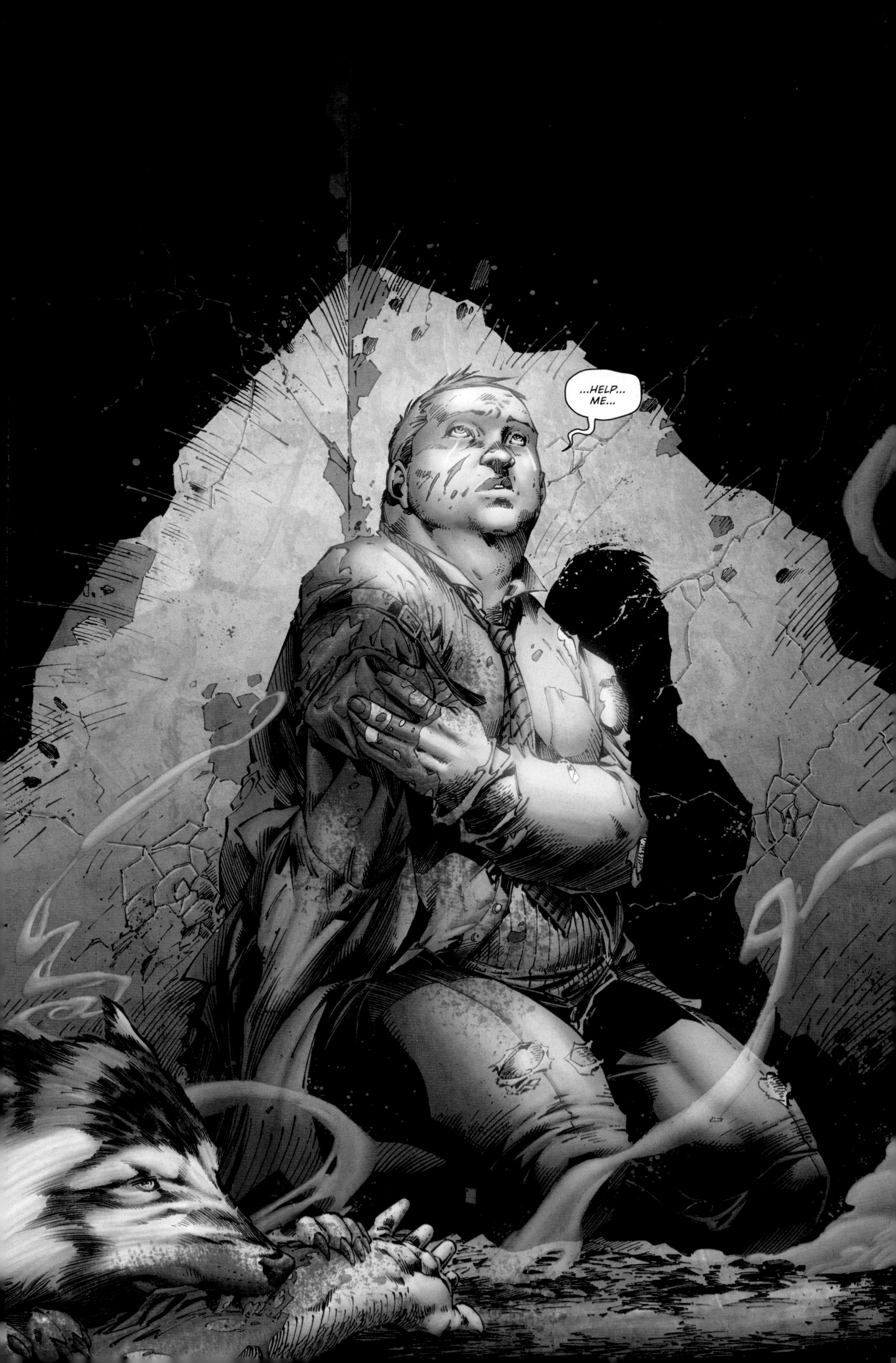
...HELP... ME...

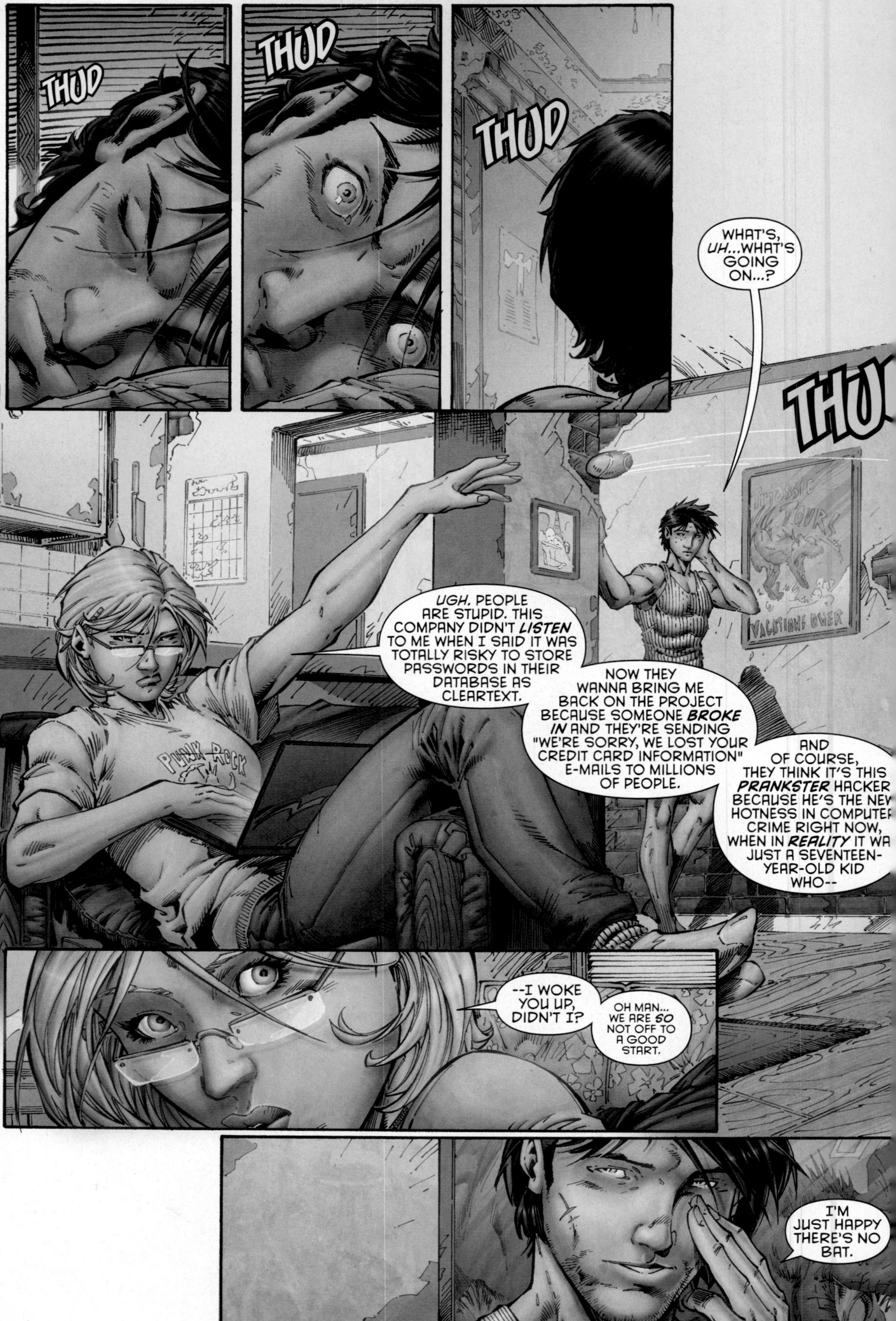
THUD
THUD
THUD
WHAT'S, UH...WHAT'S GOING ON...?
THUD
UGH. PEOPLE ARE STUPID. THIS COMPANY DIDN'T LISTEN TO ME WHEN I SAID IT WAS TOTALLY RISKY TO STORE PASSWORDS IN THEIR DATABASE AS CLEARTEXT.
NOW THEY WANNA BRING ME BACK ON THE PROJECT BECAUSE SOMEONE BROKE IN AND THEY'RE SENDING "WE'RE SORRY, WE LOST YOUR CREDIT CARD INFORMATION" E-MAILS TO MILLIONS OF PEOPLE.
AND OF COURSE, THEY THINK IT'S THIS PRANKSTER HACKER BECAUSE HE'S THE NEW HOTNESS IN COMPUTER CRIME RIGHT NOW, WHEN IN REALITY IT WA JUST A SEVENTEEN-YEAR-OLD KID WHO--
--I WOKE YOU UP, DIDN'T I?
OH MAN... WE ARE SO NOT OFF TO A GOOD START.
I'M JUST HAPPY THERE'S NO BAT.

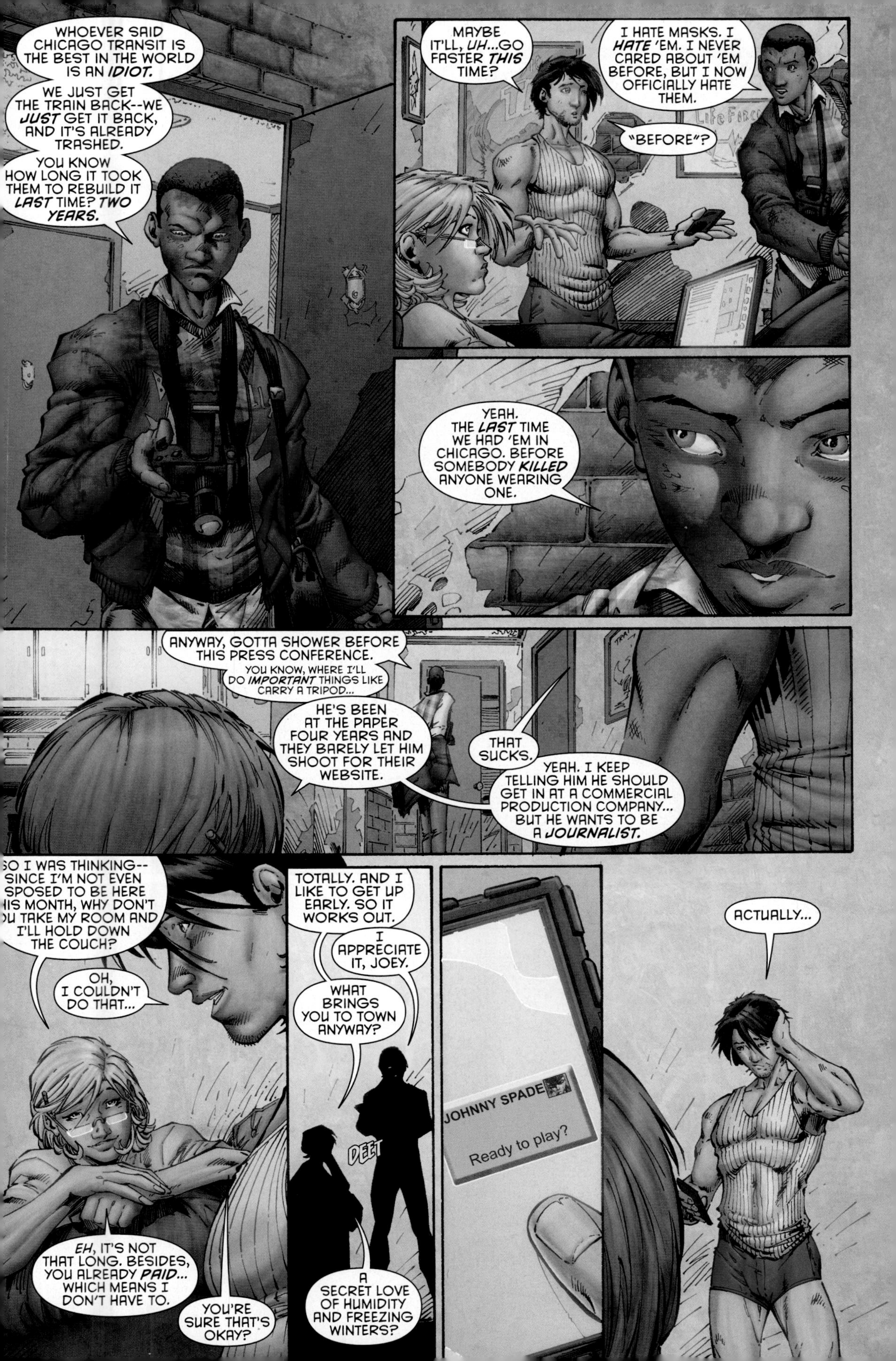
WHOEVER SAID CHICAGO TRANSIT IS THE BEST IN THE WORLD IS AN IDIOT.
WE JUST GET THE TRAIN BACK--WE JUST GET IT BACK, AND IT'S ALREADY TRASHED.
YOU KNOW HOW LONG IT TOOK THEM TO REBUILD IT LAST TIME? TWO YEARS.
MAYBE IT'LL, UH...GO FASTER THIS TIME?
I HATE MASKS. I HATE 'EM. I NEVER CARED ABOUT 'EM BEFORE, BUT I NOW OFFICIALLY HATE THEM.
"BEFORE"?
YEAH. THE LAST TIME WE HAD 'EM IN CHICAGO. BEFORE SOMEBODY KILLED ANYONE WEARING ONE.
ANYWAY, GOTTA SHOWER BEFORE THIS PRESS CONFERENCE.
YOU KNOW, WHERE I'LL DO IMPORTANT THINGS LIKE CARRY A TRIPOD...
HE'S BEEN AT THE PAPER FOUR YEARS AND THEY BARELY LET HIM SHOOT FOR THEIR WEBSITE.
THAT SUCKS.
YEAH. I KEEP TELLING HIM HE SHOULD GET IN AT A COMMERCIAL PRODUCTION COMPANY... BUT HE WANTS TO BE A JOURNALIST.
SO I WAS THINKING-- SINCE I'M NOT EVEN 'SPOSED TO BE HERE THIS MONTH, WHY DON'T YOU TAKE MY ROOM AND I'LL HOLD DOWN THE COUCH?
OH, I COULDN'T DO THAT...
EH, IT'S NOT THAT LONG. BESIDES, YOU ALREADY PAID... WHICH MEANS I DON'T HAVE TO.
YOU'RE SURE THAT'S OKAY?
TOTALLY. AND I LIKE TO GET UP EARLY. SO IT WORKS OUT.
I APPRECIATE IT, JOEY.
WHAT BRINGS YOU TO TOWN ANYWAY?
DEET
A SECRET LOVE OF HUMIDITY AND FREEZING WINTERS?
JOHNNY SPADE
Ready to play?
ACTUALLY...

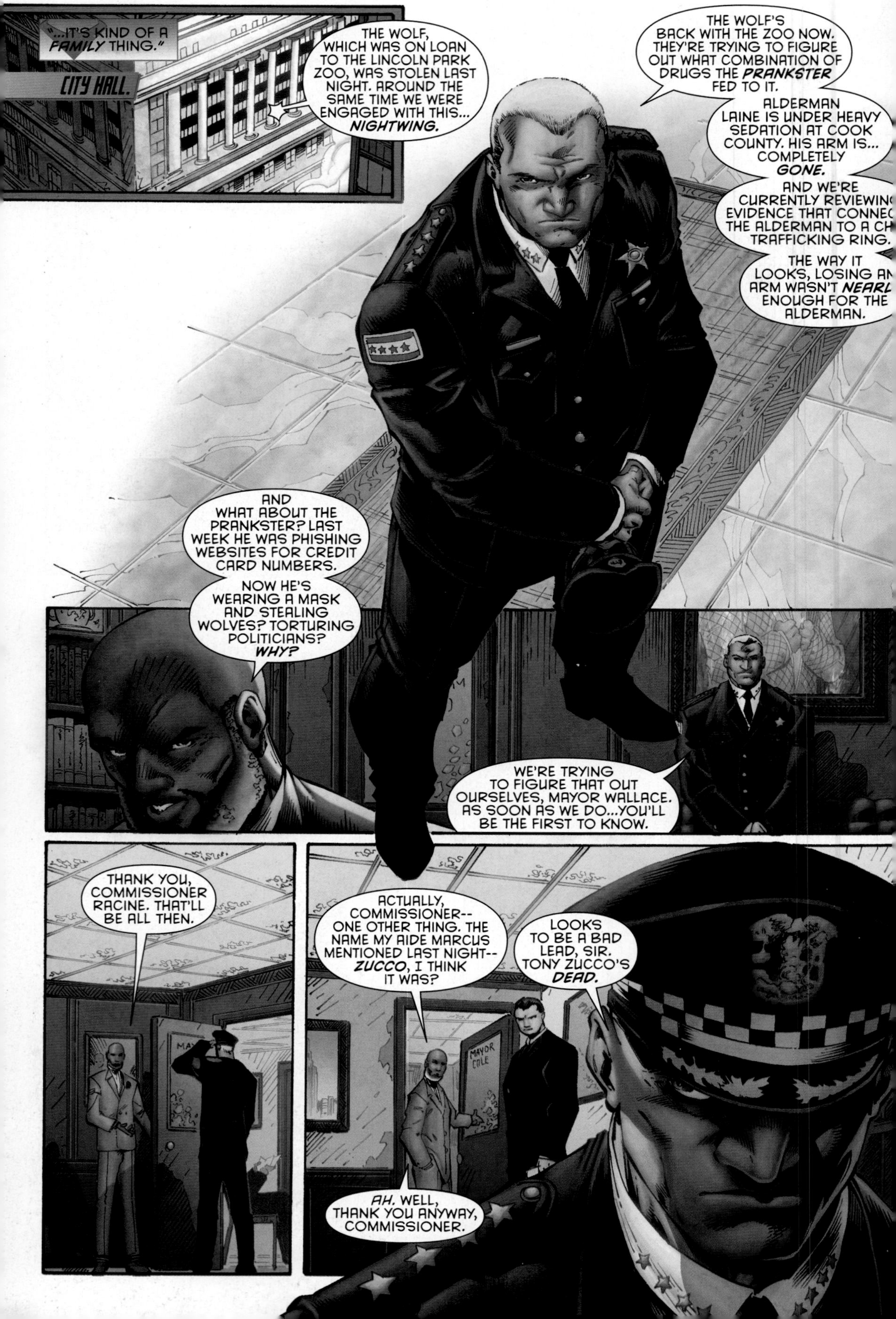
"...IT'S KIND OF A *FAMILY* THING."
CITY HALL.
THE WOLF, WHICH WAS ON LOAN TO THE LINCOLN PARK ZOO, WAS STOLEN LAST NIGHT. AROUND THE SAME TIME WE WERE ENGAGED WITH THIS... *NIGHTWING.*
THE WOLF'S BACK WITH THE ZOO NOW. THEY'RE TRYING TO FIGURE OUT WHAT COMBINATION OF DRUGS THE *PRANKSTER* FED TO IT.
ALDERMAN LAINE IS UNDER HEAVY SEDATION AT COOK COUNTY. HIS ARM IS... COMPLETELY *GONE.*
AND WE'RE CURRENTLY REVIEWIN EVIDENCE THAT CONNEC THE ALDERMAN TO A CH TRAFFICKING RING.
THE WAY IT LOOKS, LOSING AN ARM WASN'T *NEARL* ENOUGH FOR THE ALDERMAN.
AND WHAT ABOUT THE PRANKSTER? LAST WEEK HE WAS PHISHING WEBSITES FOR CREDIT CARD NUMBERS.
NOW HE'S WEARING A MASK AND STEALING WOLVES? TORTURING POLITICIANS? *WHY?*
WE'RE TRYING TO FIGURE THAT OUT OURSELVES, MAYOR WALLACE. AS SOON AS WE DO...YOU'LL BE THE FIRST TO KNOW.
THANK YOU, COMMISSIONER RACINE. THAT'LL BE ALL THEN.
ACTUALLY, COMMISSIONER-- ONE OTHER THING. THE NAME MY AIDE MARCUS MENTIONED LAST NIGHT-- *ZUCCO*, I THINK IT WAS?
LOOKS TO BE A BAD LEAD, SIR. TONY ZUCCO'S *DEAD.*
AH. WELL, THANK YOU ANYWAY, COMMISSIONER.
MAYOR COLE

HAVE YOU SLEPT? YOU LOOK *TERRIBLE.*

I GOT A FEW HOURS. BUT THIS WHOLE THING...

IT'LL BE *FINE.*

YOU HEARD RACINE--EVEN *HE* COULDN'T FIND ANYTHING. YOU'RE STILL *DEAD,* TONY.

I TOLD YOU, STOP *CALLING* ME THAT.

TONY... THIS WHOLE SITUATION IS *HARD,* I UNDERSTAND THAT. BUT THE LAST THING WE SHOULD DO IS LEAP TO ANY--

--WHAT ARE YOU CARRYING?

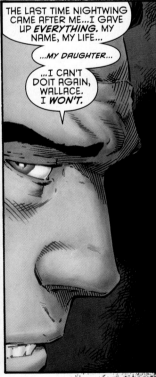

THE LAST TIME NIGHTWING CAME AFTER ME...I GAVE UP *EVERYTHING.* MY NAME, MY LIFE...

...MY DAUGHTER...

...I CAN'T DO IT AGAIN, WALLACE. I *WON'T.*

IF YOU'RE *THAT* WORRIED, THEN TAKE NANCY AND BRIAN AND GET AWAY FOR A FEW WEEKS. CLEAR YOUR HEAD.

BY THE TIME YOU COME BACK, I PROMISE...

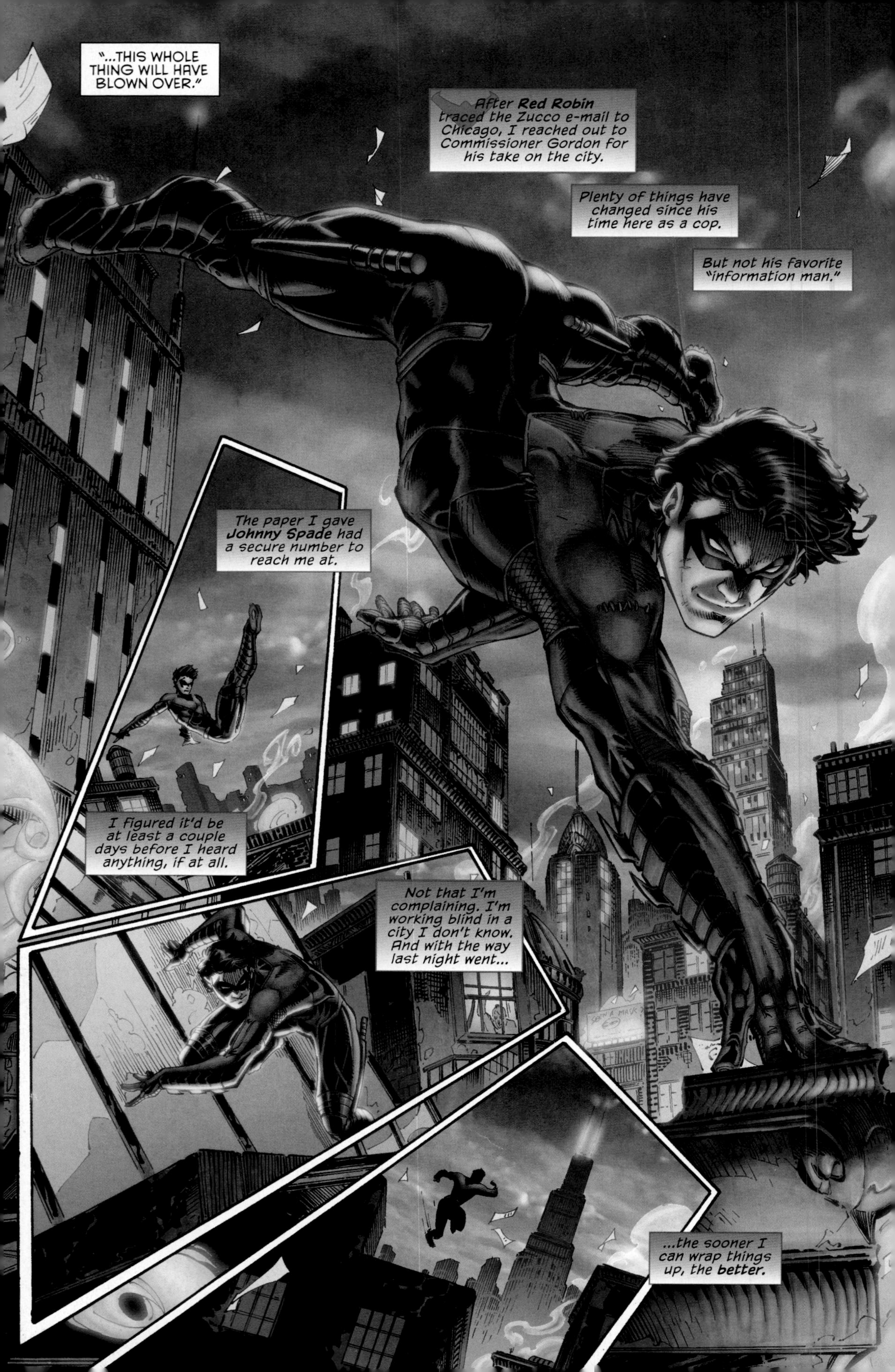
"...THIS WHOLE THING WILL HAVE BLOWN OVER."
After **Red Robin** traced the Zucco e-mail to Chicago, I reached out to Commissioner Gordon for his take on the city.
Plenty of things have changed since his time here as a cop.
But not his favorite "information man."
The paper I gave **Johnny Spade** had a secure number to reach me at.
I figured it'd be at least a couple days before I heard anything, if at all.
Not that I'm complaining. I'm working blind in a city I don't know. And with the way last night went...
...the sooner I can wrap things up, the **better**.

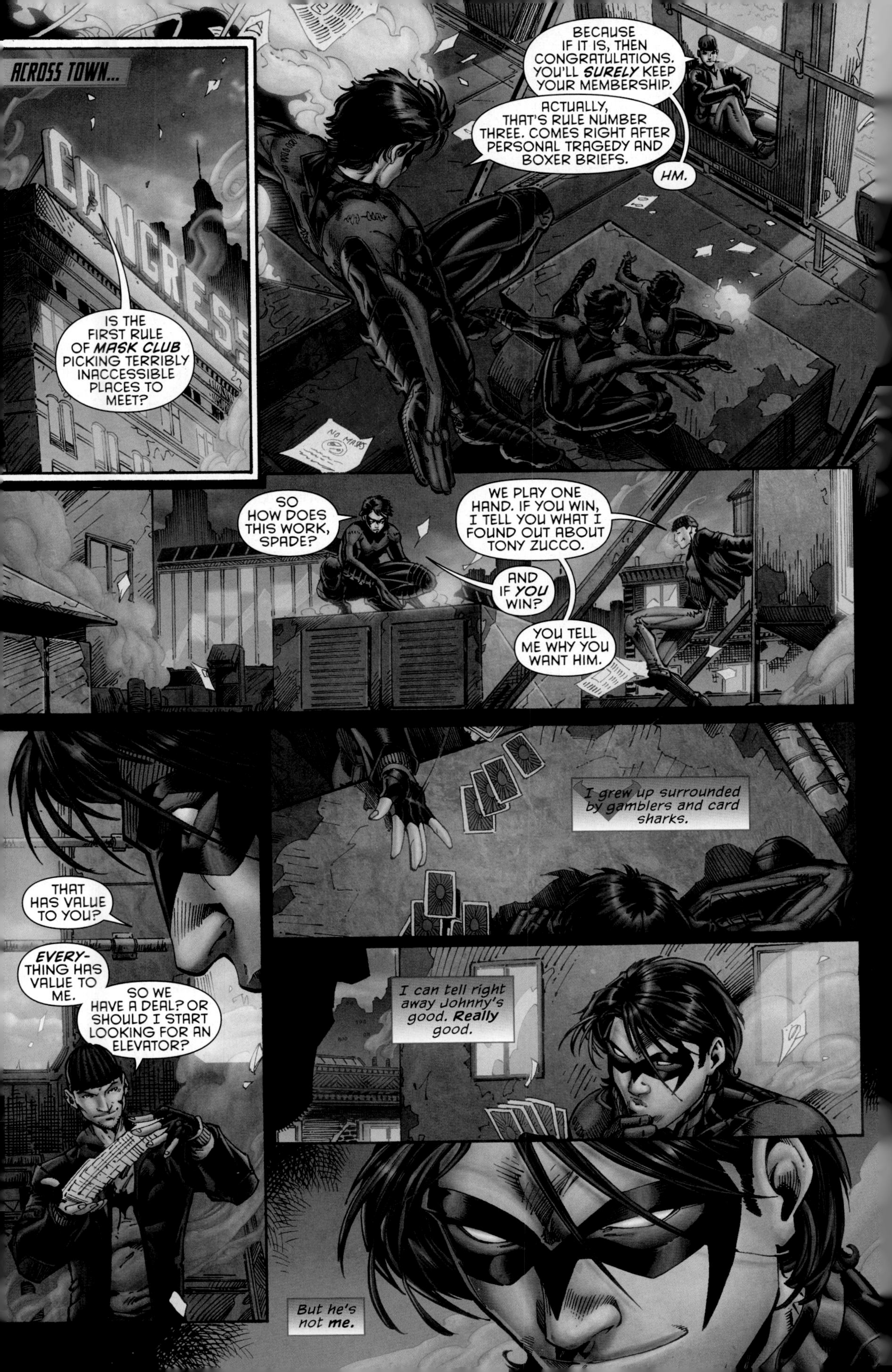
ACROSS TOWN...
CONGRESS
IS THE FIRST RULE OF MASK CLUB PICKING TERRIBLY INACCESSIBLE PLACES TO MEET?
BECAUSE IF IT IS, THEN CONGRATULATIONS. YOU'LL SURELY KEEP YOUR MEMBERSHIP.
ACTUALLY, THAT'S RULE NUMBER THREE. COMES RIGHT AFTER PERSONAL TRAGEDY AND BOXER BRIEFS.
HM.
NO MASKS
SO HOW DOES THIS WORK, SPADE?
WE PLAY ONE HAND. IF YOU WIN, I TELL YOU WHAT I FOUND OUT ABOUT TONY ZUCCO.
AND IF YOU WIN?
YOU TELL ME WHY YOU WANT HIM.
THAT HAS VALUE TO YOU?
EVERYTHING HAS VALUE TO ME.
SO WE HAVE A DEAL? OR SHOULD I START LOOKING FOR AN ELEVATOR?
I grew up surrounded by gamblers and card sharks.
I can tell right away Johnny's good. Really good.
But he's not me.

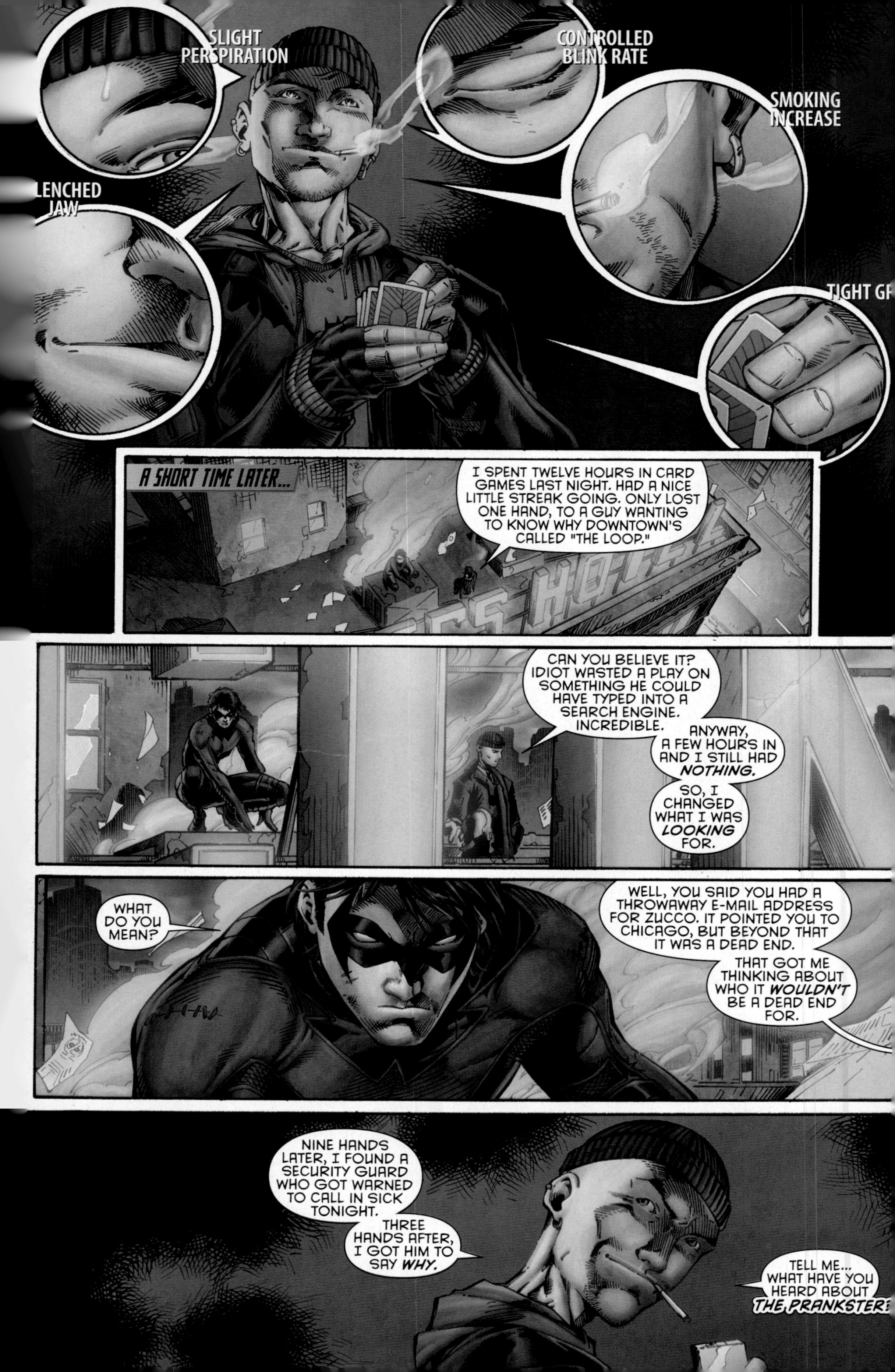
SLIGHT PERSPIRATION
CONTROLLED BLINK RATE
SMOKING INCREASE
LENCHED JAW
TIGHT GR
A SHORT TIME LATER...
I SPENT TWELVE HOURS IN CARD GAMES LAST NIGHT. HAD A NICE LITTLE STREAK GOING. ONLY LOST ONE HAND, TO A GUY WANTING TO KNOW WHY DOWNTOWN'S CALLED "THE LOOP."
CAN YOU BELIEVE IT? IDIOT WASTED A PLAY ON SOMETHING HE COULD HAVE TYPED INTO A SEARCH ENGINE. INCREDIBLE.
ANYWAY, A FEW HOURS IN AND I STILL HAD NOTHING.
SO, I CHANGED WHAT I WAS LOOKING FOR.
WHAT DO YOU MEAN?
WELL, YOU SAID YOU HAD A THROWAWAY E-MAIL ADDRESS FOR ZUCCO. IT POINTED YOU TO CHICAGO, BUT BEYOND THAT IT WAS A DEAD END.
THAT GOT ME THINKING ABOUT WHO IT WOULDN'T BE A DEAD END FOR.
NINE HANDS LATER, I FOUND A SECURITY GUARD WHO GOT WARNED TO CALL IN SICK TONIGHT.
THREE HANDS AFTER, I GOT HIM TO SAY WHY.
TELL ME... WHAT HAVE YOU HEARD ABOUT THE PRANKSTER?

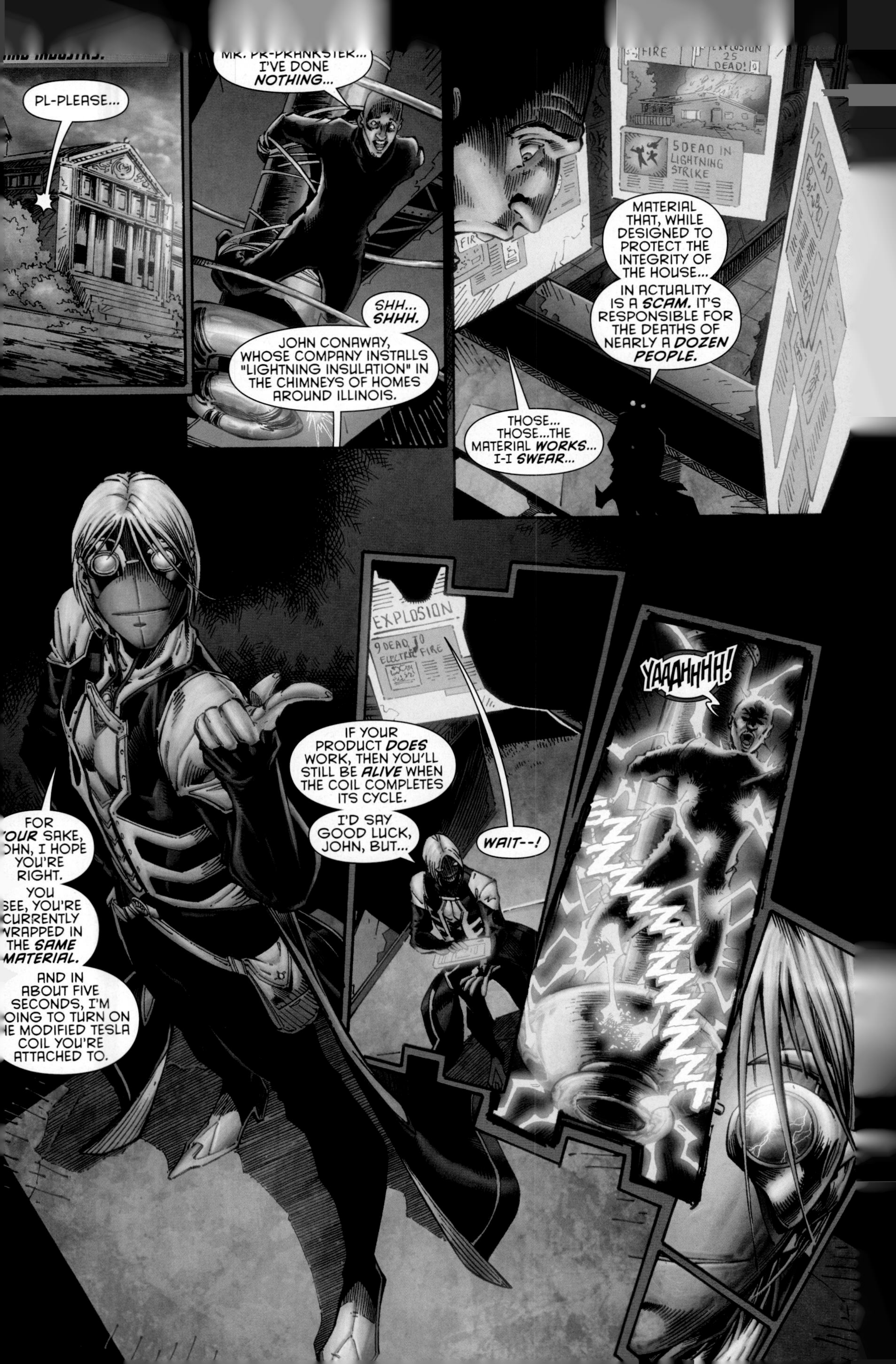
PL-PLEASE...
MR. PR-PRANKSTER... I'VE DONE NOTHING...
SHH... SHHH.
JOHN CONAWAY, WHOSE COMPANY INSTALLS "LIGHTNING INSULATION" IN THE CHIMNEYS OF HOMES AROUND ILLINOIS.
FIRE
EXPLOSION 25 DEAD!
5 DEAD IN LIGHTNING STRIKE
17 DEAD
MATERIAL THAT, WHILE DESIGNED TO PROTECT THE INTEGRITY OF THE HOUSE...
IN ACTUALITY IS A SCAM. IT'S RESPONSIBLE FOR THE DEATHS OF NEARLY A DOZEN PEOPLE.
THOSE... THOSE...THE MATERIAL WORKS... I-I SWEAR...
FOR OUR SAKE, OHN, I HOPE YOU'RE RIGHT.
YOU EE, YOU'RE CURRENTLY VRAPPED IN THE SAME MATERIAL.
AND IN ABOUT FIVE SECONDS, I'M OING TO TURN ON E MODIFIED TESLA COIL YOU'RE ATTACHED TO.
EXPLOSION
9 DEAD TO ELECTRIC FIRE
IF YOUR PRODUCT DOES WORK, THEN YOU'LL STILL BE ALIVE WHEN THE COIL COMPLETES ITS CYCLE.
I'D SAY GOOD LUCK, JOHN, BUT...
WAIT--!
YAAAHHHH!
ZZZZZZZZZZZZT

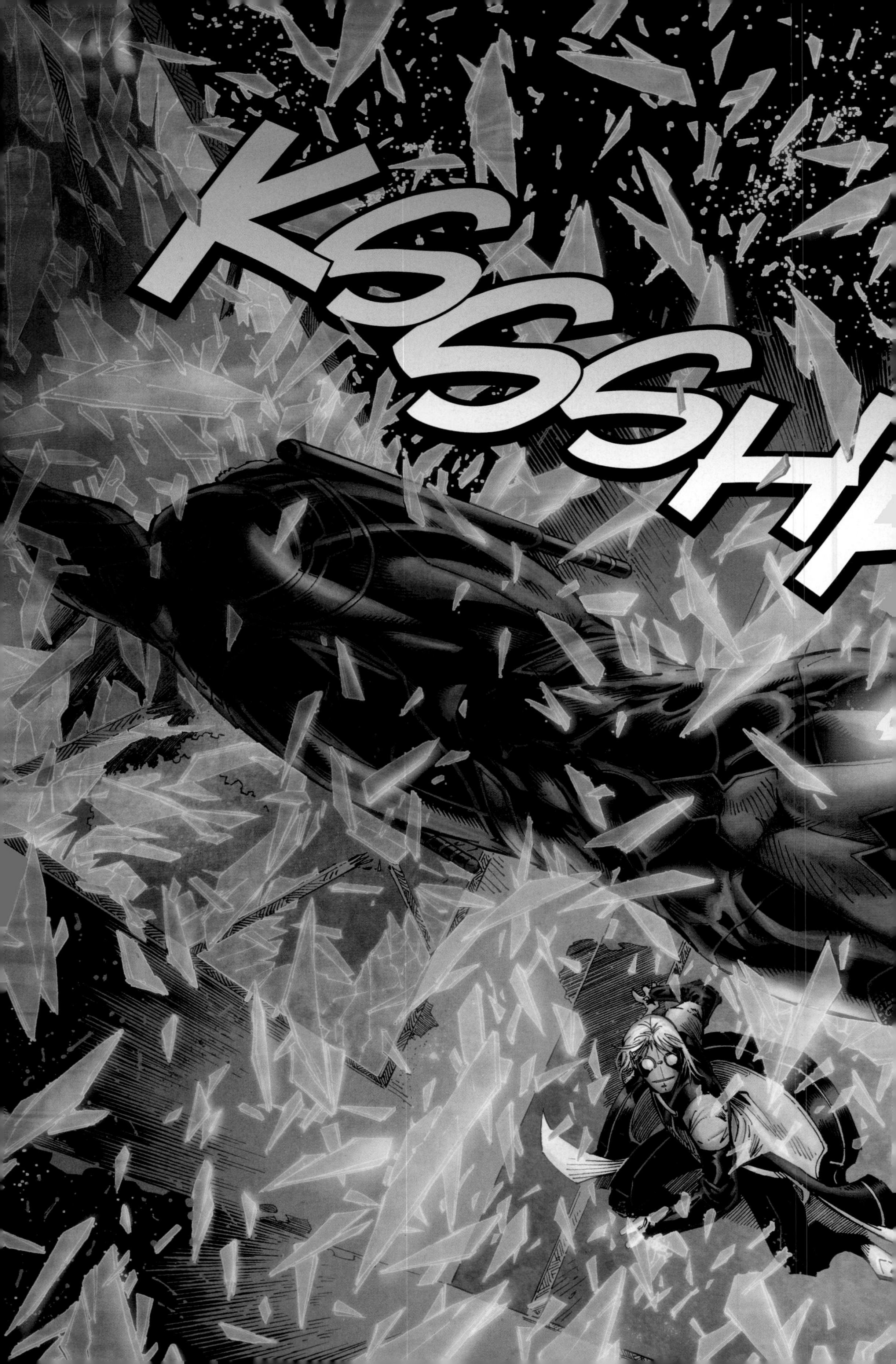
KSSSH

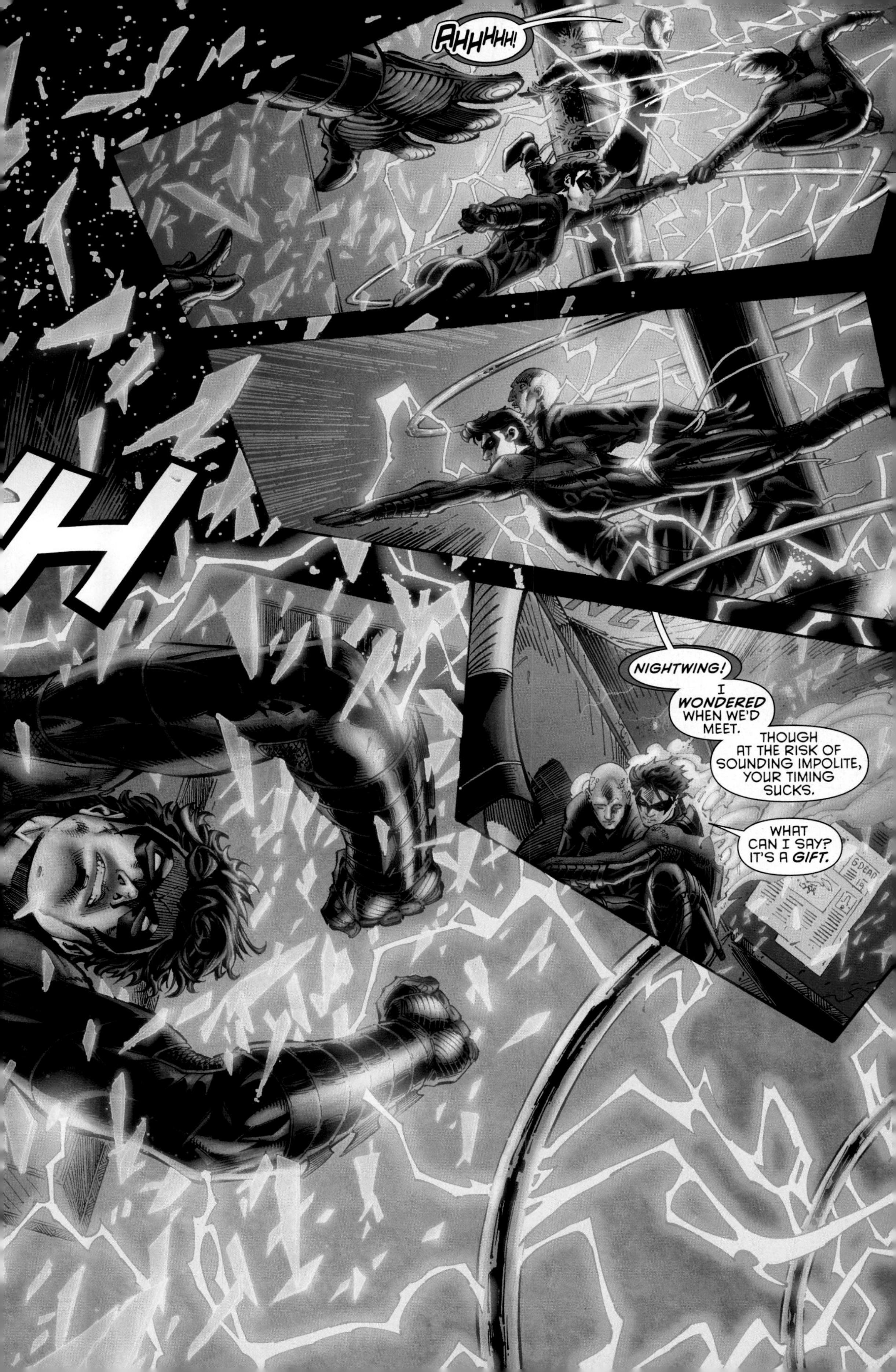

AHHHHH!
H
NIGHTWING!
I WONDERED WHEN WE'D MEET.
THOUGH AT THE RISK OF SOUNDING IMPOLITE, YOUR TIMING SUCKS.
WHAT CAN I SAY? IT'S A GIFT.

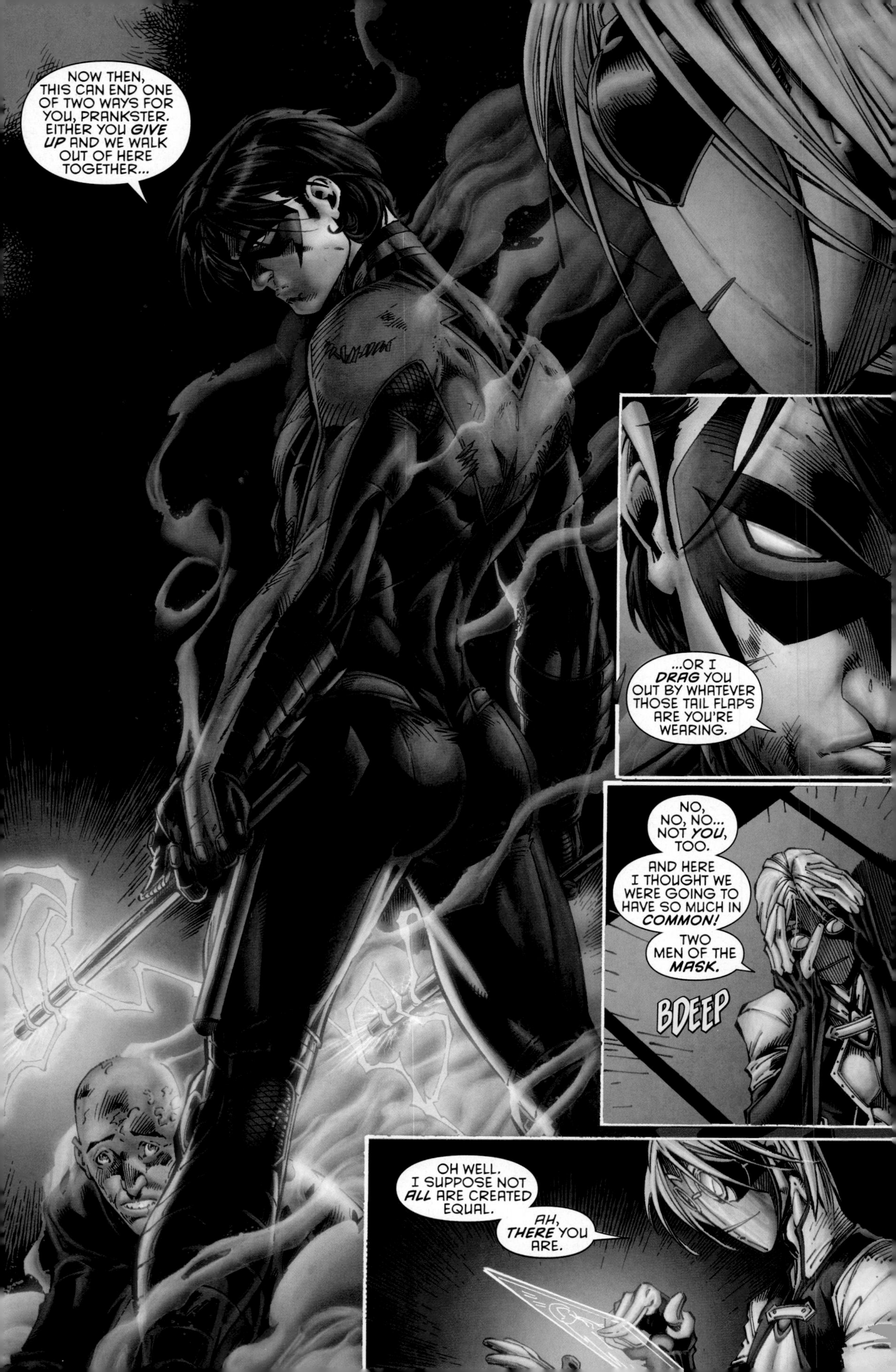
NOW THEN, THIS CAN END ONE OF TWO WAYS FOR YOU, PRANKSTER. EITHER YOU GIVE UP AND WE WALK OUT OF HERE TOGETHER...
...OR I DRAG YOU OUT BY WHATEVER THOSE TAIL FLAPS ARE YOU'RE WEARING.
NO, NO, NO... NOT YOU, TOO.
AND HERE I THOUGHT WE WERE GOING TO HAVE SO MUCH IN COMMON!
TWO MEN OF THE MASK.
BDEEP
OH WELL. I SUPPOSE NOT ALL ARE CREATED EQUAL.
AH, THERE YOU ARE.

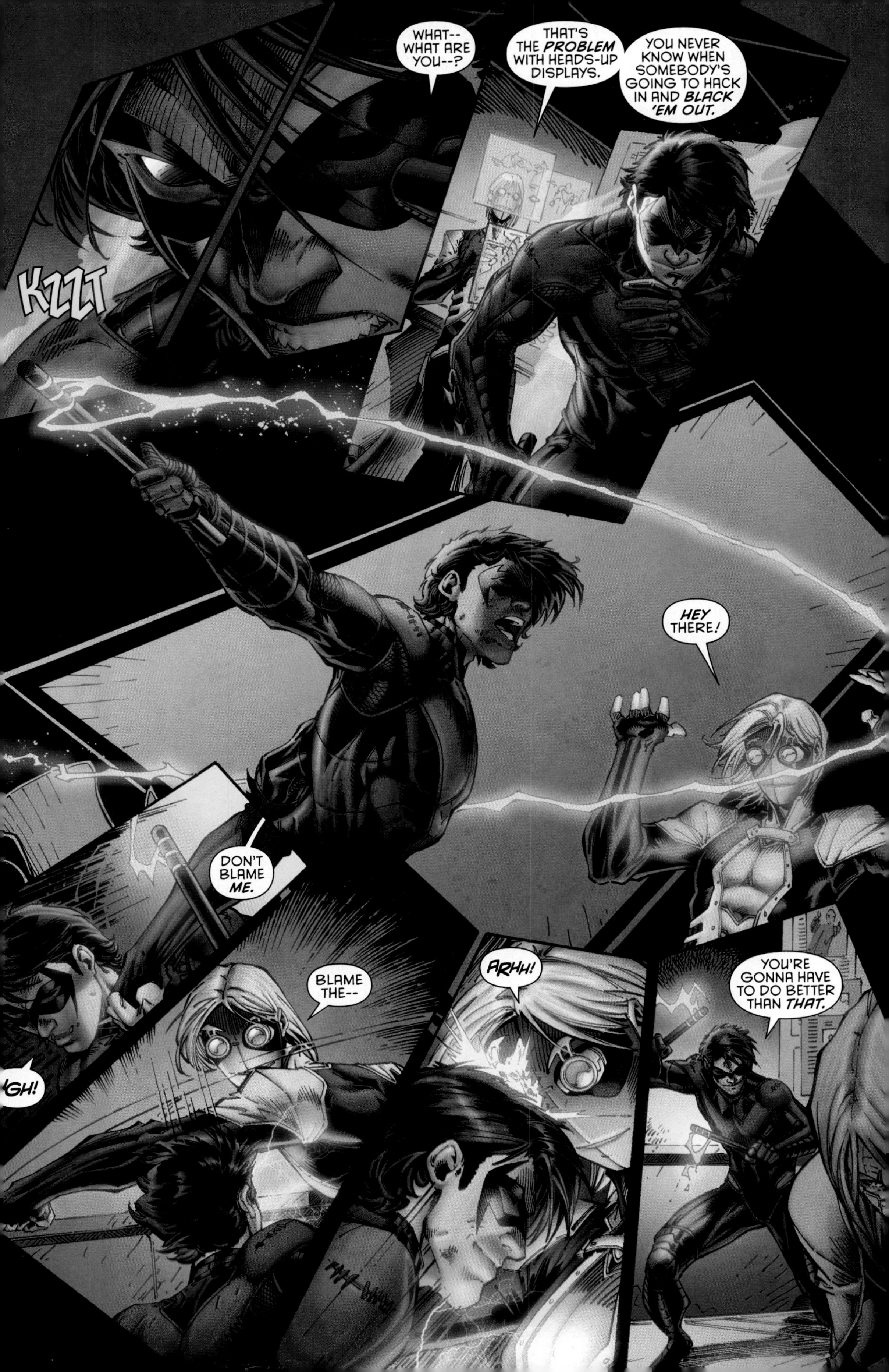

WHAT-- WHAT ARE YOU--?
THAT'S THE PROBLEM WITH HEADS-UP DISPLAYS.
YOU NEVER KNOW WHEN SOMEBODY'S GOING TO HACK IN AND BLACK 'EM OUT.
KZZZT
HEY THERE!
DON'T BLAME ME.
BLAME THE--
ARHH!
YOU'RE GONNA HAVE TO DO BETTER THAN THAT.
GH!

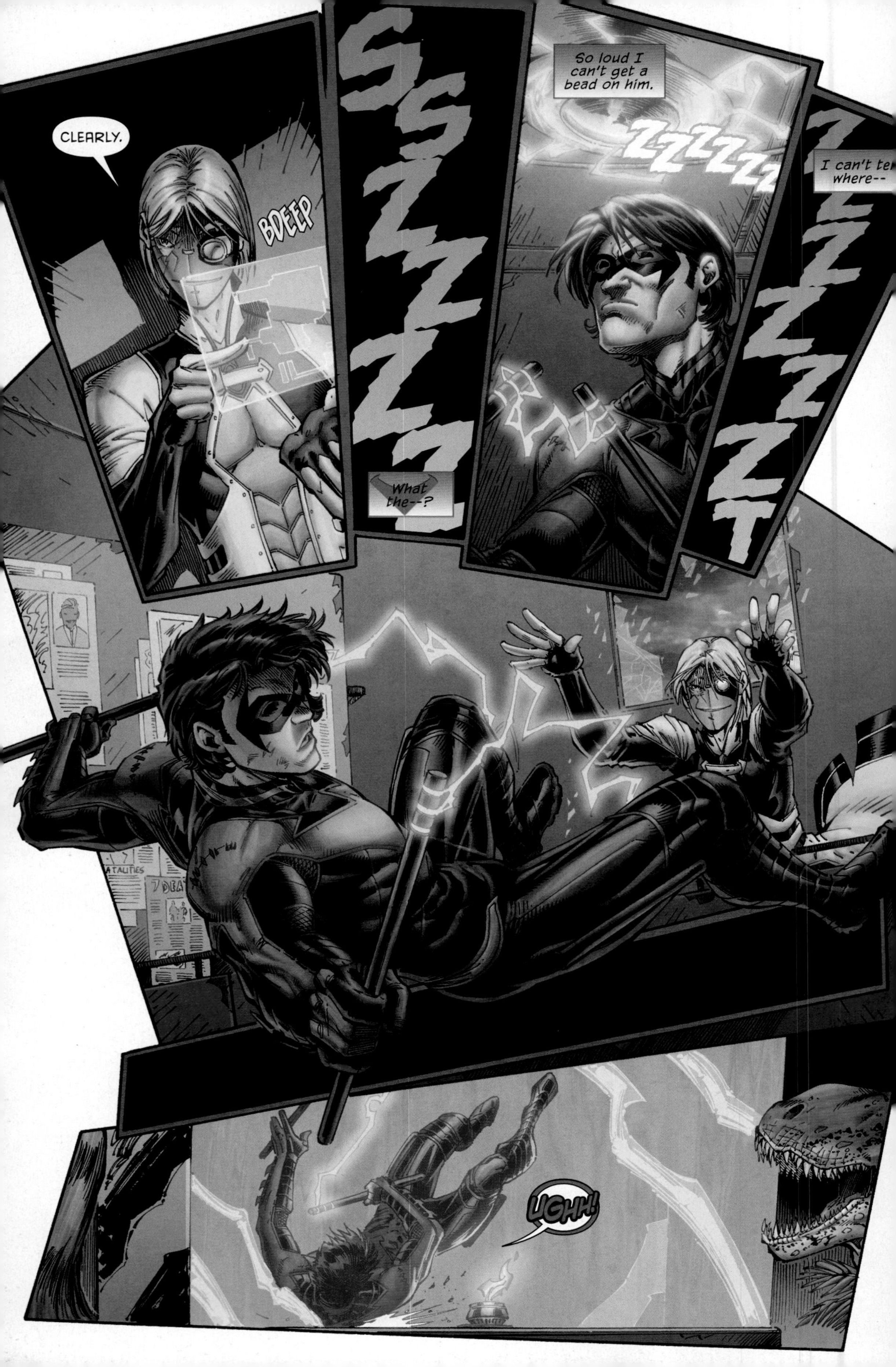
CLEARLY.
BDEEP
SSZZZZ
What the--?
So loud I can't get a bead on him.
ZZZZZZ
I can't te
where--
ZZZZZT
UGHH!

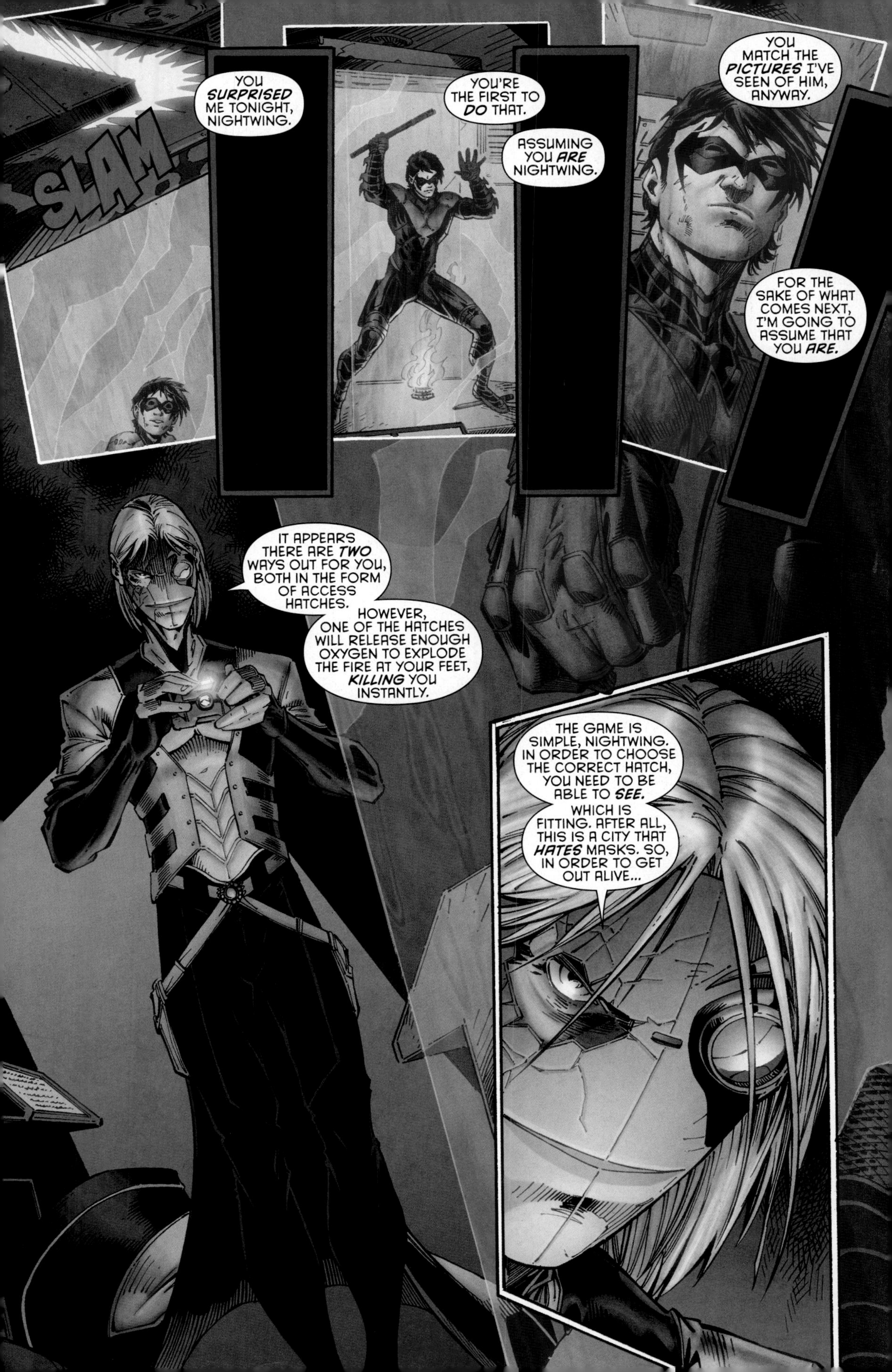
SLAM!
YOU SURPRISED ME TONIGHT, NIGHTWING.
YOU'RE THE FIRST TO DO THAT.
ASSUMING YOU ARE NIGHTWING.
YOU MATCH THE PICTURES I'VE SEEN OF HIM, ANYWAY.
FOR THE SAKE OF WHAT COMES NEXT, I'M GOING TO ASSUME THAT YOU ARE.
IT APPEARS THERE ARE TWO WAYS OUT FOR YOU, BOTH IN THE FORM OF ACCESS HATCHES.
HOWEVER, ONE OF THE HATCHES WILL RELEASE ENOUGH OXYGEN TO EXPLODE THE FIRE AT YOUR FEET, KILLING YOU INSTANTLY.
THE GAME IS SIMPLE, NIGHTWING. IN ORDER TO CHOOSE THE CORRECT HATCH, YOU NEED TO BE ABLE TO SEE.
WHICH IS FITTING. AFTER ALL, THIS IS A CITY THAT HATES MASKS. SO, IN ORDER TO GET OUT ALIVE...

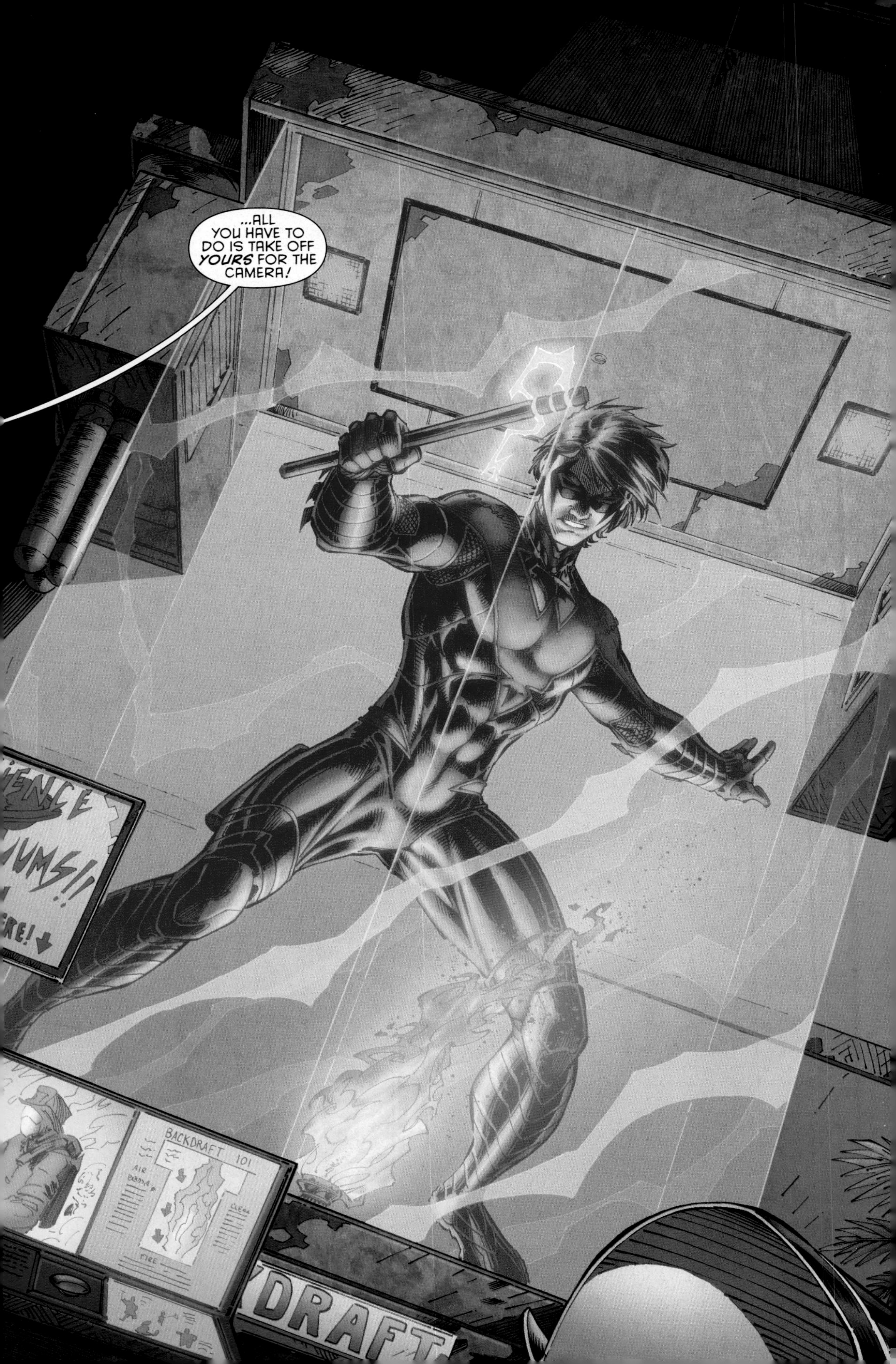
...ALL YOU HAVE TO DO IS TAKE OFF *YOURS* FOR THE CAMERA!
BACKDRAFT 101
AIR
FIRE
DRAFT

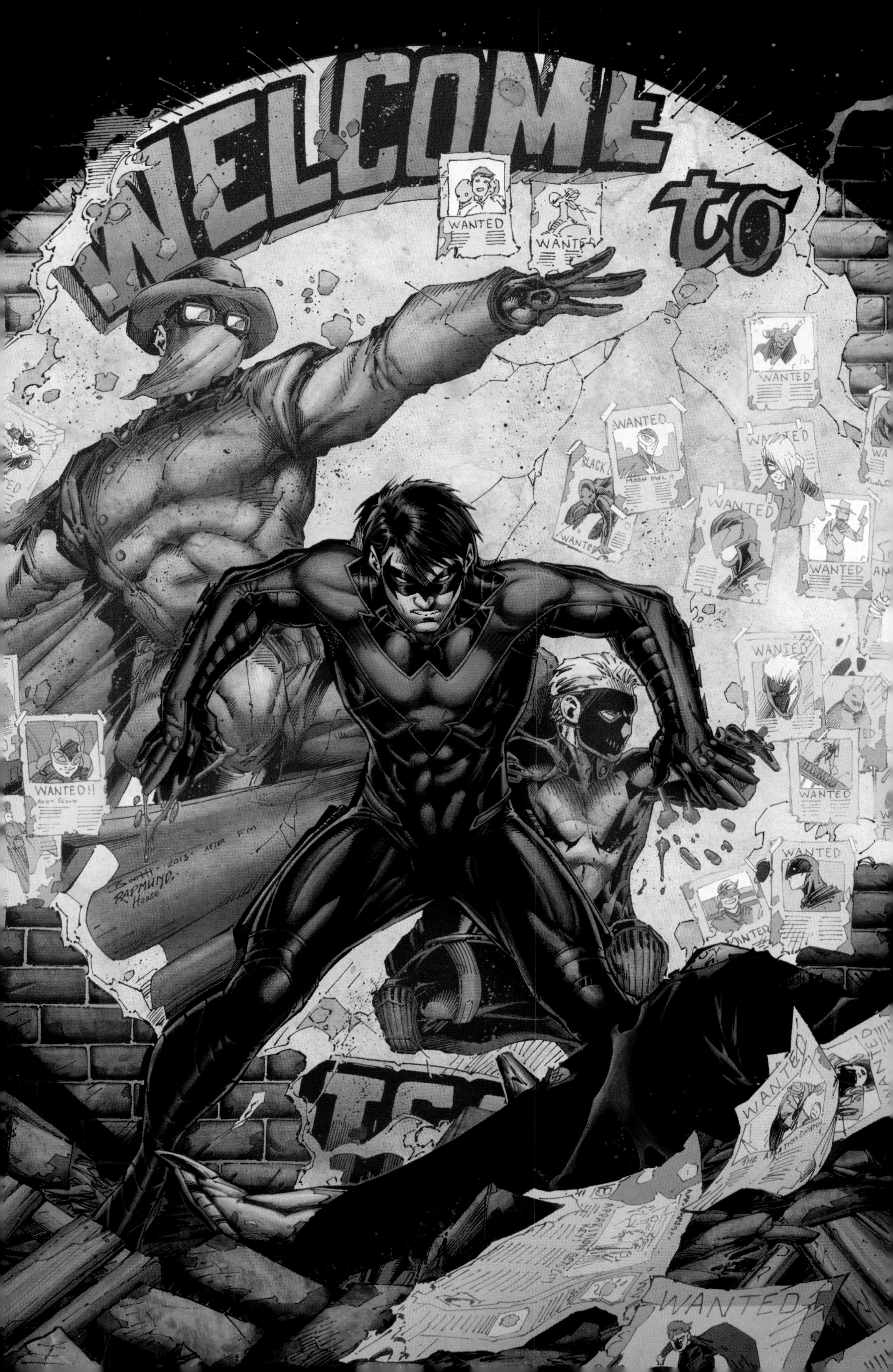
WELCOME
to
WANTED
WANTED
WANTED
MOON OWL
BLACK
WANTED
WANTED
WANTED
WANTED
WANTED
WANTED
WANTED!!
WANTED
WANTED
WANTED
WANTED
Booth 2013 AFTER FM
RAPMUND
House

KYLE HIGGINS writer BRETT BOOTH penciller NORM RAPMUND inker cover art by BRETT BOOTH, NORM RAPMUND & ANDREW DALHOUSE

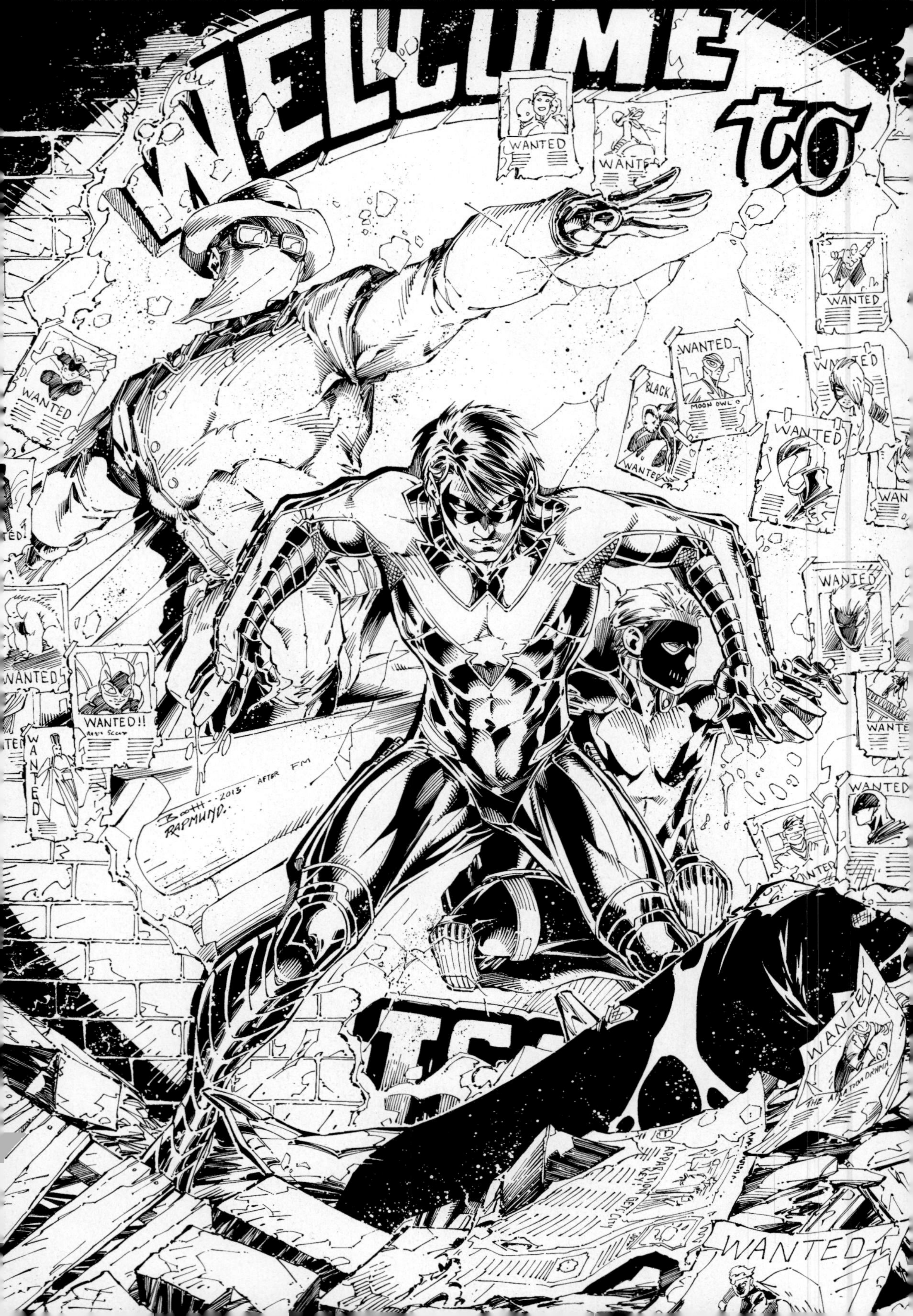
WELCOME
to
WANTED
WANTED
WANTED
WANTED
BLACK
MOON OWL
WANTED
WANTED
WANTED
WANTED!!
WANTED
WANTED
WANTED
BOOTH - 2013 - AFTER FM
RAPMUND.
WANTED
THE APPARITION
APPARITION
WANTED

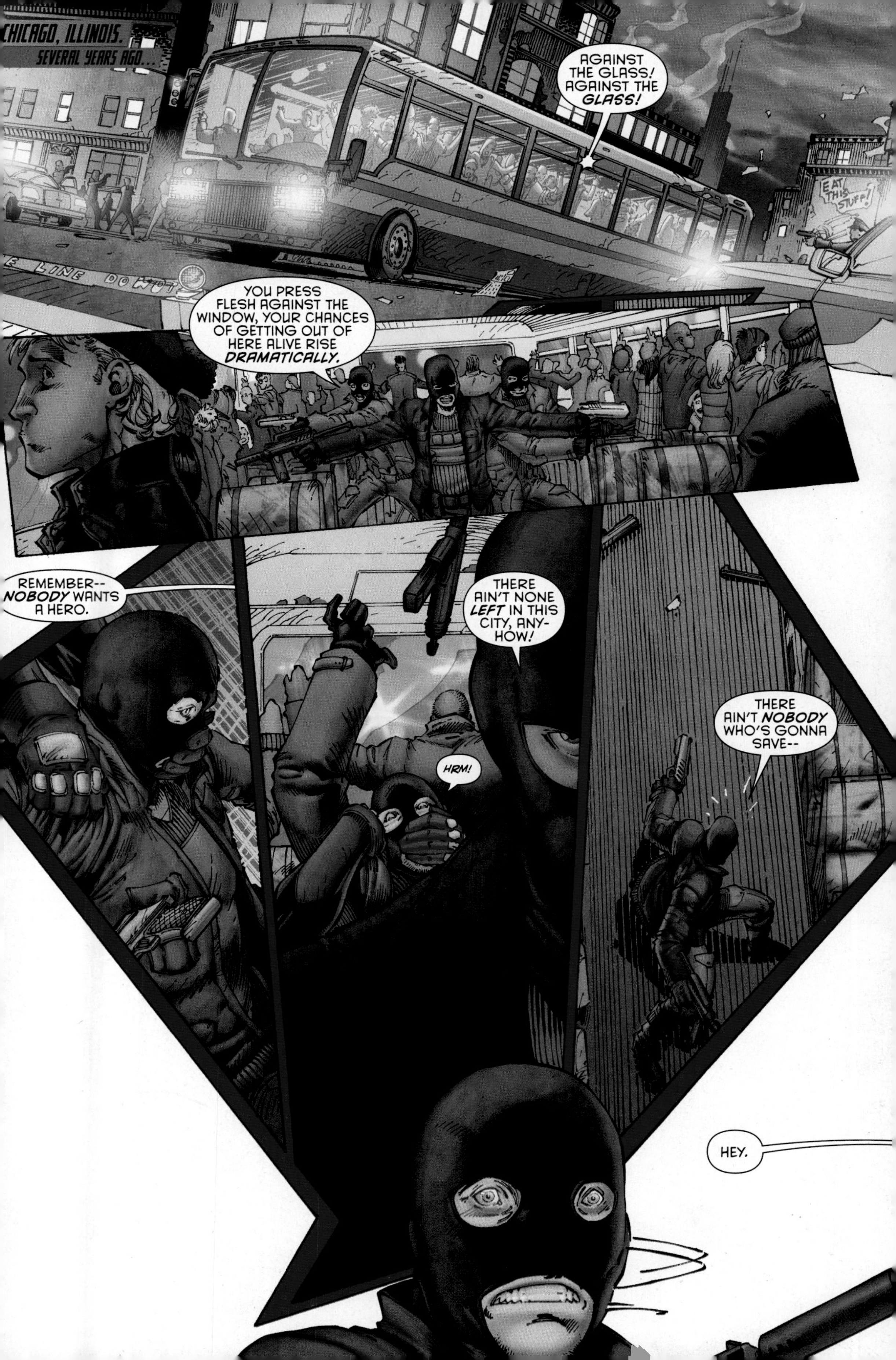
CHICAGO, ILLINOIS.
SEVERAL YEARS AGO...
AGAINST THE GLASS! AGAINST THE GLASS!
EAT THIS STUFF!
YOU PRESS FLESH AGAINST THE WINDOW, YOUR CHANCES OF GETTING OUT OF HERE ALIVE RISE DRAMATICALLY.
REMEMBER-- NOBODY WANTS A HERO.
THERE AIN'T NONE LEFT IN THIS CITY, ANY-HOW!
HRM!
THERE AIN'T NOBODY WHO'S GONNA SAVE--
HEY.

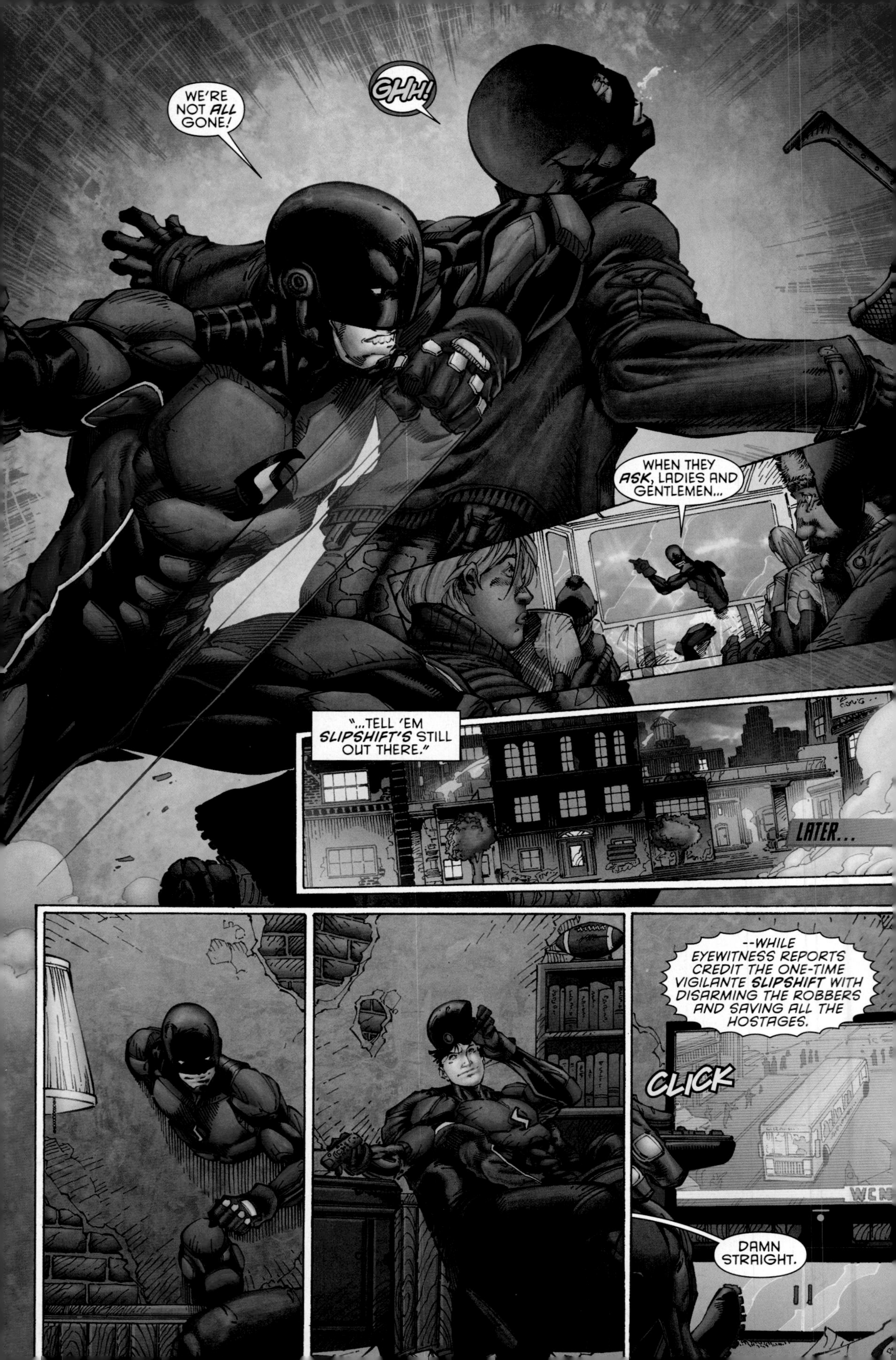
WE'RE NOT ALL GONE!
GHH!
WHEN THEY ASK, LADIES AND GENTLEMEN...
"...TELL 'EM SLIPSHIFT'S STILL OUT THERE."
LATER...
--WHILE EYEWITNESS REPORTS CREDIT THE ONE-TIME VIGILANTE SLIPSHIFT WITH DISARMING THE ROBBERS AND SAVING ALL THE HOSTAGES.
CLICK
DAMN STRAIGHT.

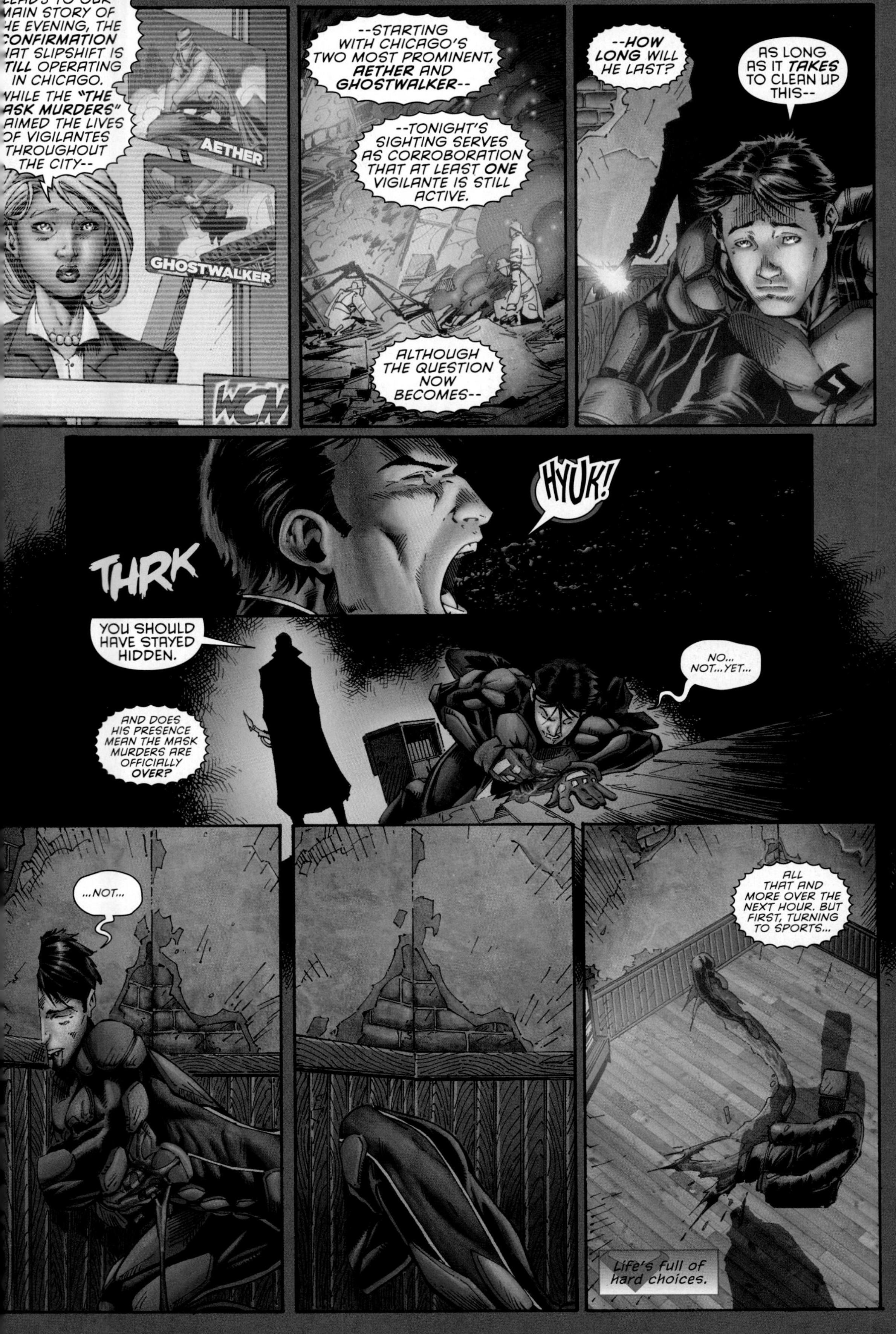
WHICH LEADS TO OUR MAIN STORY OF HE EVENING, THE CONFIRMATION HAT SLIPSHIFT IS TILL OPERATING IN CHICAGO. WHILE THE "THE ASK MURDERS" AIMED THE LIVES OF VIGILANTES THROUGHOUT THE CITY--
AETHER
GHOSTWALKER
--STARTING WITH CHICAGO'S TWO MOST PROMINENT, AETHER AND GHOSTWALKER--
--TONIGHT'S SIGHTING SERVES AS CORROBORATION THAT AT LEAST ONE VIGILANTE IS STILL ACTIVE.
ALTHOUGH THE QUESTION NOW BECOMES--
--HOW LONG WILL HE LAST?
AS LONG AS IT TAKES TO CLEAN UP THIS--
HYUK!
THRK
YOU SHOULD HAVE STAYED HIDDEN.
NO... NOT...YET...
AND DOES HIS PRESENCE MEAN THE MASK MURDERS ARE OFFICIALLY OVER?
...NOT...
ALL THAT AND MORE OVER THE NEXT HOUR. BUT FIRST, TURNING TO SPORTS...
Life's full of hard choices.

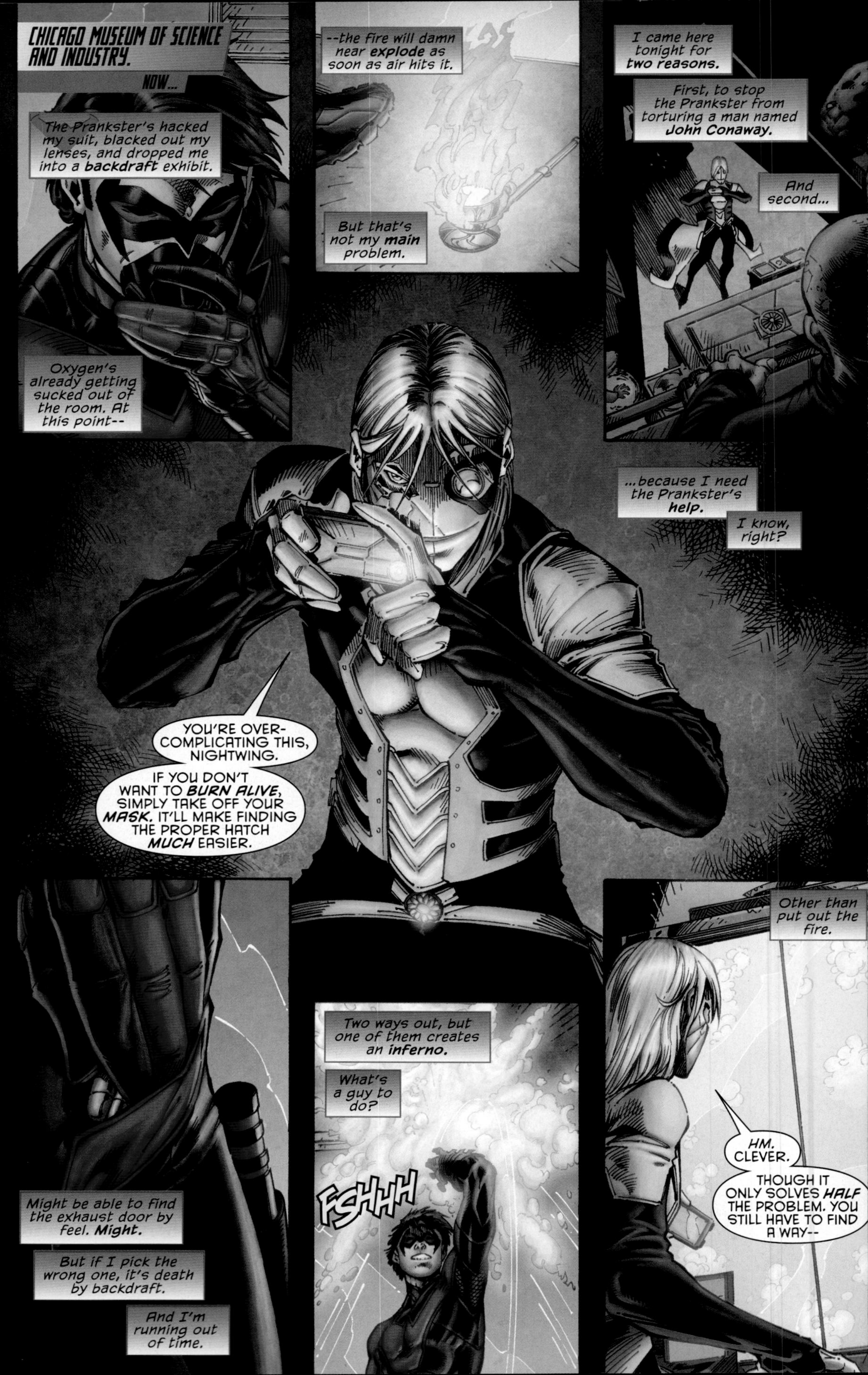
CHICAGO MUSEUM OF SCIENCE AND INDUSTRY.
NOW...
The Prankster's hacked my suit, blacked out my lenses, and dropped me into a backdraft exhibit.
Oxygen's already getting sucked out of the room. At this point--
--the fire will damn near explode as soon as air hits it.
But that's not my main problem.
I came here tonight for two reasons.
First, to stop the Prankster from torturing a man named John Conaway.
And second...
...because I need the Prankster's help.
I know, right?
YOU'RE OVER-COMPLICATING THIS, NIGHTWING.
IF YOU DON'T WANT TO BURN ALIVE, SIMPLY TAKE OFF YOUR MASK. IT'LL MAKE FINDING THE PROPER HATCH MUCH EASIER.
Might be able to find the exhaust door by feel. Might.
But if I pick the wrong one, it's death by backdraft.
And I'm running out of time.
Two ways out, but one of them creates an inferno.
What's a guy to do?
FSHHH
Other than put out the fire.
HM. CLEVER.
THOUGH IT ONLY SOLVES HALF THE PROBLEM. YOU STILL HAVE TO FIND A WAY--

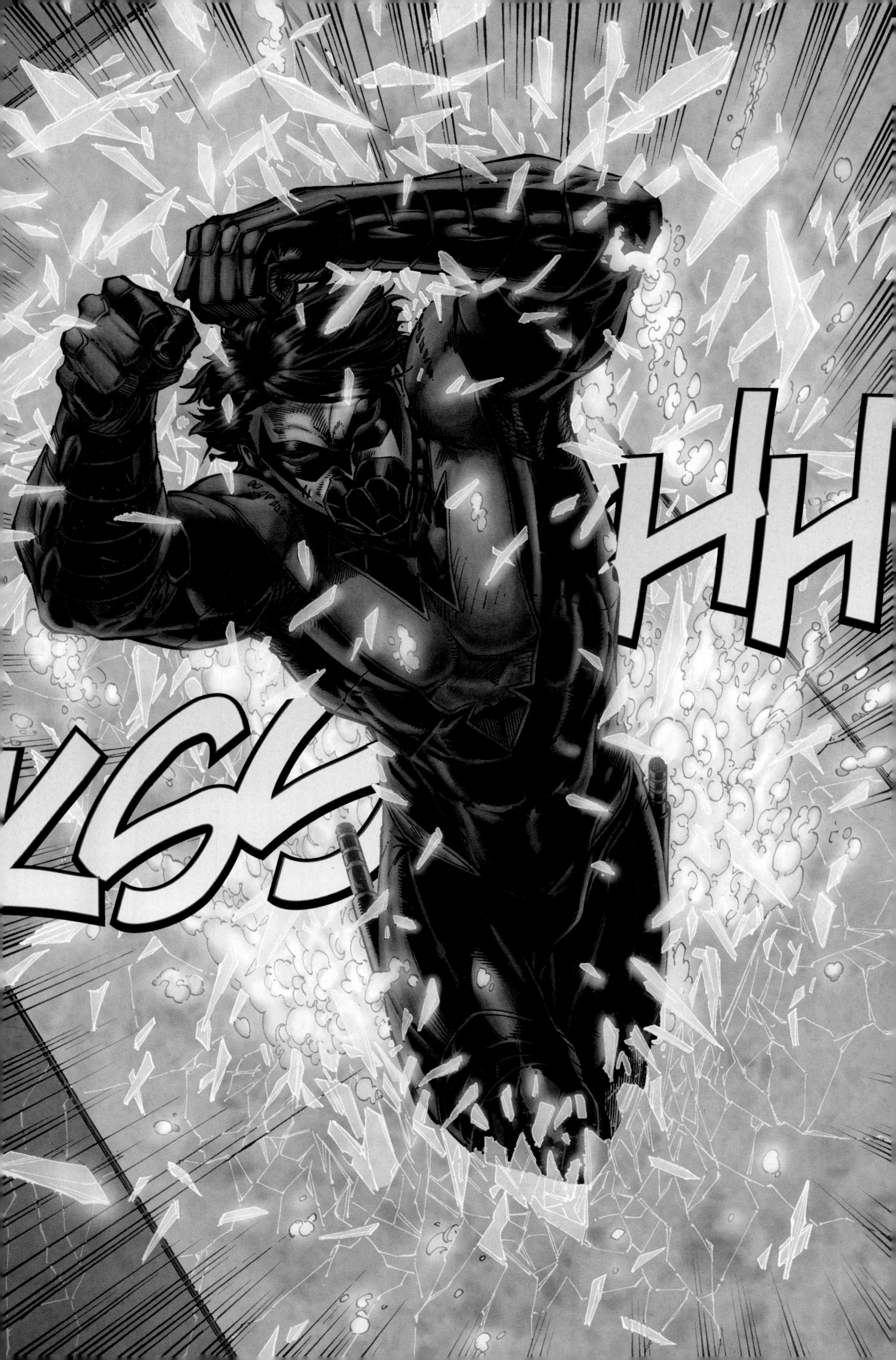

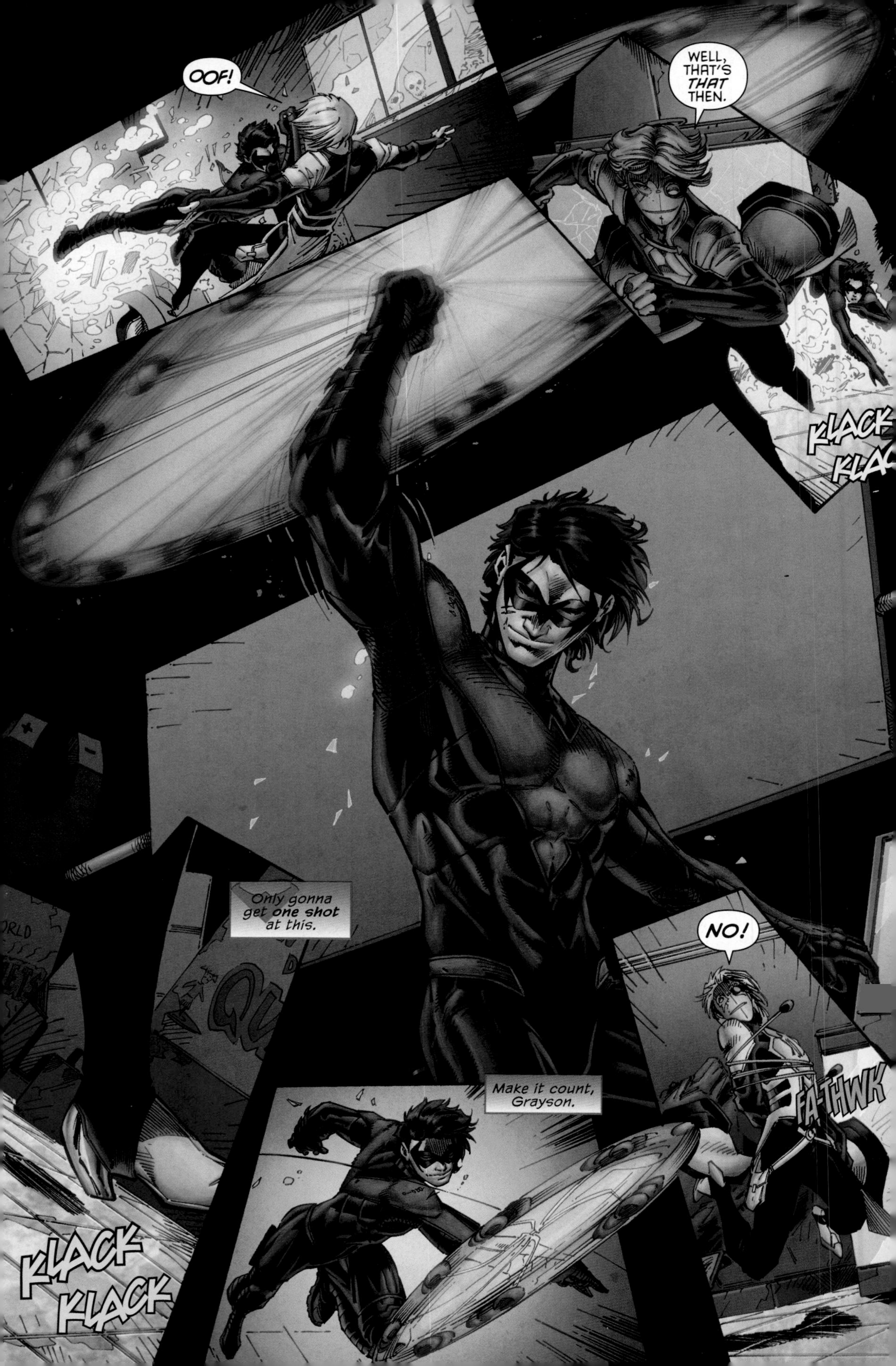
OOF!
WELL, THAT'S THAT THEN.
KLACK KLAC
Only gonna get one shot at this.
NO!
Make it count, Grayson.
FA-THWK
KLACK KLACK

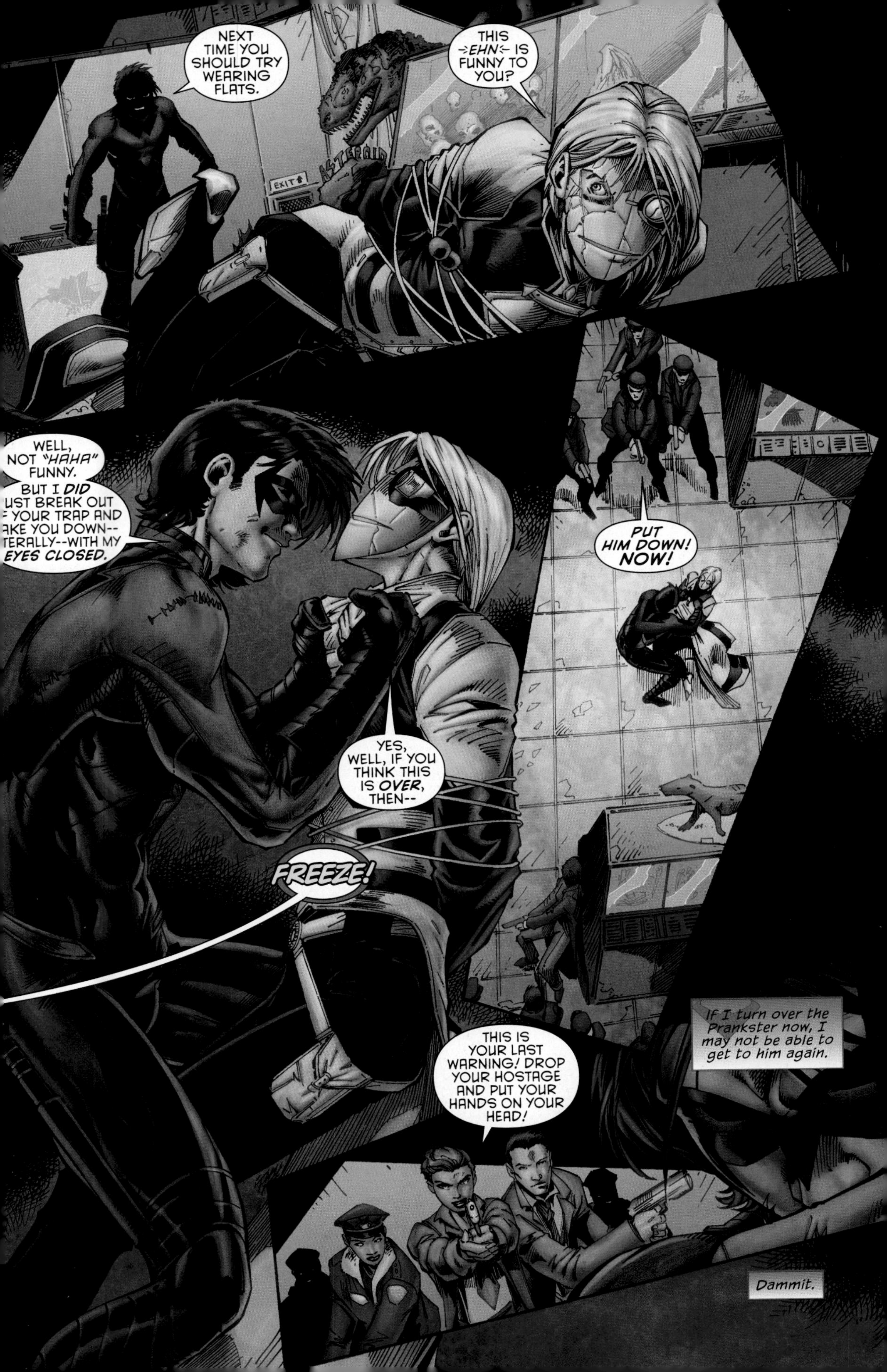

NEXT TIME YOU SHOULD TRY WEARING FLATS.
THIS -EHN- IS FUNNY TO YOU?
WELL, NOT "HAHA" FUNNY.
BUT I DID
UST BREAK OUT
F YOUR TRAP AND
AKE YOU DOWN--
TERALLY--WITH MY
EYES CLOSED.
PUT HIM DOWN! NOW!
YES, WELL, IF YOU THINK THIS IS OVER, THEN--
FREEZE!
THIS IS YOUR LAST WARNING! DROP YOUR HOSTAGE AND PUT YOUR HANDS ON YOUR HEAD!
If I turn over the Prankster now, I may not be able to get to him again.
Dammit.

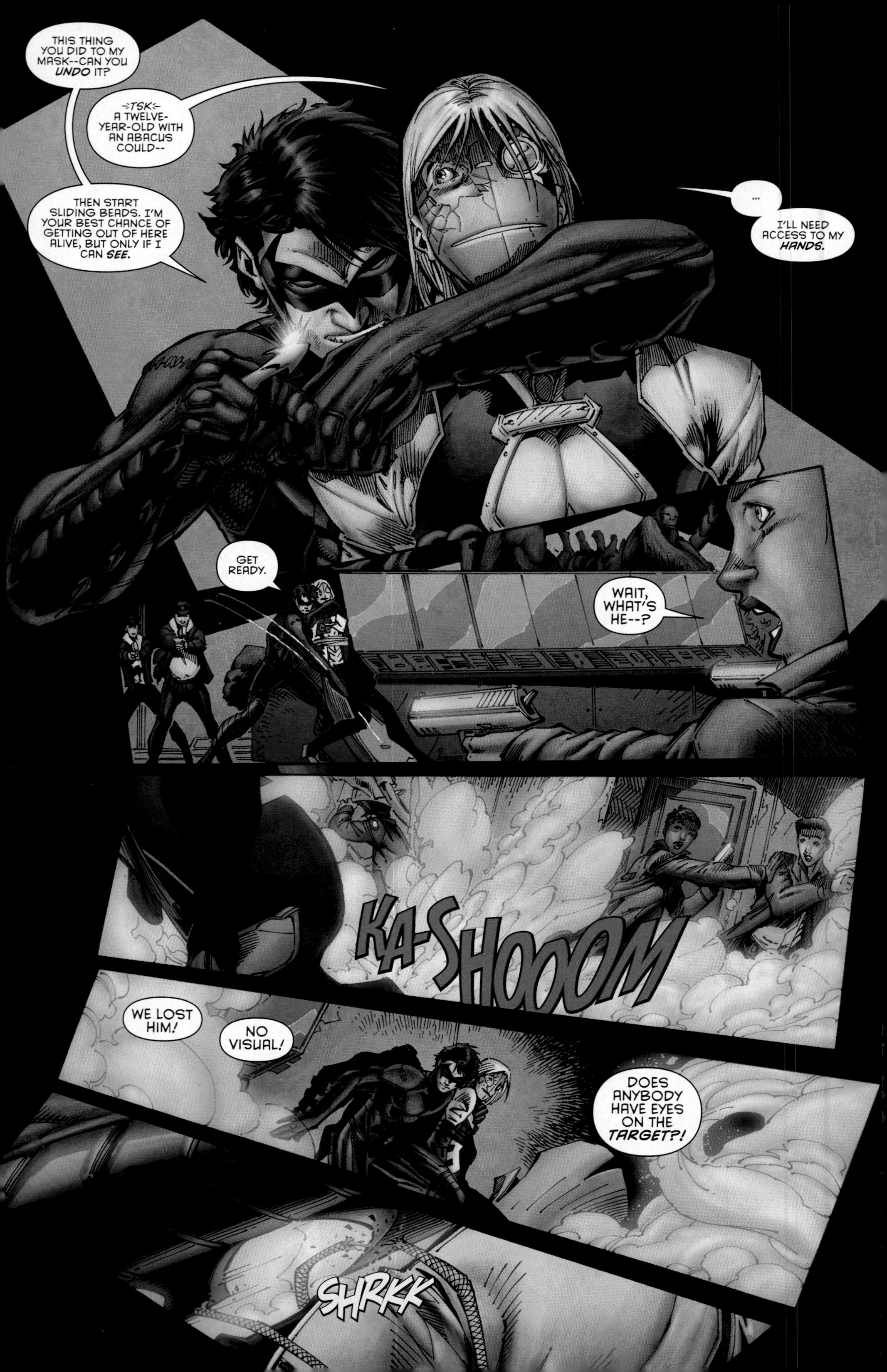
THIS THING YOU DID TO MY MASK--CAN YOU UNDO IT?
⇒TSK⇐ A TWELVE-YEAR-OLD WITH AN ABACUS COULD--
THEN START SLIDING BEADS. I'M YOUR BEST CHANCE OF GETTING OUT OF HERE ALIVE, BUT ONLY IF I CAN SEE.
...
I'LL NEED ACCESS TO MY HANDS.
GET READY.
WAIT, WHAT'S HE--?
KA-SHOOOM
WE LOST HIM!
NO VISUAL!
DOES ANYBODY HAVE EYES ON THE TARGET?!
SHRKK

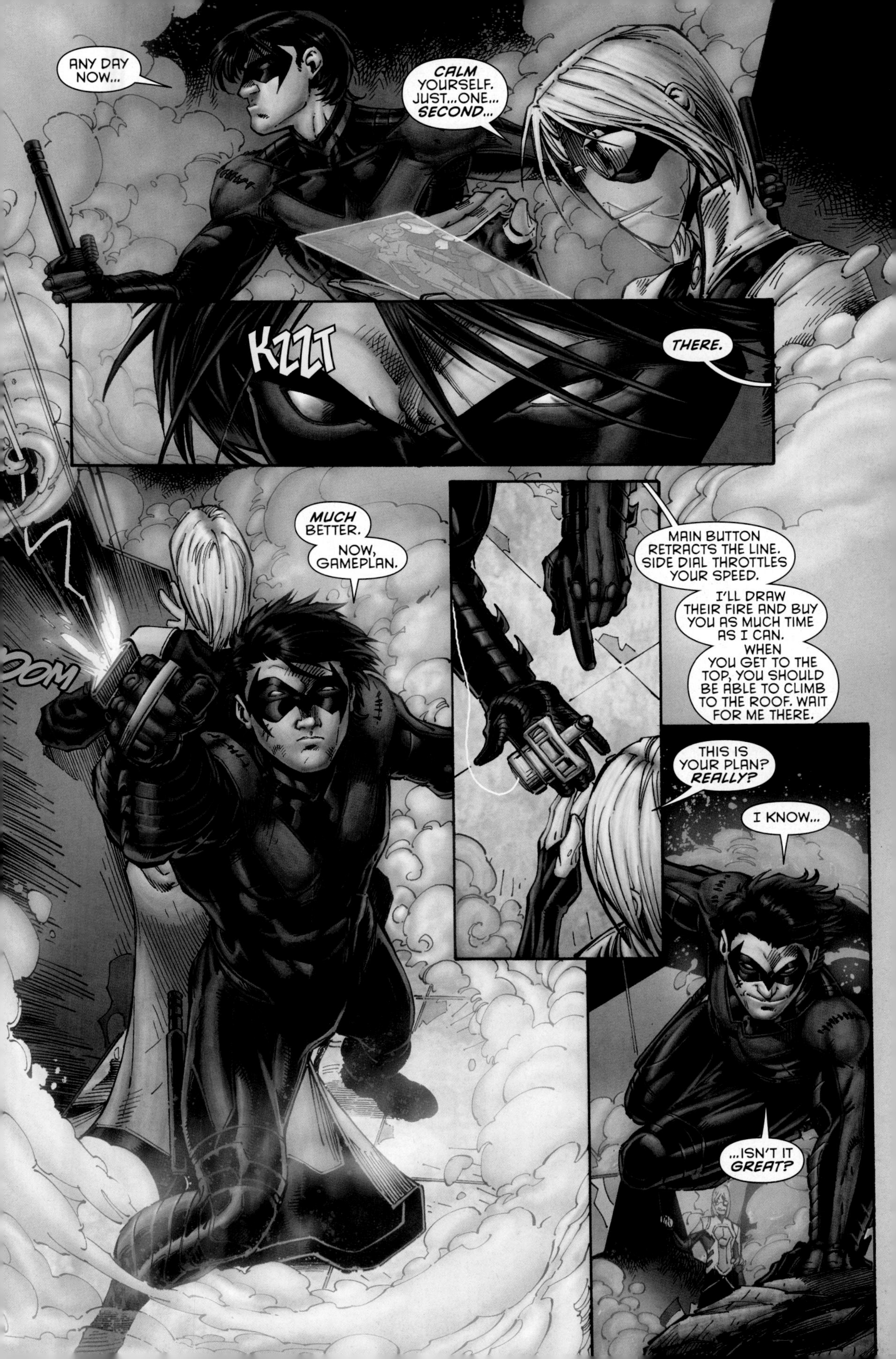
ANY DAY NOW...
CALM YOURSELF. JUST...ONE... SECOND...
KZZT
THERE.
MUCH BETTER.
NOW, GAMEPLAN.
MAIN BUTTON RETRACTS THE LINE. SIDE DIAL THROTTLES YOUR SPEED.
I'LL DRAW THEIR FIRE AND BUY YOU AS MUCH TIME AS I CAN.
WHEN YOU GET TO THE TOP, YOU SHOULD BE ABLE TO CLIMB TO THE ROOF. WAIT FOR ME THERE.
THIS IS YOUR PLAN? REALLY?
I KNOW...
...ISN'T IT GREAT?

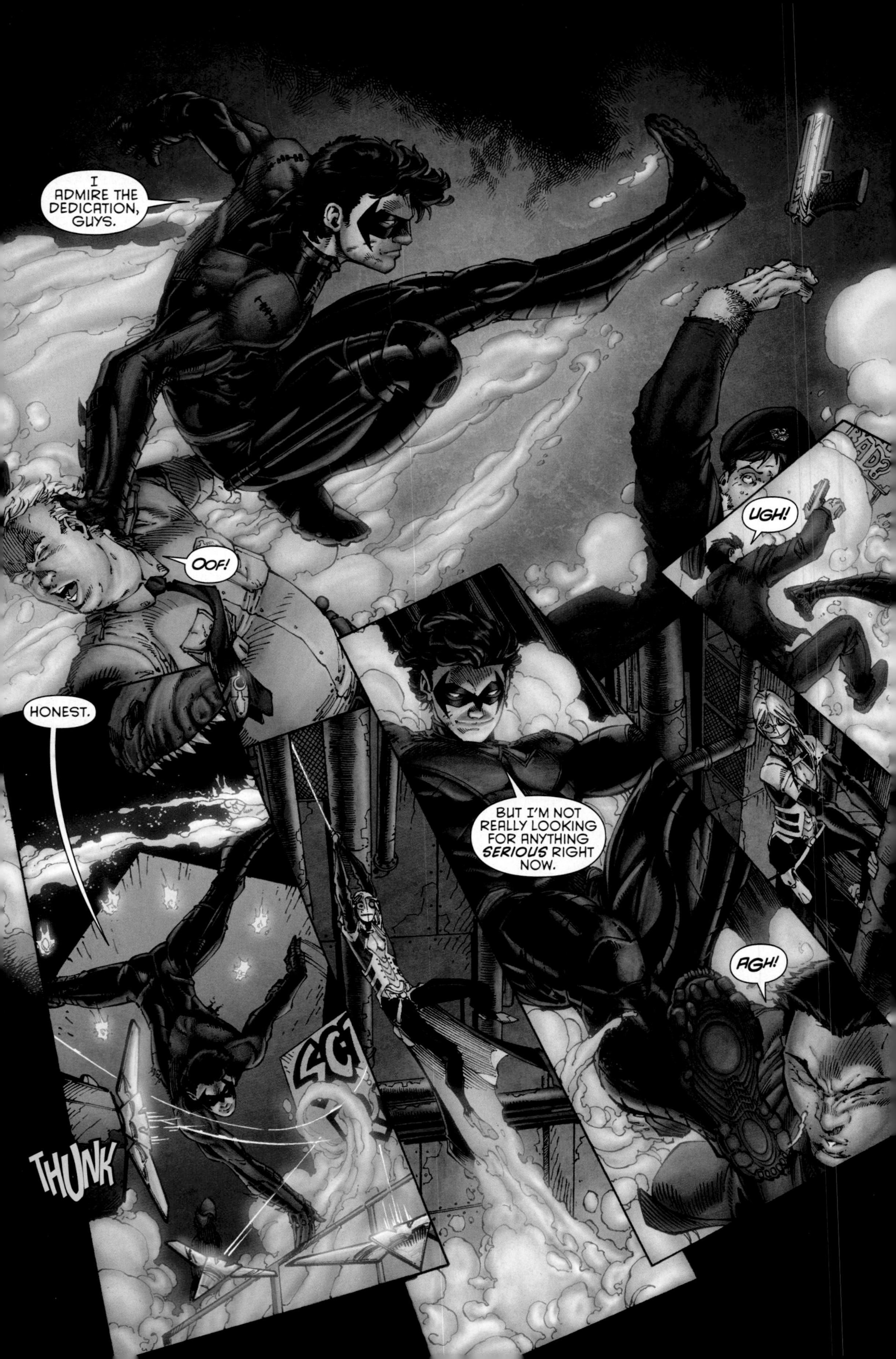
I ADMIRE THE DEDICATION, GUYS.
OOF!
UGH!
HONEST.
BUT I'M NOT REALLY LOOKING FOR ANYTHING *SERIOUS* RIGHT NOW.
AGH!
THUNK

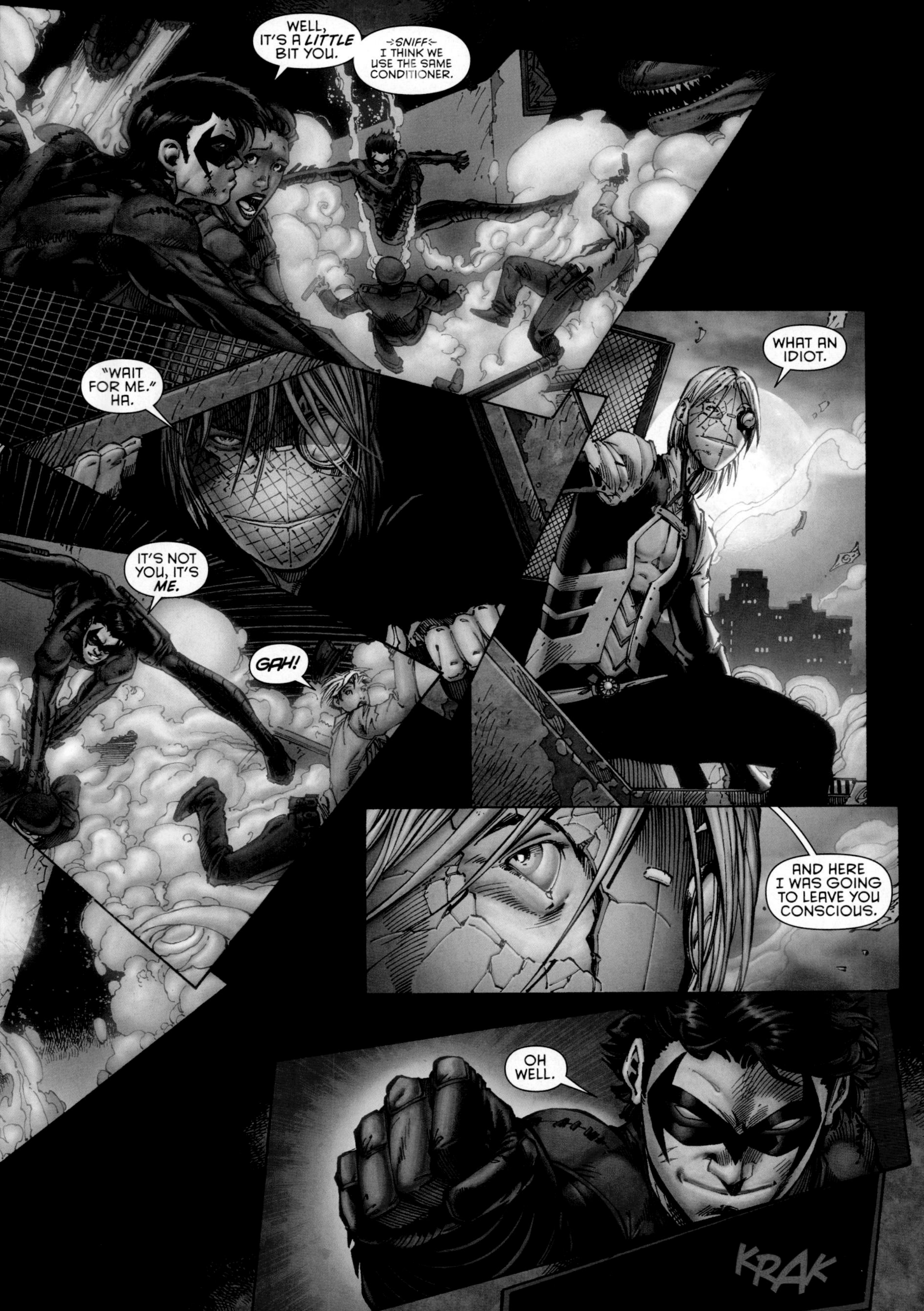

WELL, IT'S A LITTLE BIT YOU.
SNIFF I THINK WE USE THE SAME CONDITIONER.
"WAIT FOR ME." HA.
WHAT AN IDIOT.
IT'S NOT YOU, IT'S ME.
GAH!
AND HERE I WAS GOING TO LEAVE YOU CONSCIOUS.
OH WELL.
KRAK

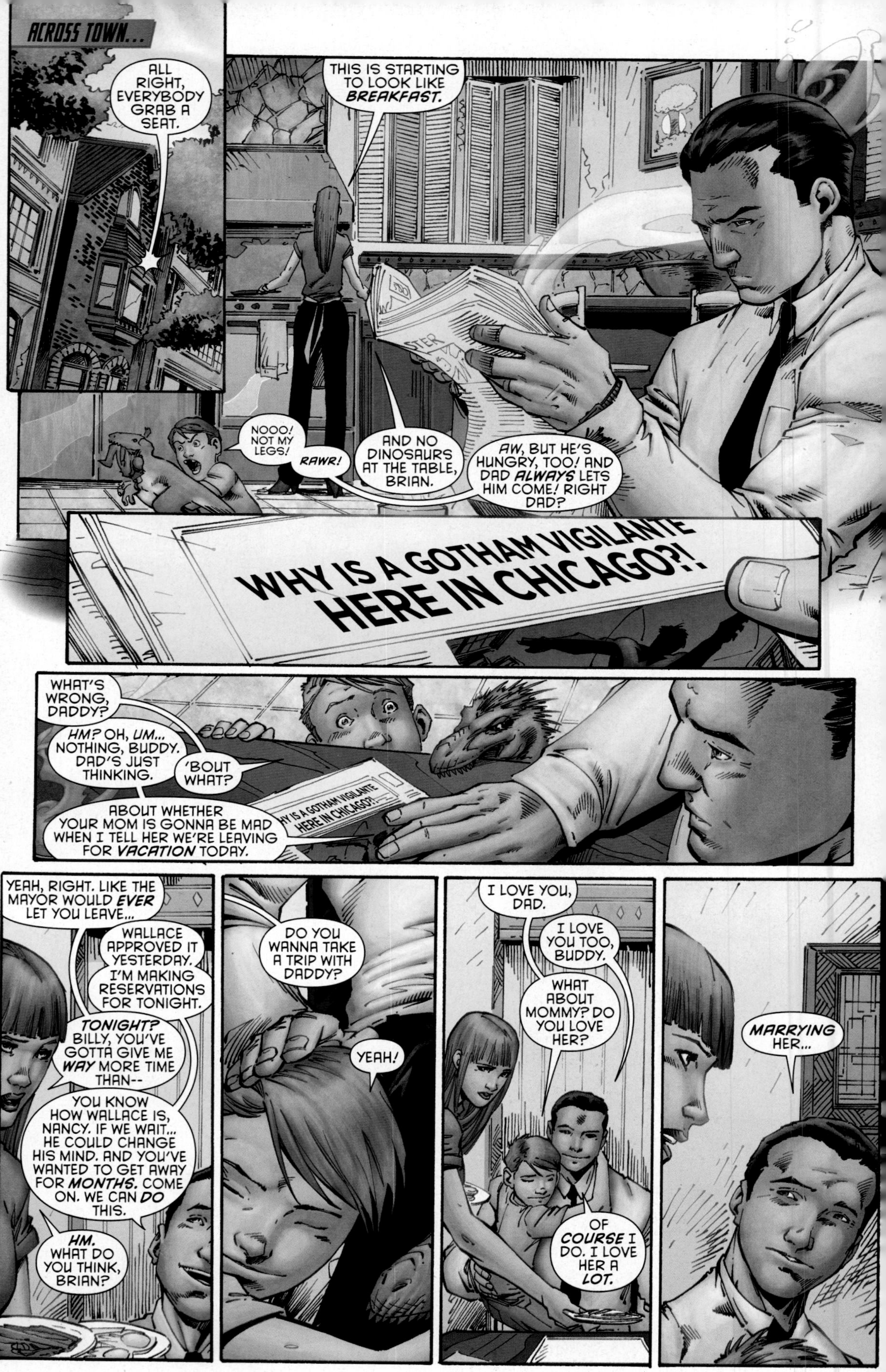
ACROSS TOWN...
ALL RIGHT, EVERYBODY GRAB A SEAT.
THIS IS STARTING TO LOOK LIKE BREAKFAST.
NOOO! NOT MY LEGS!
RAWR!
AND NO DINOSAURS AT THE TABLE, BRIAN.
AW, BUT HE'S HUNGRY, TOO! AND DAD ALWAYS LETS HIM COME! RIGHT DAD?
WHY IS A GOTHAM VIGILANTE HERE IN CHICAGO?!
WHAT'S WRONG, DADDY?
HM? OH, UM... NOTHING, BUDDY. DAD'S JUST THINKING.
'BOUT WHAT?
ABOUT WHETHER YOUR MOM IS GONNA BE MAD WHEN I TELL HER WE'RE LEAVING FOR VACATION TODAY.
WHY IS A GOTHAM VIGILANTE HERE IN CHICAGO?!
YEAH, RIGHT. LIKE THE MAYOR WOULD EVER LET YOU LEAVE...
WALLACE APPROVED IT YESTERDAY. I'M MAKING RESERVATIONS FOR TONIGHT.
TONIGHT? BILLY, YOU'VE GOTTA GIVE ME WAY MORE TIME THAN--
YOU KNOW HOW WALLACE IS, NANCY. IF WE WAIT... HE COULD CHANGE HIS MIND. AND YOU'VE WANTED TO GET AWAY FOR MONTHS. COME ON. WE CAN DO THIS.
HM. WHAT DO YOU THINK, BRIAN?
DO YOU WANNA TAKE A TRIP WITH DADDY?
YEAH!
I LOVE YOU, DAD.
I LOVE YOU TOO, BUDDY.
WHAT ABOUT MOMMY? DO YOU LOVE HER?
OF COURSE I DO. I LOVE HER A LOT.
MARRYING HER...

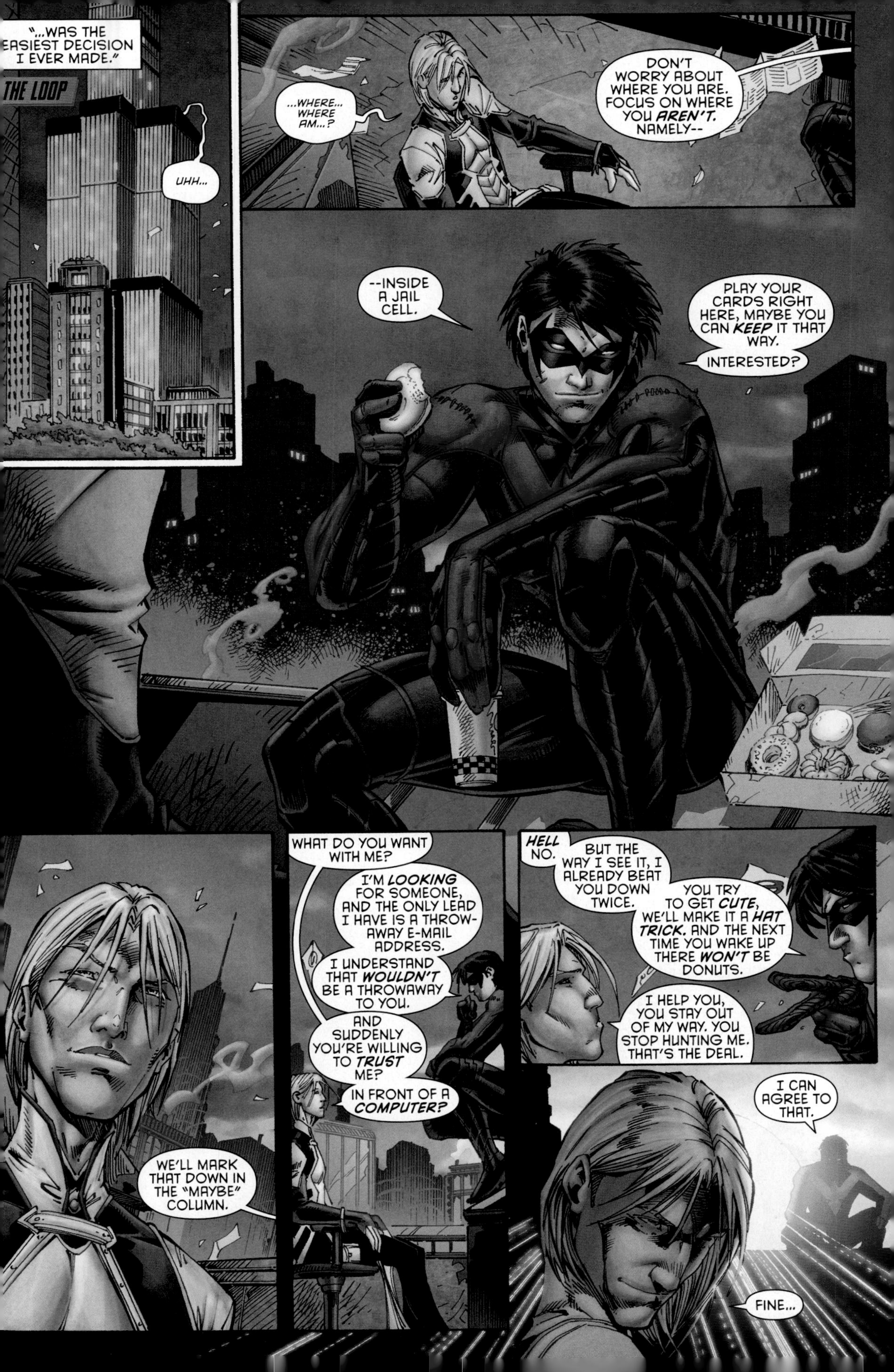
"...WAS THE EASIEST DECISION I EVER MADE."
THE LOOP
UHH...
...WHERE... WHERE AM...?
DON'T WORRY ABOUT WHERE YOU ARE. FOCUS ON WHERE YOU AREN'T. NAMELY--
--INSIDE A JAIL CELL.
PLAY YOUR CARDS RIGHT HERE, MAYBE YOU CAN KEEP IT THAT WAY.
INTERESTED?
WE'LL MARK THAT DOWN IN THE "MAYBE" COLUMN.
WHAT DO YOU WANT WITH ME?
I'M LOOKING FOR SOMEONE, AND THE ONLY LEAD I HAVE IS A THROW-AWAY E-MAIL ADDRESS.
I UNDERSTAND THAT WOULDN'T BE A THROWAWAY TO YOU.
AND SUDDENLY YOU'RE WILLING TO TRUST ME?
IN FRONT OF A COMPUTER?
HELL NO.
BUT THE WAY I SEE IT, I ALREADY BEAT YOU DOWN TWICE.
YOU TRY TO GET CUTE, WE'LL MAKE IT A HAT TRICK. AND THE NEXT TIME YOU WAKE UP THERE WON'T BE DONUTS.
I HELP YOU, YOU STAY OUT OF MY WAY. YOU STOP HUNTING ME. THAT'S THE DEAL.
I CAN AGREE TO THAT.
FINE...

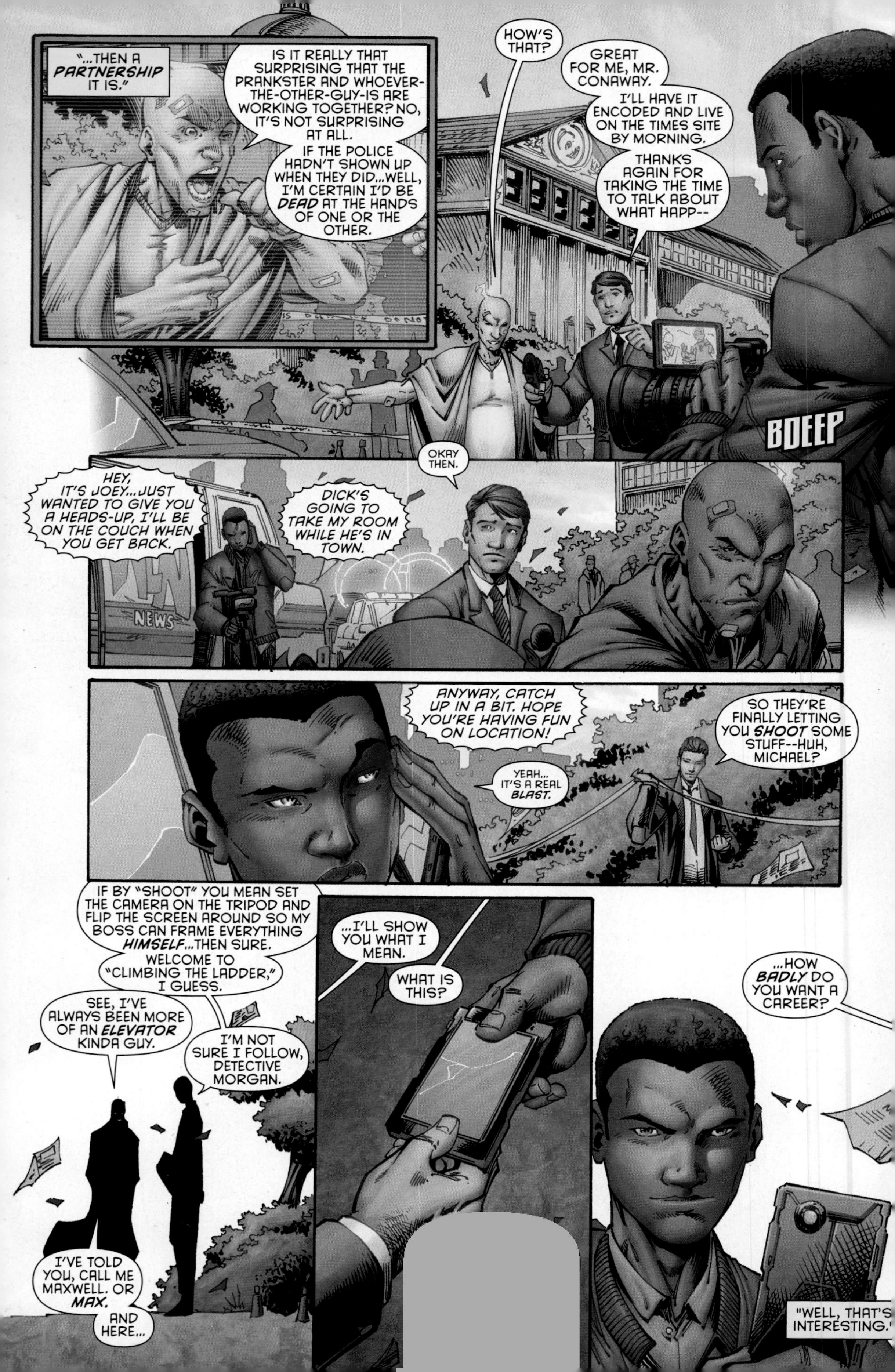
"...THEN A *PARTNERSHIP* IT IS."
IS IT REALLY THAT SURPRISING THAT THE PRANKSTER AND WHOEVER-THE-OTHER-GUY-IS ARE WORKING TOGETHER? NO, IT'S NOT SURPRISING AT ALL.
IF THE POLICE HADN'T SHOWN UP WHEN THEY DID...WELL, I'M CERTAIN I'D BE *DEAD* AT THE HANDS OF ONE OR THE OTHER.
HOW'S THAT?
GREAT FOR ME, MR. CONAWAY.
I'LL HAVE IT ENCODED AND LIVE ON THE TIMES SITE BY MORNING.
THANKS AGAIN FOR TAKING THE TIME TO TALK ABOUT WHAT HAPP--
BDEEP
OKAY THEN.
HEY, IT'S JOEY...JUST WANTED TO GIVE YOU A HEADS-UP, I'LL BE ON THE COUCH WHEN YOU GET BACK.
DICK'S GOING TO TAKE MY ROOM WHILE HE'S IN TOWN.
NEWS
ANYWAY, CATCH UP IN A BIT. HOPE YOU'RE HAVING FUN ON LOCATION!
YEAH... IT'S A REAL *BLAST.*
SO THEY'RE FINALLY LETTING YOU *SHOOT* SOME STUFF--HUH, MICHAEL?
IF BY "SHOOT" YOU MEAN SET THE CAMERA ON THE TRIPOD AND FLIP THE SCREEN AROUND SO MY BOSS CAN FRAME EVERYTHING *HIMSELF*...THEN SURE.
WELCOME TO "CLIMBING THE LADDER," I GUESS.
SEE, I'VE ALWAYS BEEN MORE OF AN *ELEVATOR* KINDA GUY.
I'M NOT SURE I FOLLOW, DETECTIVE MORGAN.
I'VE TOLD YOU, CALL ME MAXWELL. OR *MAX.*
AND HERE...
...I'LL SHOW YOU WHAT I MEAN.
WHAT IS THIS?
...HOW *BADLY* DO YOU WANT A CAREER?
"WELL, THAT'S INTERESTING."

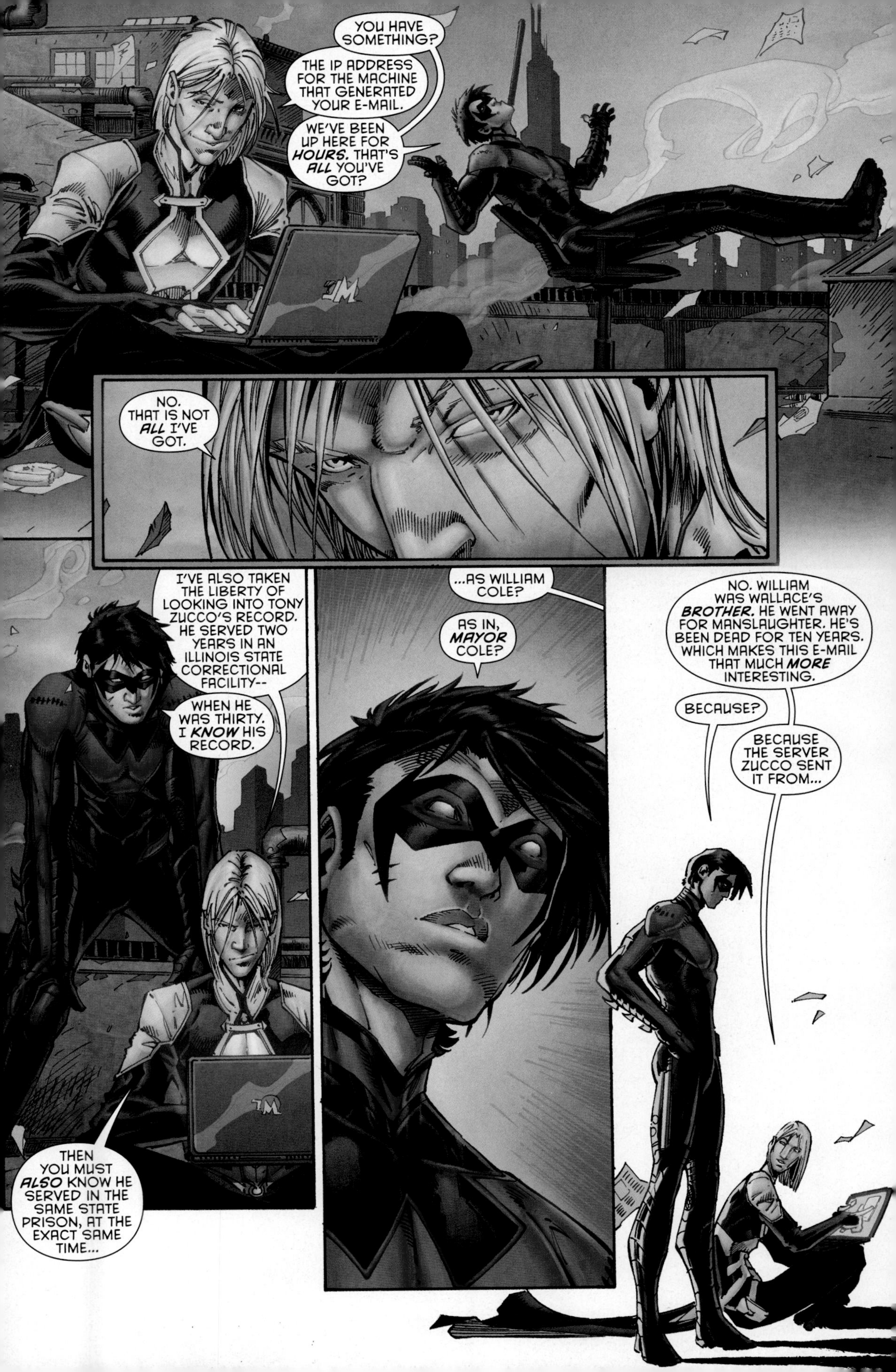
YOU HAVE SOMETHING?
THE IP ADDRESS FOR THE MACHINE THAT GENERATED YOUR E-MAIL.
WE'VE BEEN UP HERE FOR HOURS. THAT'S ALL YOU'VE GOT?
NO. THAT IS NOT ALL I'VE GOT.
I'VE ALSO TAKEN THE LIBERTY OF LOOKING INTO TONY ZUCCO'S RECORD. HE SERVED TWO YEARS IN AN ILLINOIS STATE CORRECTIONAL FACILITY--
WHEN HE WAS THIRTY. I KNOW HIS RECORD.
THEN YOU MUST ALSO KNOW HE SERVED IN THE SAME STATE PRISON, AT THE EXACT SAME TIME...
...AS WILLIAM COLE?
AS IN, MAYOR COLE?
NO. WILLIAM WAS WALLACE'S BROTHER. HE WENT AWAY FOR MANSLAUGHTER. HE'S BEEN DEAD FOR TEN YEARS. WHICH MAKES THIS E-MAIL THAT MUCH MORE INTERESTING.
BECAUSE?
BECAUSE THE SERVER ZUCCO SENT IT FROM...

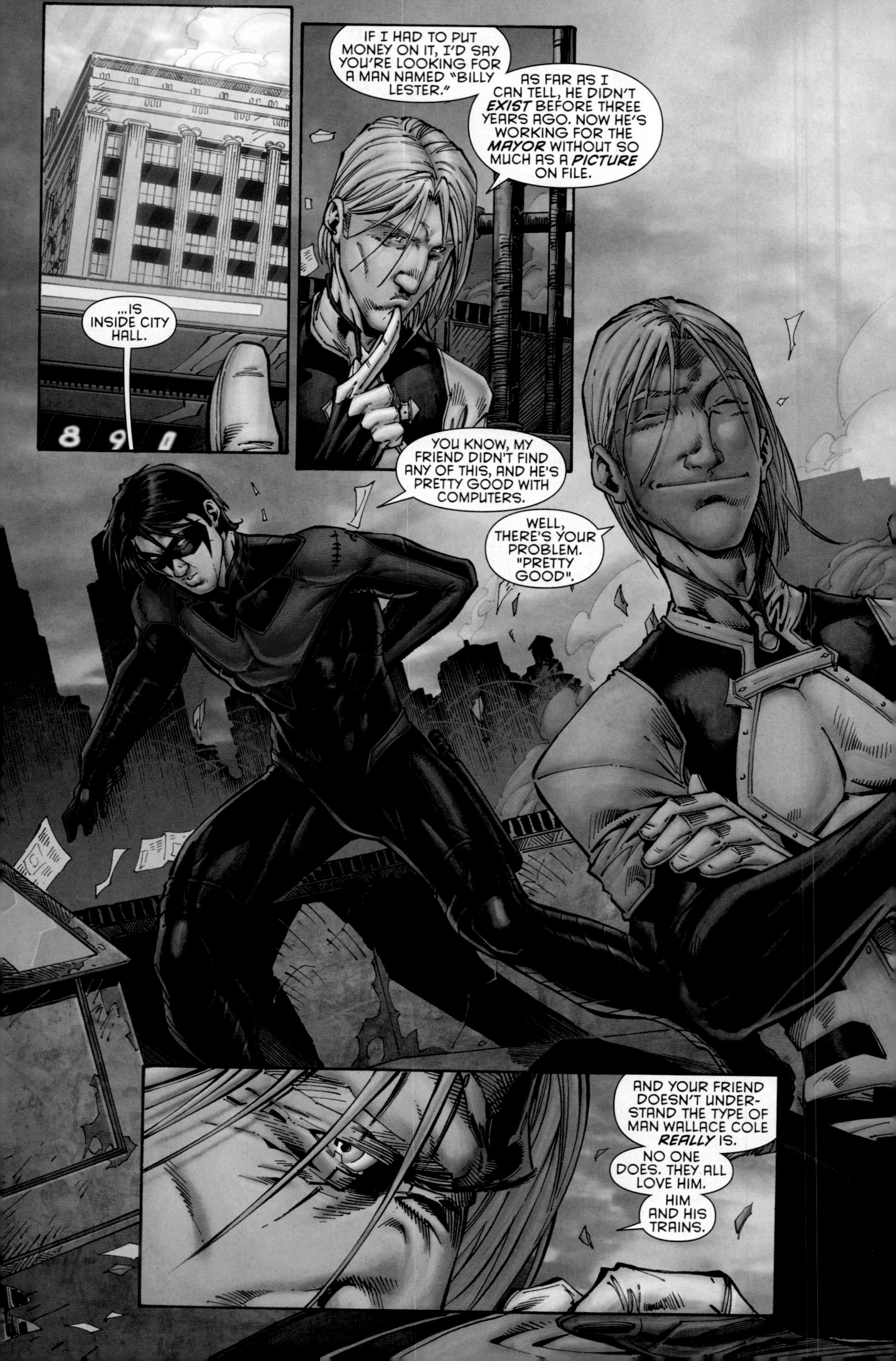
...IS INSIDE CITY HALL.
8 9 0
IF I HAD TO PUT MONEY ON IT, I'D SAY YOU'RE LOOKING FOR A MAN NAMED "BILLY LESTER."
AS FAR AS I CAN TELL, HE DIDN'T EXIST BEFORE THREE YEARS AGO. NOW HE'S WORKING FOR THE MAYOR WITHOUT SO MUCH AS A PICTURE ON FILE.
YOU KNOW, MY FRIEND DIDN'T FIND ANY OF THIS, AND HE'S PRETTY GOOD WITH COMPUTERS.
WELL, THERE'S YOUR PROBLEM. "PRETTY GOOD".
AND YOUR FRIEND DOESN'T UNDER-STAND THE TYPE OF MAN WALLACE COLE REALLY IS.
NO ONE DOES. THEY ALL LOVE HIM.
HIM AND HIS TRAINS.

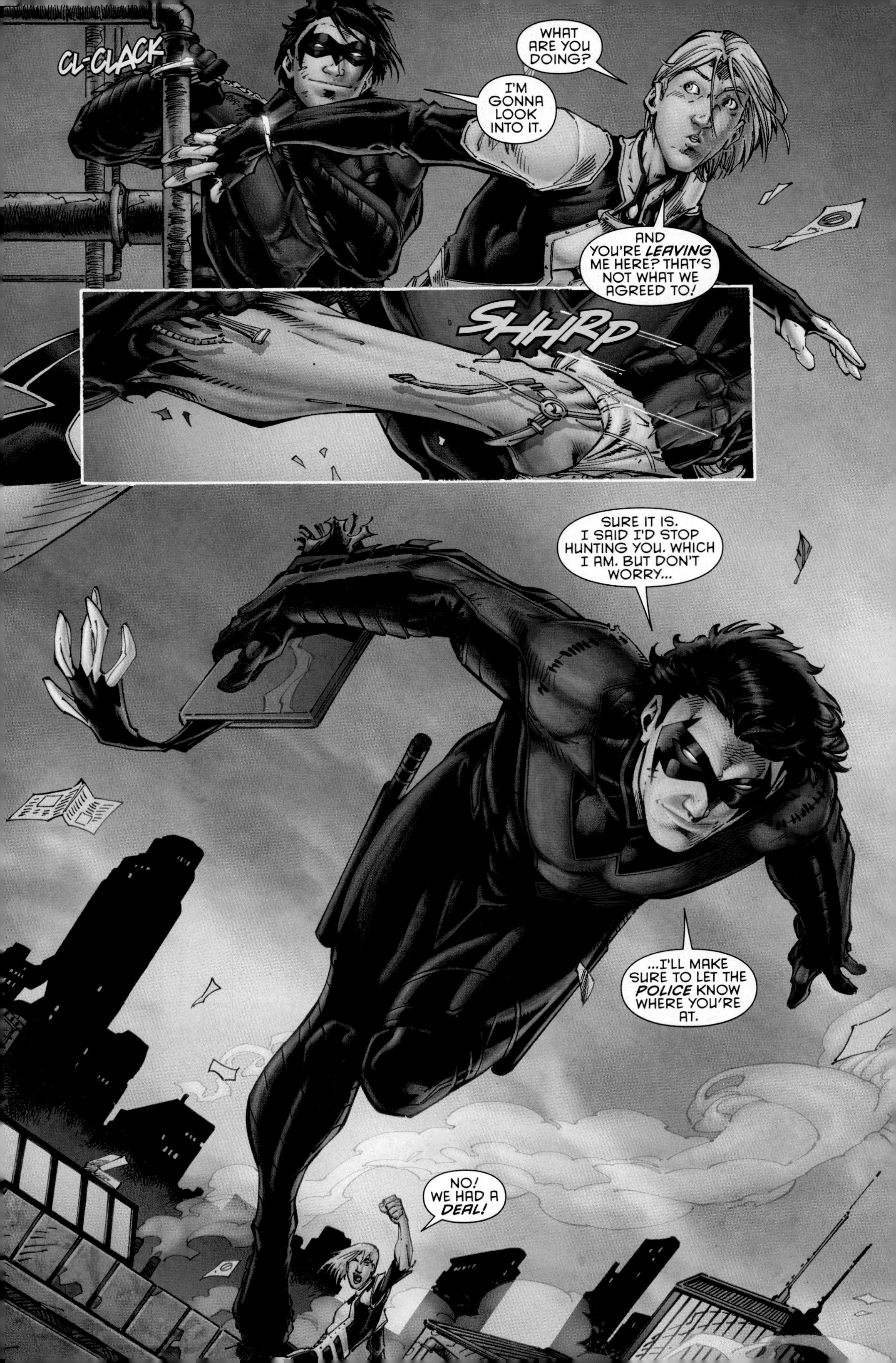
CL-CLACK
WHAT ARE YOU DOING?
I'M GONNA LOOK INTO IT.
AND YOU'RE *LEAVING* ME HERE? THAT'S NOT WHAT WE AGREED TO!
SHHRP
SURE IT IS. I SAID I'D STOP HUNTING YOU. WHICH I AM. BUT DON'T WORRY...
...I'LL MAKE SURE TO LET THE *POLICE* KNOW WHERE YOU'RE AT.
NO! WE HAD A *DEAL*!

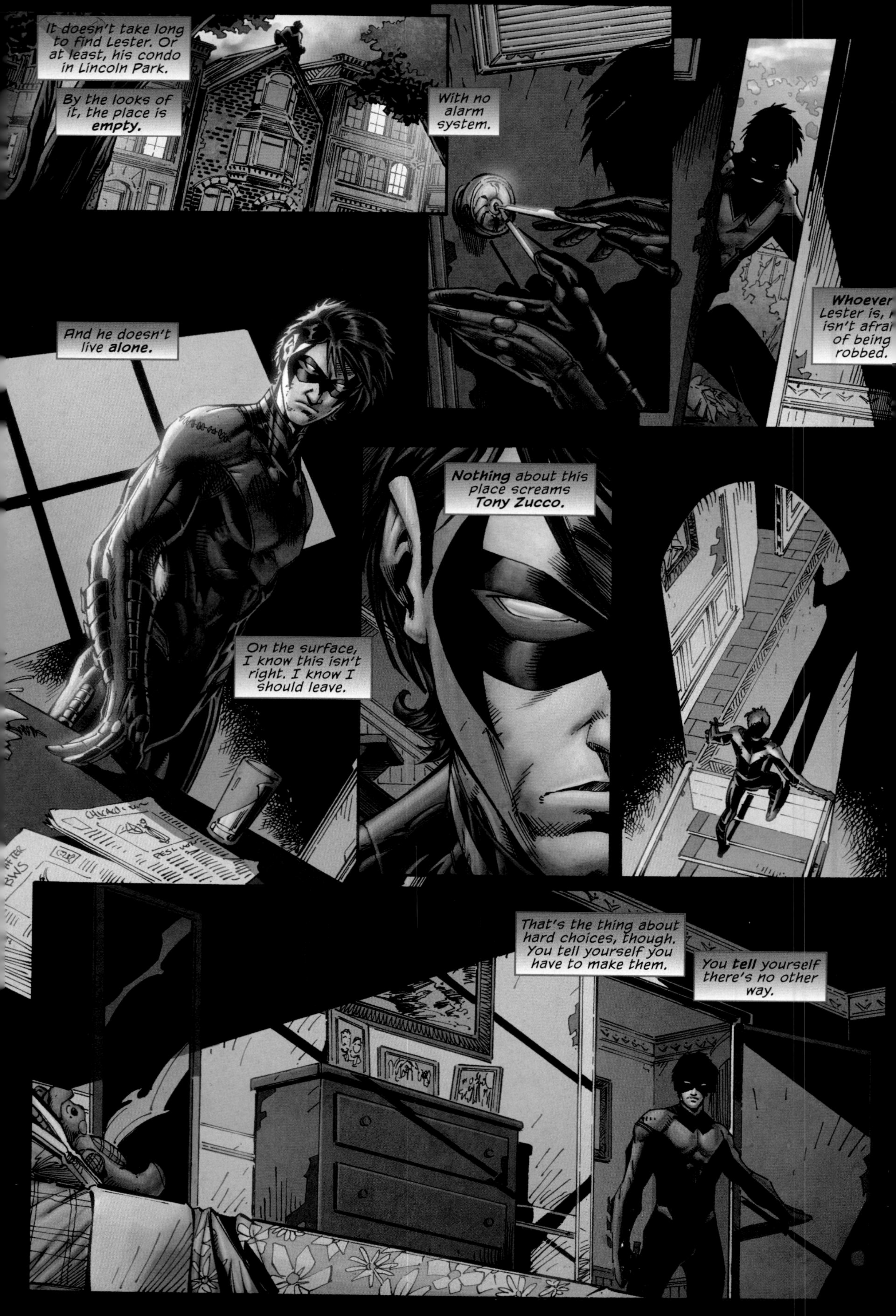
It doesn't take long to find Lester. Or at least, his condo in Lincoln Park.
By the looks of it, the place is empty.
With no alarm system.
Whoever Lester is,
isn't afrai
of being
robbed.
And he doesn't live alone.
On the surface, I know this isn't right. I know I should leave.
Nothing about this place screams Tony Zucco.
That's the thing about hard choices, though. You tell yourself you have to make them.
You tell yourself there's no other way.

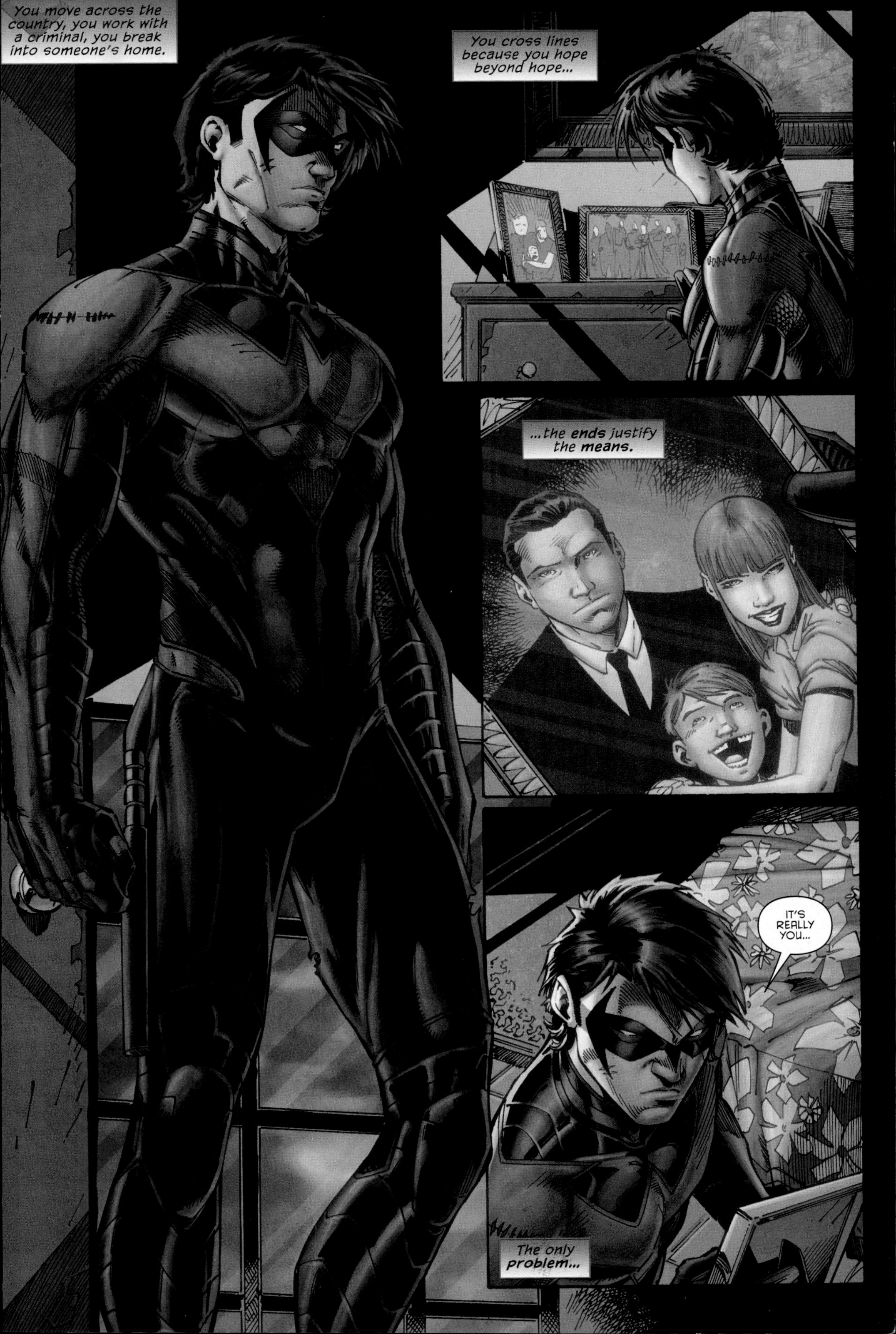
You move across the country, you work with a criminal, you break into someone's home.
You cross lines because you hope beyond hope...
...the **ends** justify the **means.**
IT'S REALLY YOU...
The only **problem...**

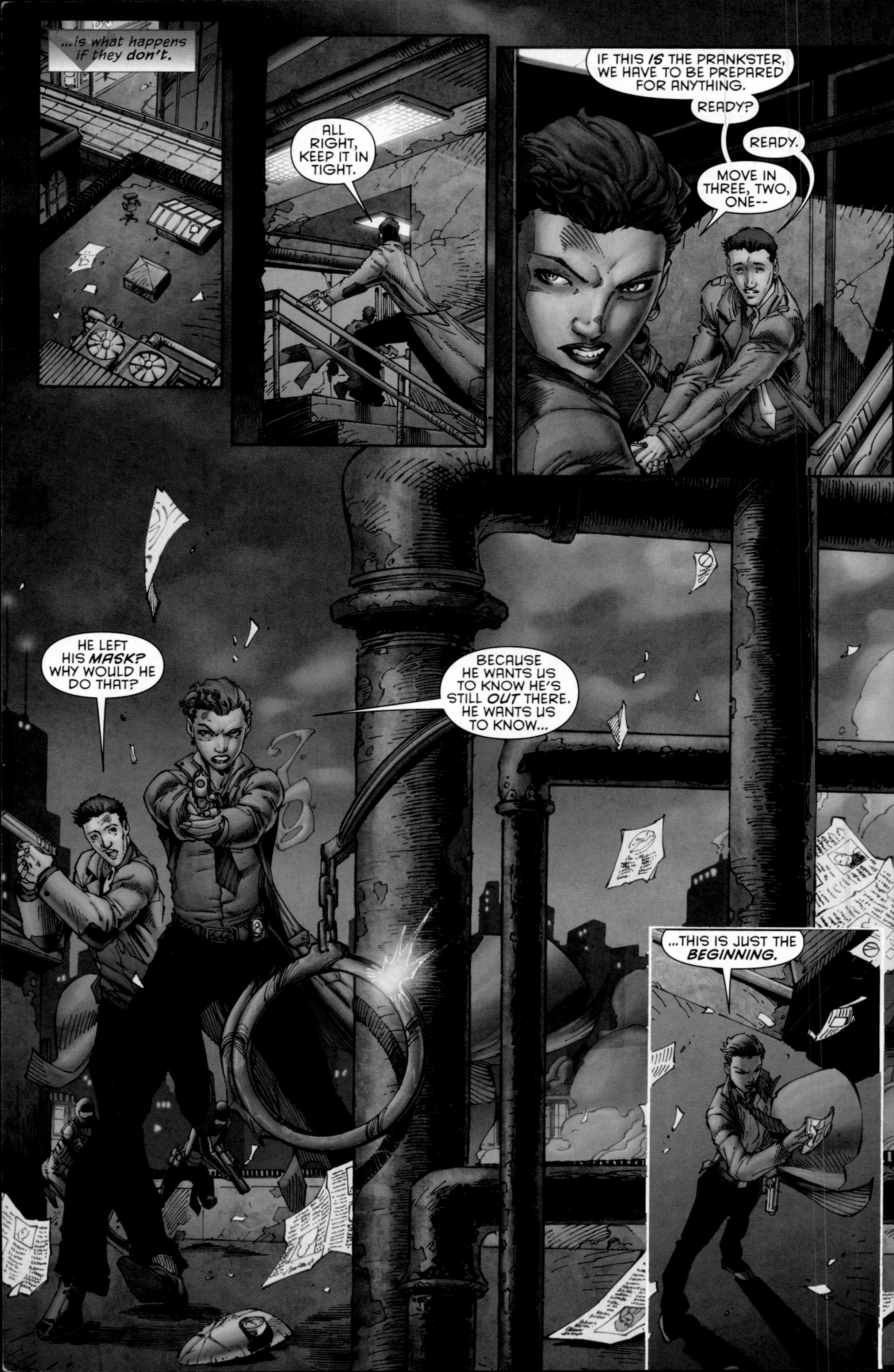
...is what happens if they **don't.**
ALL RIGHT, KEEP IT IN TIGHT.
IF THIS *IS* THE PRANKSTER, WE HAVE TO BE PREPARED FOR ANYTHING.
READY?
READY.
MOVE IN THREE, TWO, ONE--
HE LEFT HIS *MASK?* WHY WOULD HE DO THAT?
BECAUSE HE WANTS US TO KNOW HE'S STILL *OUT* THERE. HE WANTS US TO KNOW...
...THIS IS JUST THE *BEGINNING.*

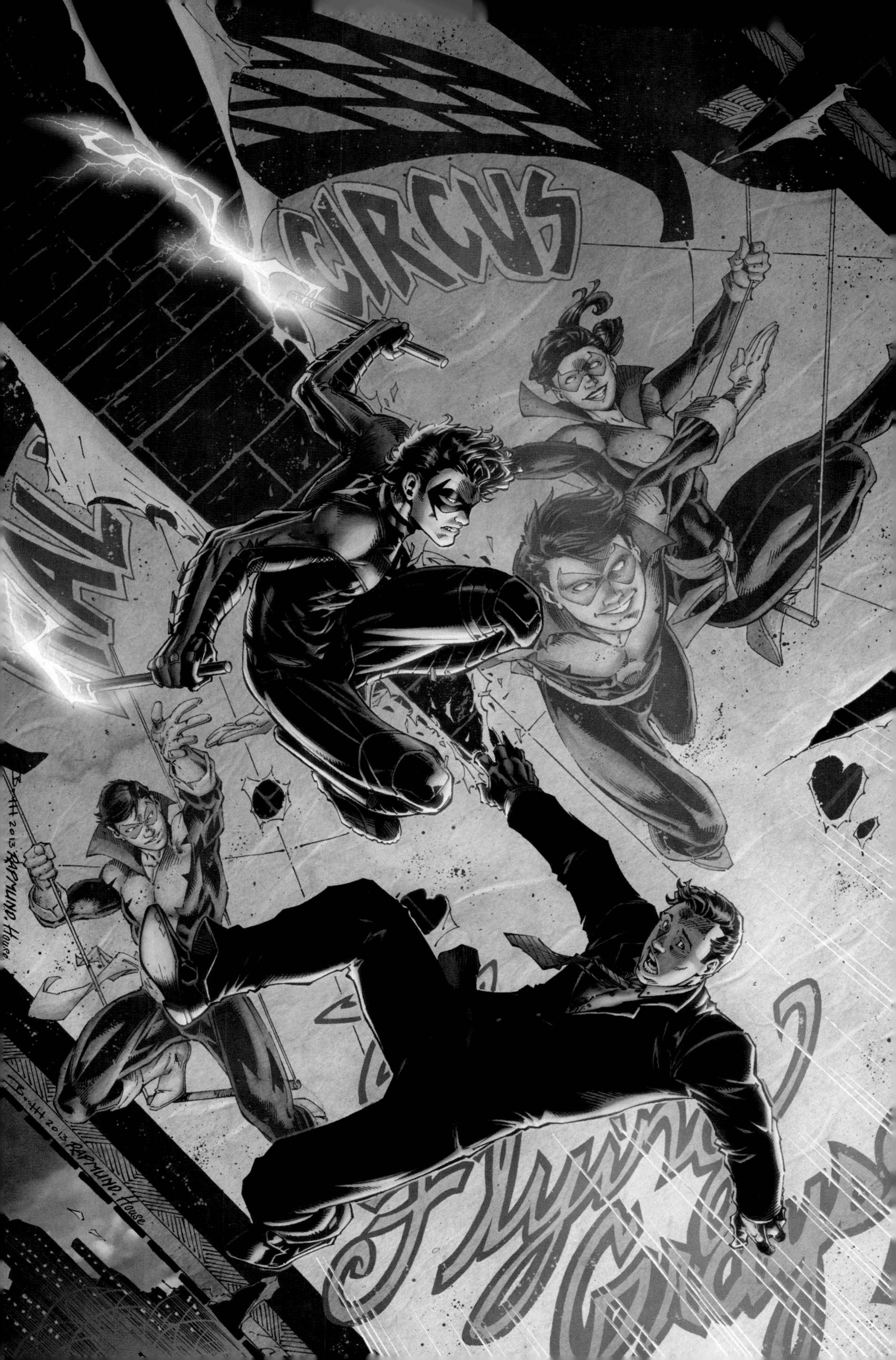
CIRCUS

SHOWTIME

KYLE HIGGINS writer **WILL CONRAD** artist cover art by **BRETT BOOTH, NORM RAPMUND & ANDREW DALHOUSE**

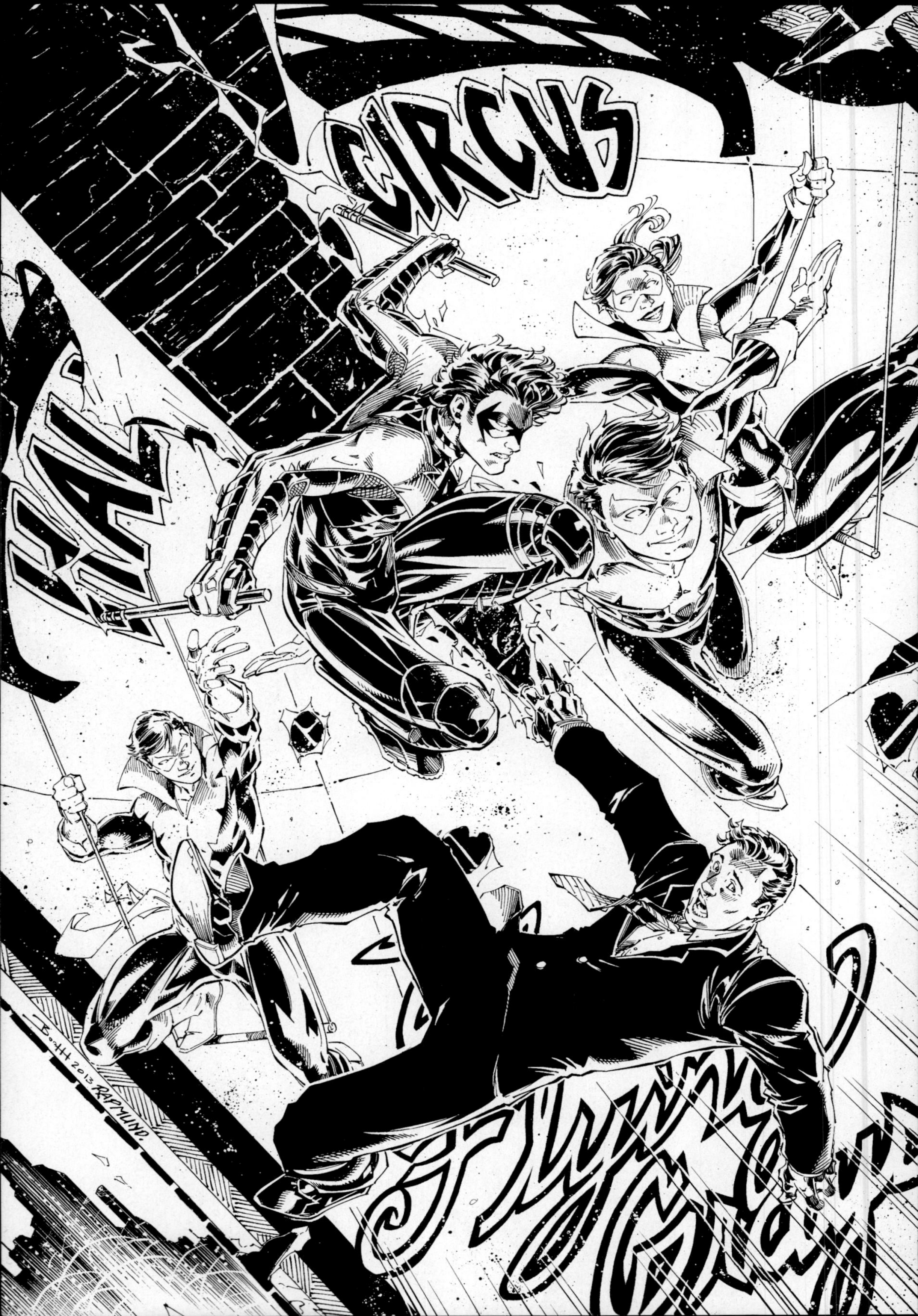
CIRCUS
Booth 2013 RAPMUND.

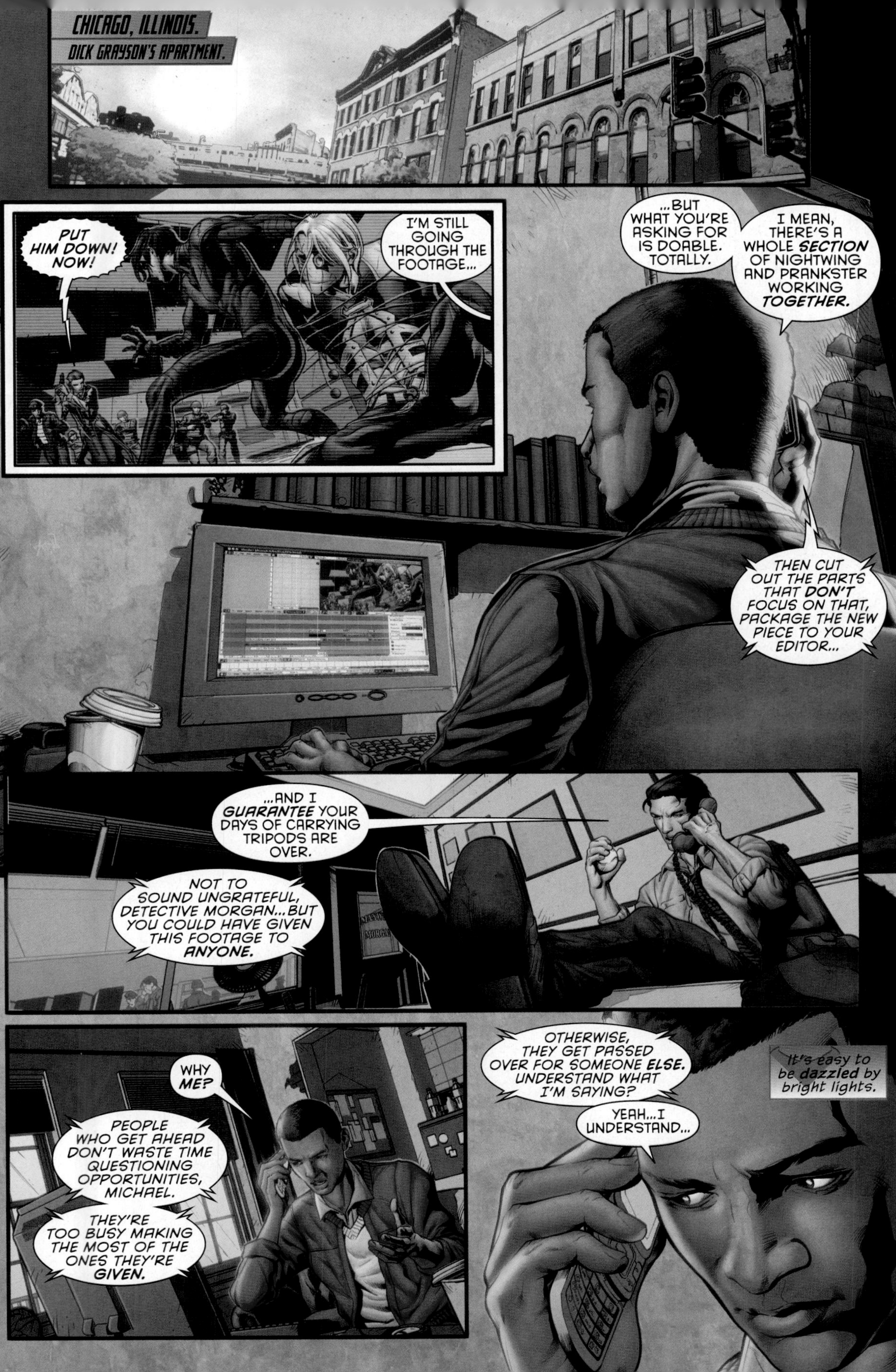
CHICAGO, ILLINOIS.
DICK GRAYSON'S APARTMENT.
PUT HIM DOWN! NOW!
I'M STILL GOING THROUGH THE FOOTAGE...
...BUT WHAT YOU'RE ASKING FOR IS DOABLE. TOTALLY.
I MEAN, THERE'S A WHOLE SECTION OF NIGHTWING AND PRANKSTER WORKING TOGETHER.
THEN CUT OUT THE PARTS THAT DON'T FOCUS ON THAT, PACKAGE THE NEW PIECE TO YOUR EDITOR...
...AND I GUARANTEE YOUR DAYS OF CARRYING TRIPODS ARE OVER.
NOT TO SOUND UNGRATEFUL, DETECTIVE MORGAN...BUT YOU COULD HAVE GIVEN THIS FOOTAGE TO ANYONE.
WHY ME?
PEOPLE WHO GET AHEAD DON'T WASTE TIME QUESTIONING OPPORTUNITIES, MICHAEL.
THEY'RE TOO BUSY MAKING THE MOST OF THE ONES THEY'RE GIVEN.
OTHERWISE, THEY GET PASSED OVER FOR SOMEONE ELSE. UNDERSTAND WHAT I'M SAYING?
YEAH...I UNDERSTAND...
It's easy to be dazzled by bright lights.

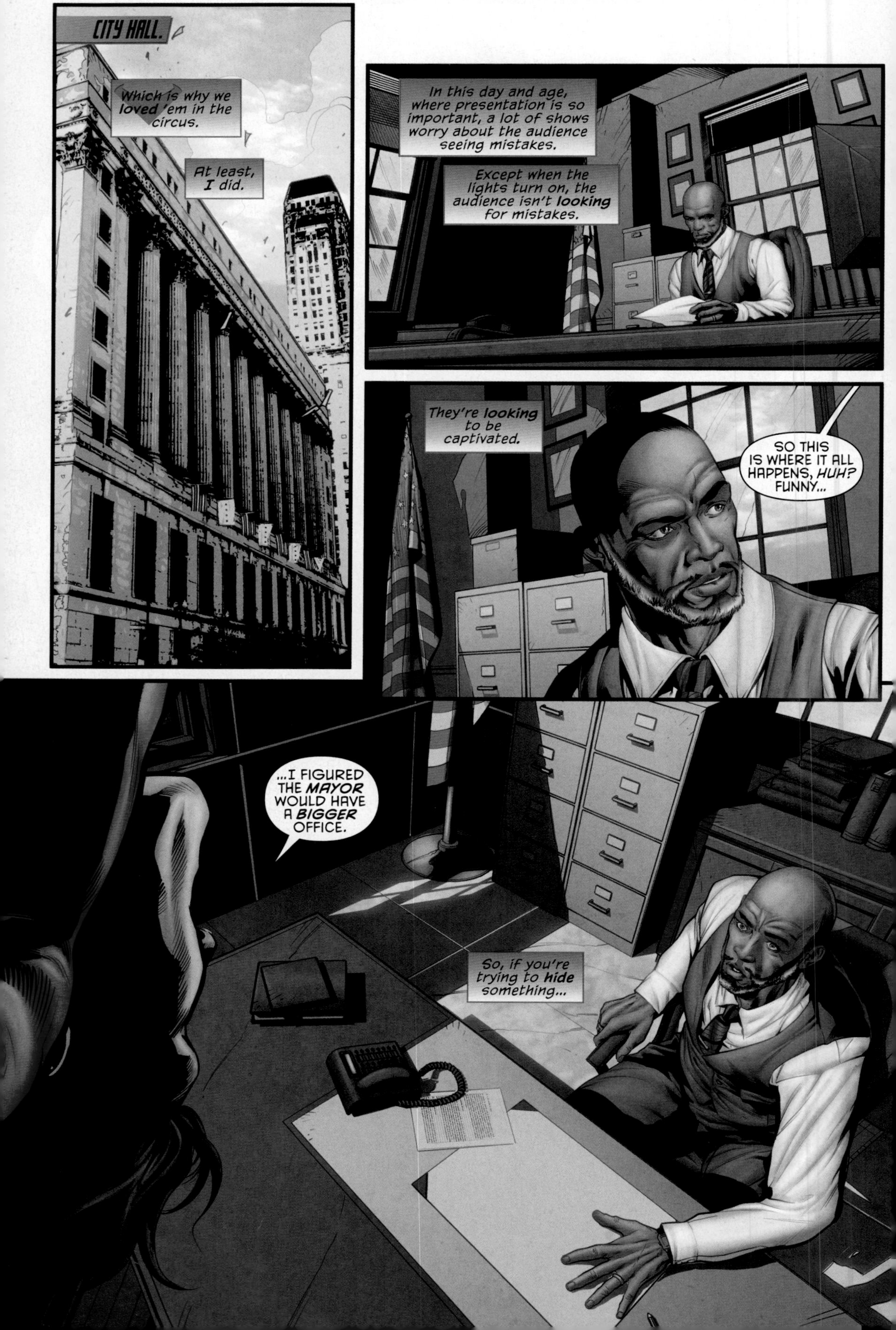
CITY HALL.
Which is why we loved 'em in the circus.
At least, I did.
In this day and age, where presentation is so important, a lot of shows worry about the audience seeing mistakes.
Except when the lights turn on, the audience isn't looking for mistakes.
They're looking to be captivated.
SO THIS IS WHERE IT ALL HAPPENS, HUH? FUNNY...
...I FIGURED THE MAYOR WOULD HAVE A BIGGER OFFICE.
So, if you're trying to hide something...

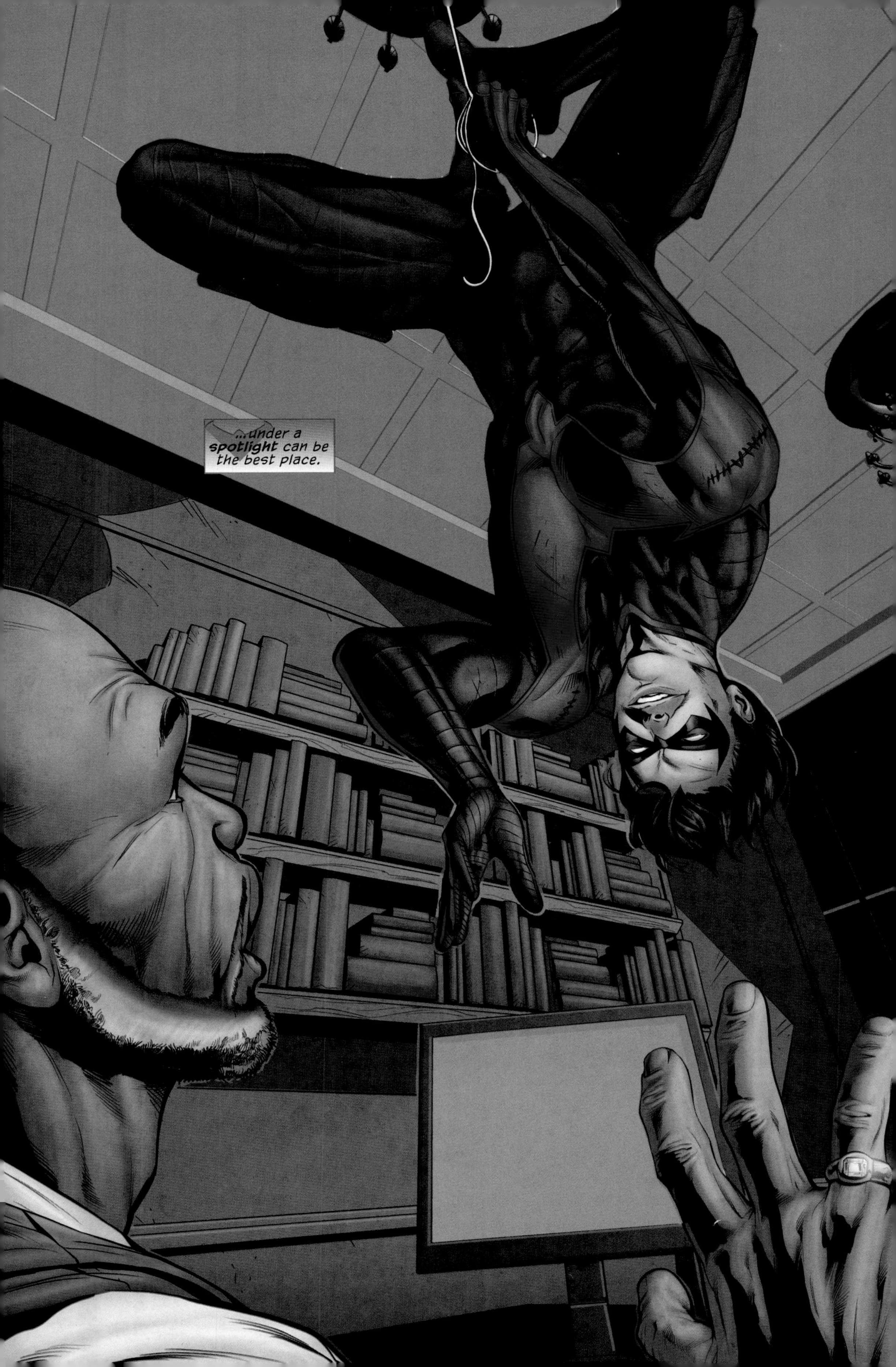
...under a spotlight can be the best place.

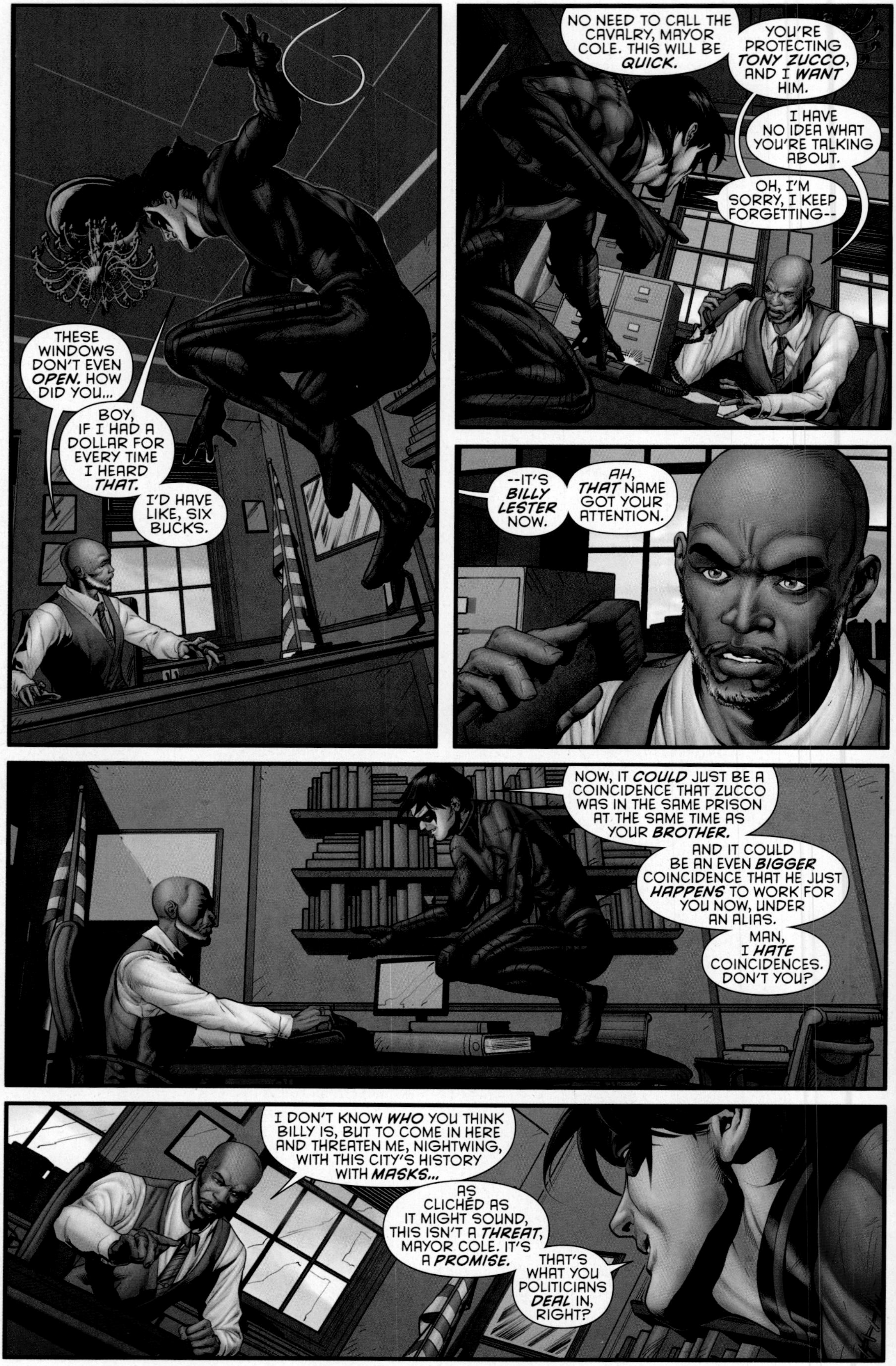
THESE WINDOWS DON'T EVEN OPEN. HOW DID YOU...
BOY, IF I HAD A DOLLAR FOR EVERY TIME I HEARD THAT.
I'D HAVE LIKE, SIX BUCKS.
NO NEED TO CALL THE CAVALRY, MAYOR COLE. THIS WILL BE QUICK.
YOU'RE PROTECTING TONY ZUCCO, AND I WANT HIM.
I HAVE NO IDEA WHAT YOU'RE TALKING ABOUT.
OH, I'M SORRY, I KEEP FORGETTING--
--IT'S BILLY LESTER NOW.
AH, THAT NAME GOT YOUR ATTENTION.
NOW, IT COULD JUST BE A COINCIDENCE THAT ZUCCO WAS IN THE SAME PRISON AT THE SAME TIME AS YOUR BROTHER.
AND IT COULD BE AN EVEN BIGGER COINCIDENCE THAT HE JUST HAPPENS TO WORK FOR YOU NOW, UNDER AN ALIAS.
MAN, I HATE COINCIDENCES. DON'T YOU?
I DON'T KNOW WHO YOU THINK BILLY IS, BUT TO COME IN HERE AND THREATEN ME, NIGHTWING, WITH THIS CITY'S HISTORY WITH MASKS...
AS CLICHÉD AS IT MIGHT SOUND, THIS ISN'T A THREAT, MAYOR COLE. IT'S A PROMISE.
THAT'S WHAT YOU POLITICIANS DEAL IN, RIGHT?

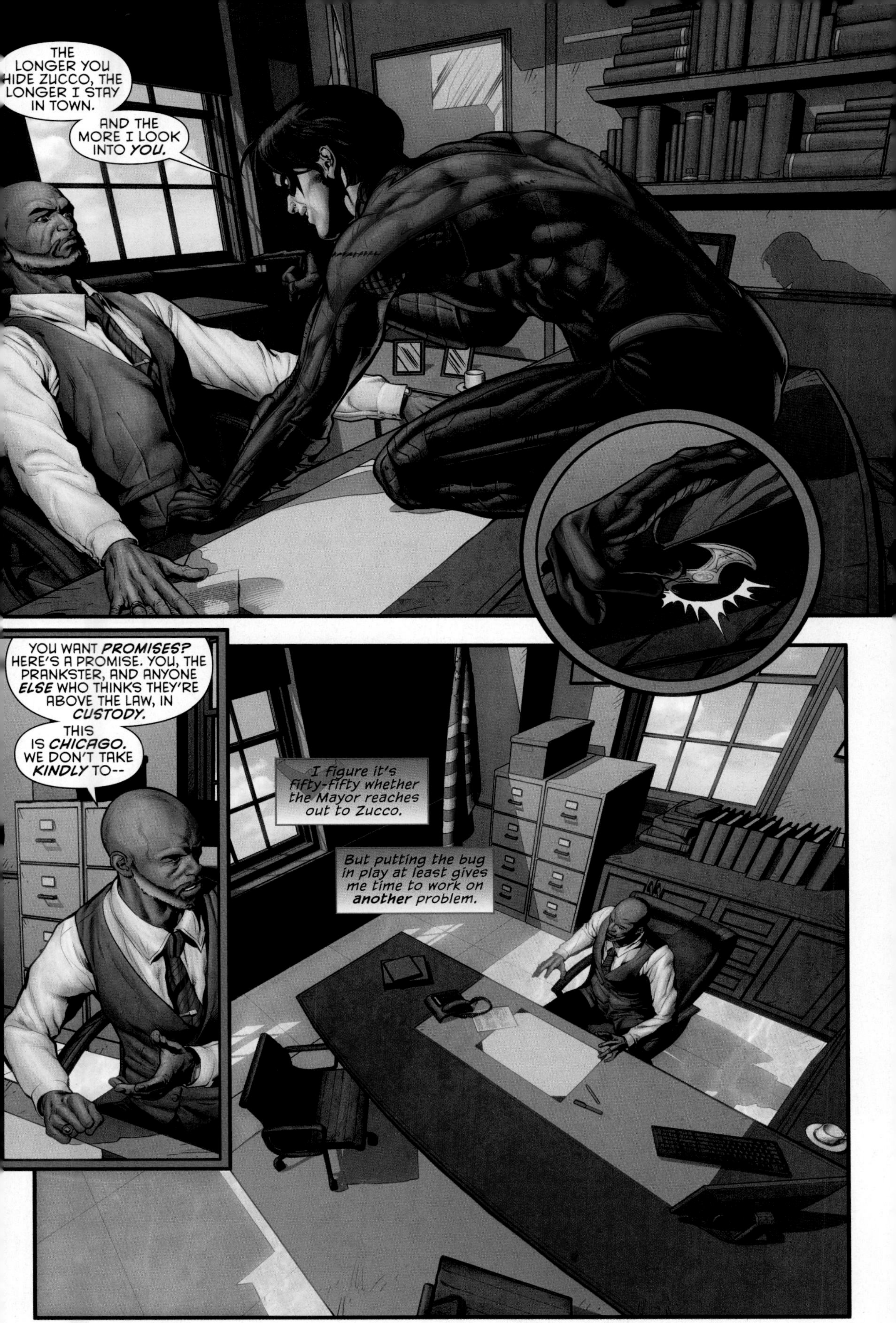
THE LONGER YOU HIDE ZUCCO, THE LONGER I STAY IN TOWN.
AND THE MORE I LOOK INTO YOU.
YOU WANT PROMISES? HERE'S A PROMISE. YOU, THE PRANKSTER, AND ANYONE ELSE WHO THINKS THEY'RE ABOVE THE LAW, IN CUSTODY.
THIS IS CHICAGO. WE DON'T TAKE KINDLY TO--
I figure it's fifty-fifty whether the Mayor reaches out to Zucco.
But putting the bug in play at least gives me time to work on another problem.

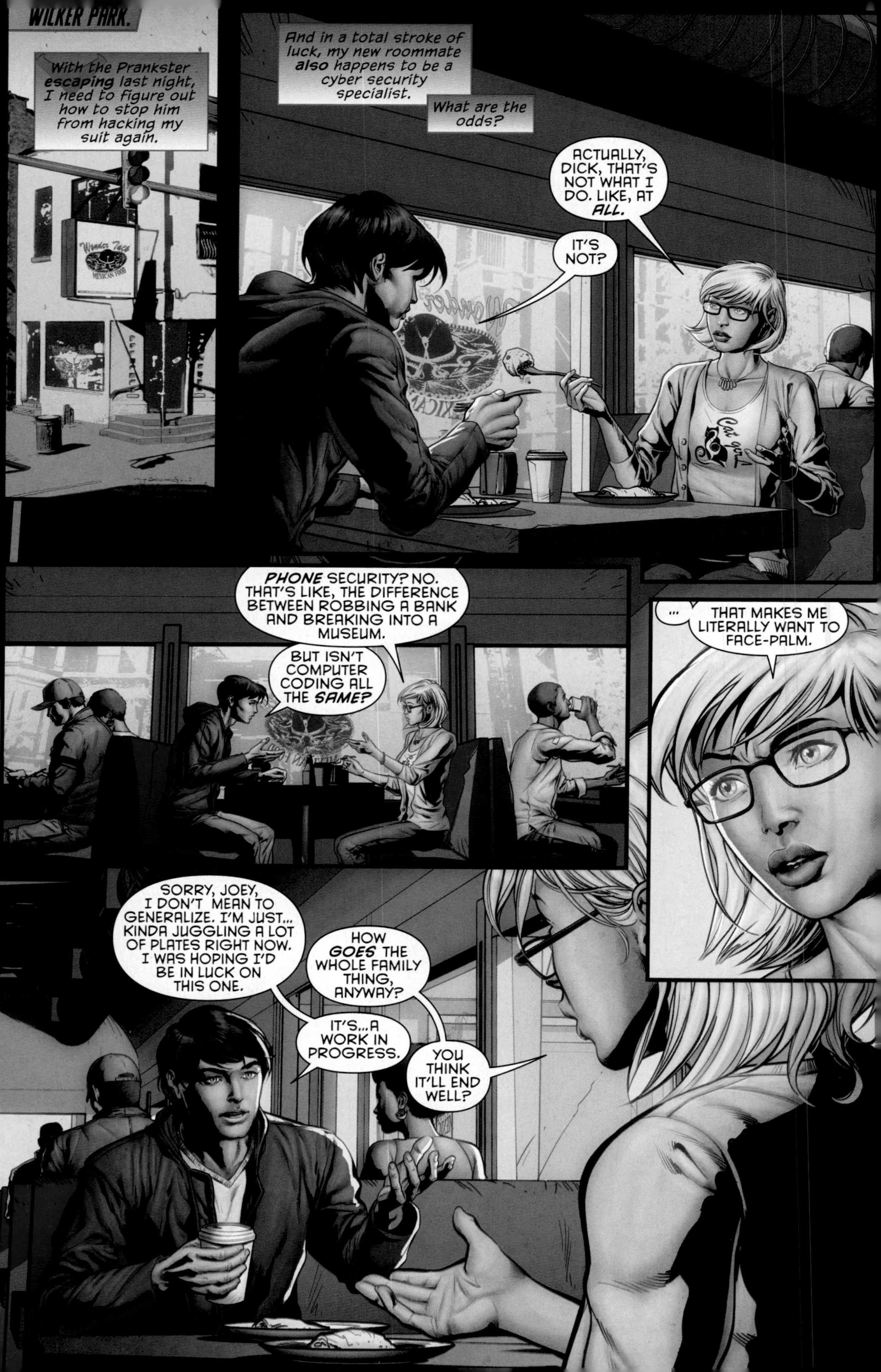
WILKER PARK.
With the Prankster escaping last night, I need to figure out how to stop him from hacking my suit again.
And in a total stroke of luck, my new roommate also happens to be a cyber security specialist.
What are the odds?
ACTUALLY, DICK, THAT'S NOT WHAT I DO. LIKE, AT ALL.
IT'S NOT?
Wonder Taco MEXICAN FOOD
PHONE SECURITY? NO. THAT'S LIKE, THE DIFFERENCE BETWEEN ROBBING A BANK AND BREAKING INTO A MUSEUM.
BUT ISN'T COMPUTER CODING ALL THE SAME?
...
THAT MAKES ME LITERALLY WANT TO FACE-PALM.
SORRY, JOEY, I DON'T MEAN TO GENERALIZE. I'M JUST... KINDA JUGGLING A LOT OF PLATES RIGHT NOW. I WAS HOPING I'D BE IN LUCK ON THIS ONE.
HOW GOES THE WHOLE FAMILY THING, ANYWAY?
IT'S...A WORK IN PROGRESS.
YOU THINK IT'LL END WELL?

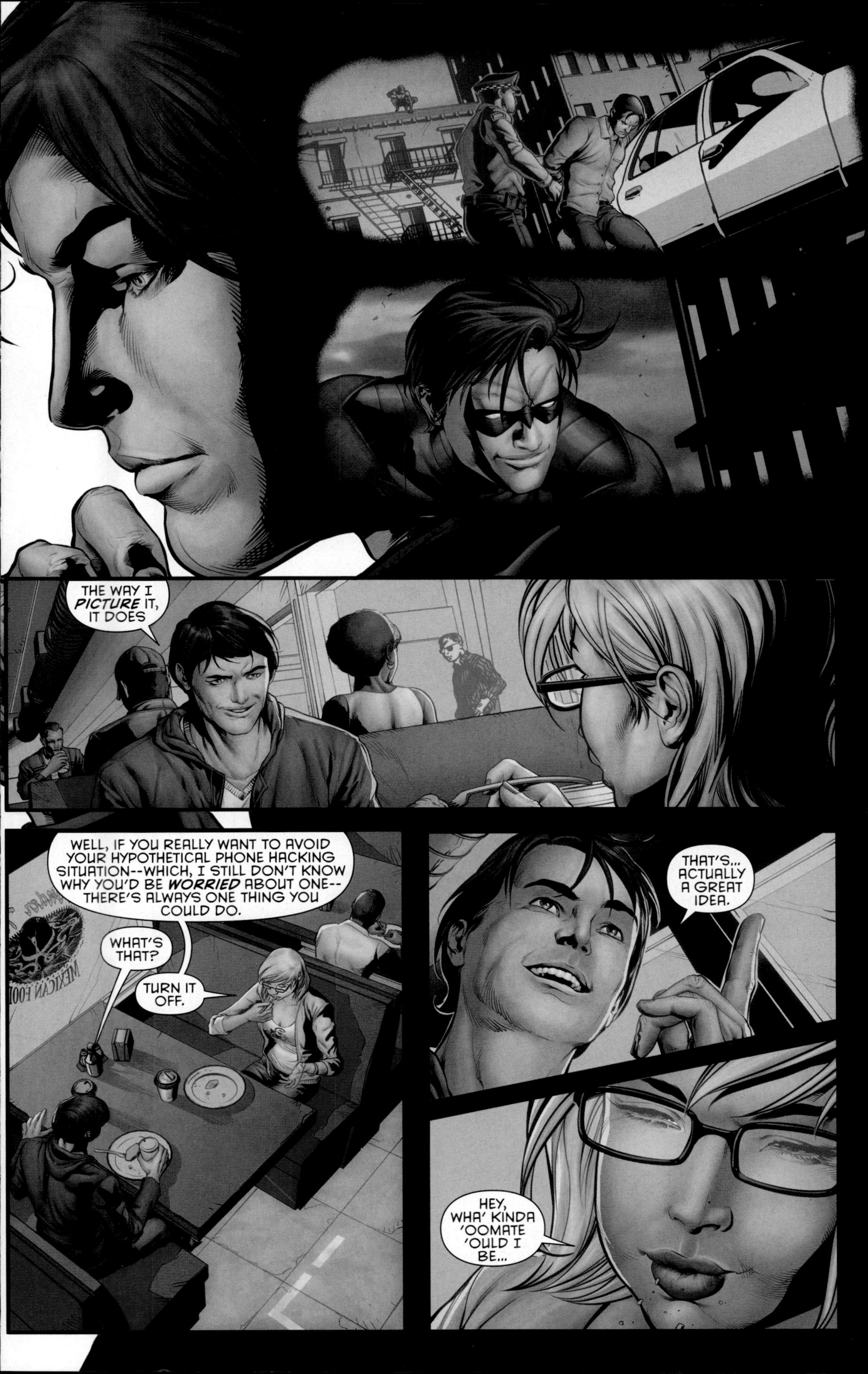
THE WAY I PICTURE IT, IT DOES
WELL, IF YOU REALLY WANT TO AVOID YOUR HYPOTHETICAL PHONE HACKING SITUATION--WHICH, I STILL DON'T KNOW WHY YOU'D BE WORRIED ABOUT ONE-- THERE'S ALWAYS ONE THING YOU COULD DO.
WHAT'S THAT?
TURN IT OFF.
MEXICAN FOOD
THAT'S... ACTUALLY A GREAT IDEA.
HEY, WHA' KINDA 'OOMATE 'OULD I BE...

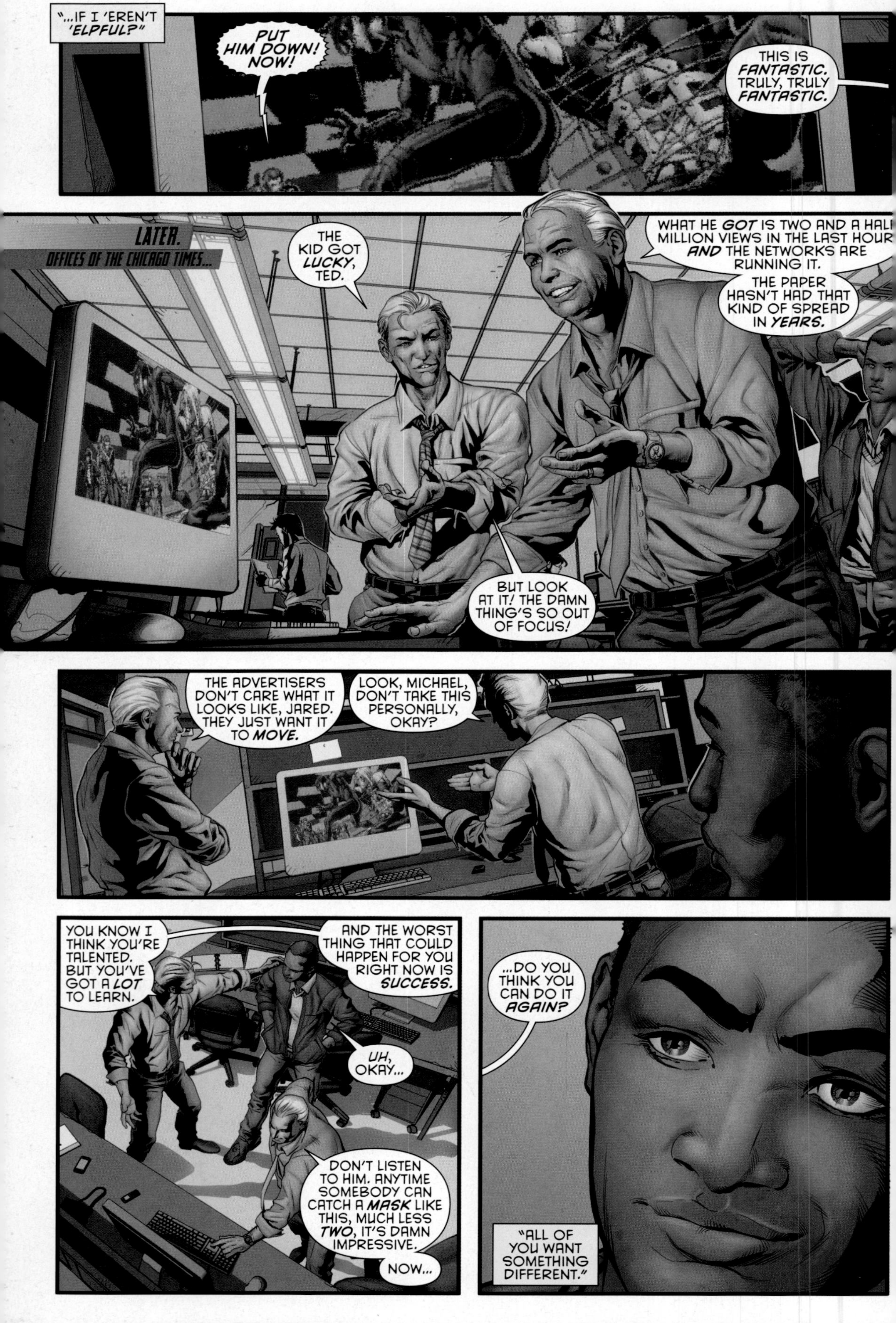
"...IF I 'EREN'T 'ELPFUL?"
PUT HIM DOWN! NOW!
THIS IS FANTASTIC. TRULY, TRULY FANTASTIC.
LATER.
OFFICES OF THE CHICAGO TIMES...
THE KID GOT LUCKY, TED.
WHAT HE GOT IS TWO AND A HALF MILLION VIEWS IN THE LAST HOUR AND THE NETWORKS ARE RUNNING IT.
THE PAPER HASN'T HAD THAT KIND OF SPREAD IN YEARS.
BUT LOOK AT IT! THE DAMN THING'S SO OUT OF FOCUS!
THE ADVERTISERS DON'T CARE WHAT IT LOOKS LIKE, JARED. THEY JUST WANT IT TO MOVE.
LOOK, MICHAEL, DON'T TAKE THIS PERSONALLY, OKAY?
YOU KNOW I THINK YOU'RE TALENTED. BUT YOU'VE GOT A LOT TO LEARN.
AND THE WORST THING THAT COULD HAPPEN FOR YOU RIGHT NOW IS SUCCESS.
UH, OKAY...
DON'T LISTEN TO HIM. ANYTIME SOMEBODY CAN CATCH A MASK LIKE THIS, MUCH LESS TWO, IT'S DAMN IMPRESSIVE.
NOW...
...DO YOU THINK YOU CAN DO IT AGAIN?
"ALL OF YOU WANT SOMETHING DIFFERENT."

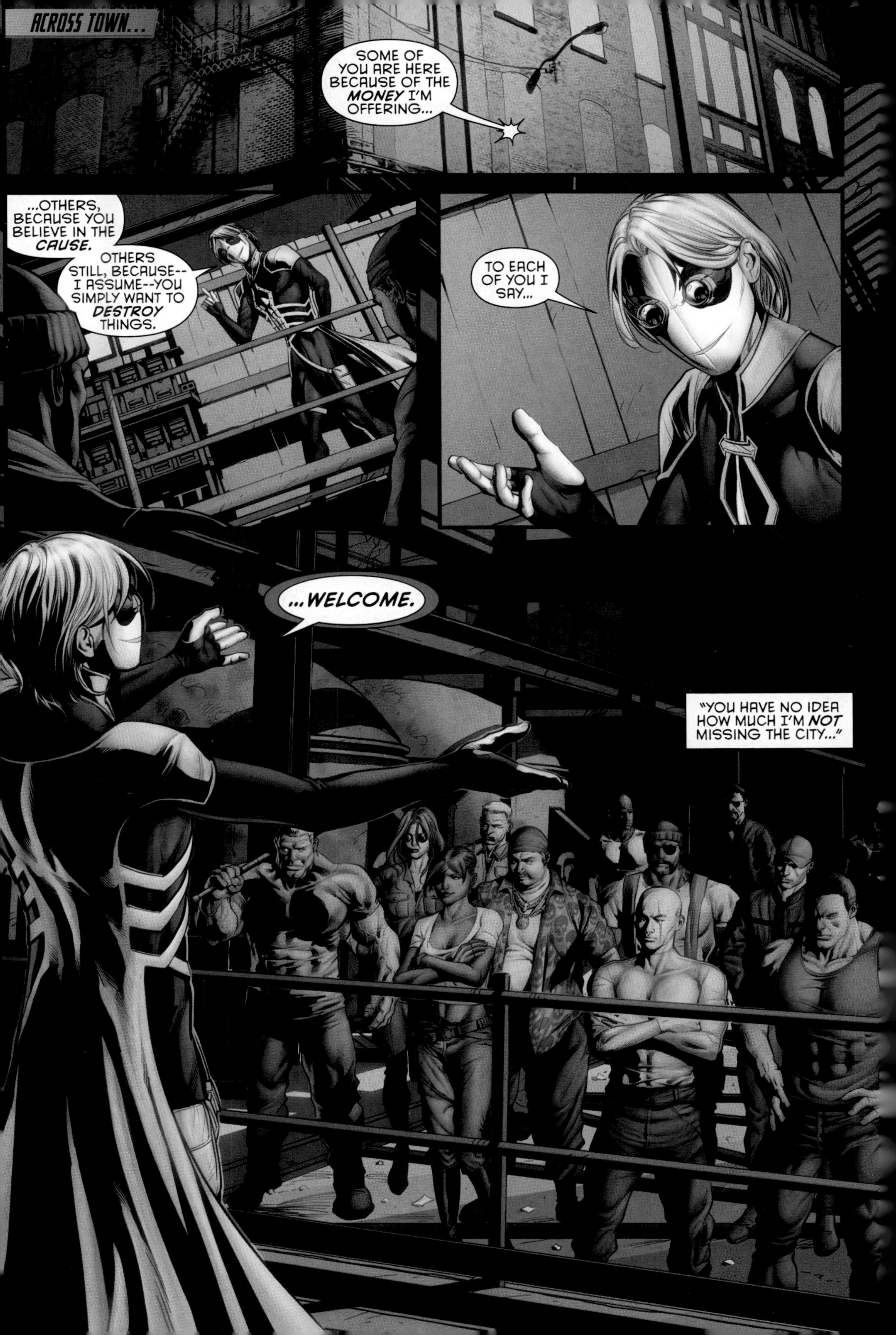
ACROSS TOWN...
SOME OF YOU ARE HERE BECAUSE OF THE *MONEY* I'M OFFERING...
...OTHERS, BECAUSE YOU BELIEVE IN THE *CAUSE.*
OTHERS STILL, BECAUSE-- I ASSUME--YOU SIMPLY WANT TO *DESTROY* THINGS.
TO EACH OF YOU I SAY...
...WELCOME.
"YOU HAVE NO IDEA HOW MUCH I'M *NOT* MISSING THE CITY..."

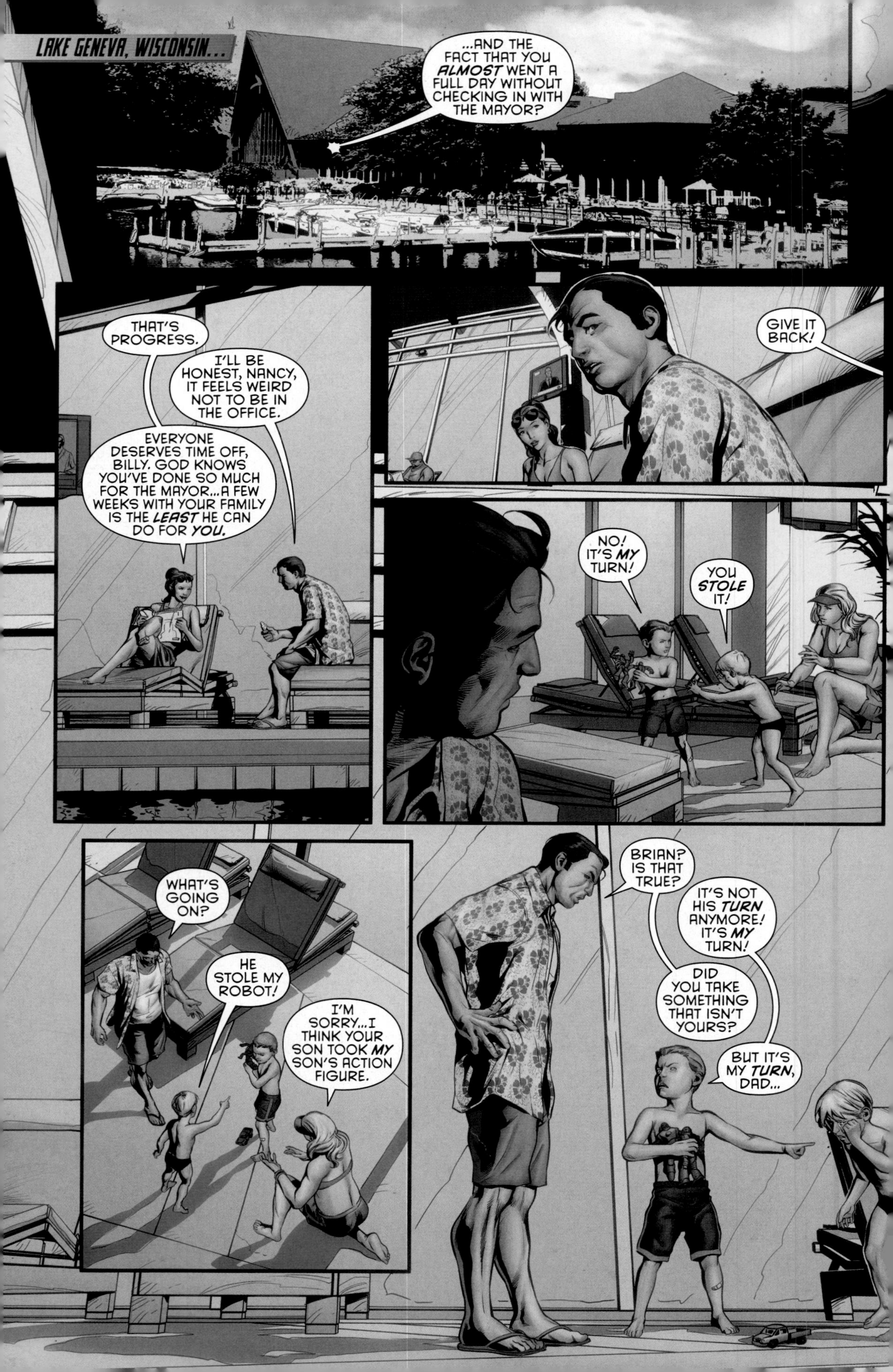
LAKE GENEVA, WISCONSIN...
...AND THE FACT THAT YOU ALMOST WENT A FULL DAY WITHOUT CHECKING IN WITH THE MAYOR?
THAT'S PROGRESS.
I'LL BE HONEST, NANCY, IT FEELS WEIRD NOT TO BE IN THE OFFICE.
EVERYONE DESERVES TIME OFF, BILLY. GOD KNOWS YOU'VE DONE SO MUCH FOR THE MAYOR...A FEW WEEKS WITH YOUR FAMILY IS THE LEAST HE CAN DO FOR YOU.
GIVE IT BACK!
NO! IT'S MY TURN!
YOU STOLE IT!
WHAT'S GOING ON?
HE STOLE MY ROBOT!
I'M SORRY...I THINK YOUR SON TOOK MY SON'S ACTION FIGURE.
BRIAN? IS THAT TRUE?
IT'S NOT HIS TURN ANYMORE! IT'S MY TURN!
DID YOU TAKE SOMETHING THAT ISN'T YOURS?
BUT IT'S MY TURN, DAD...

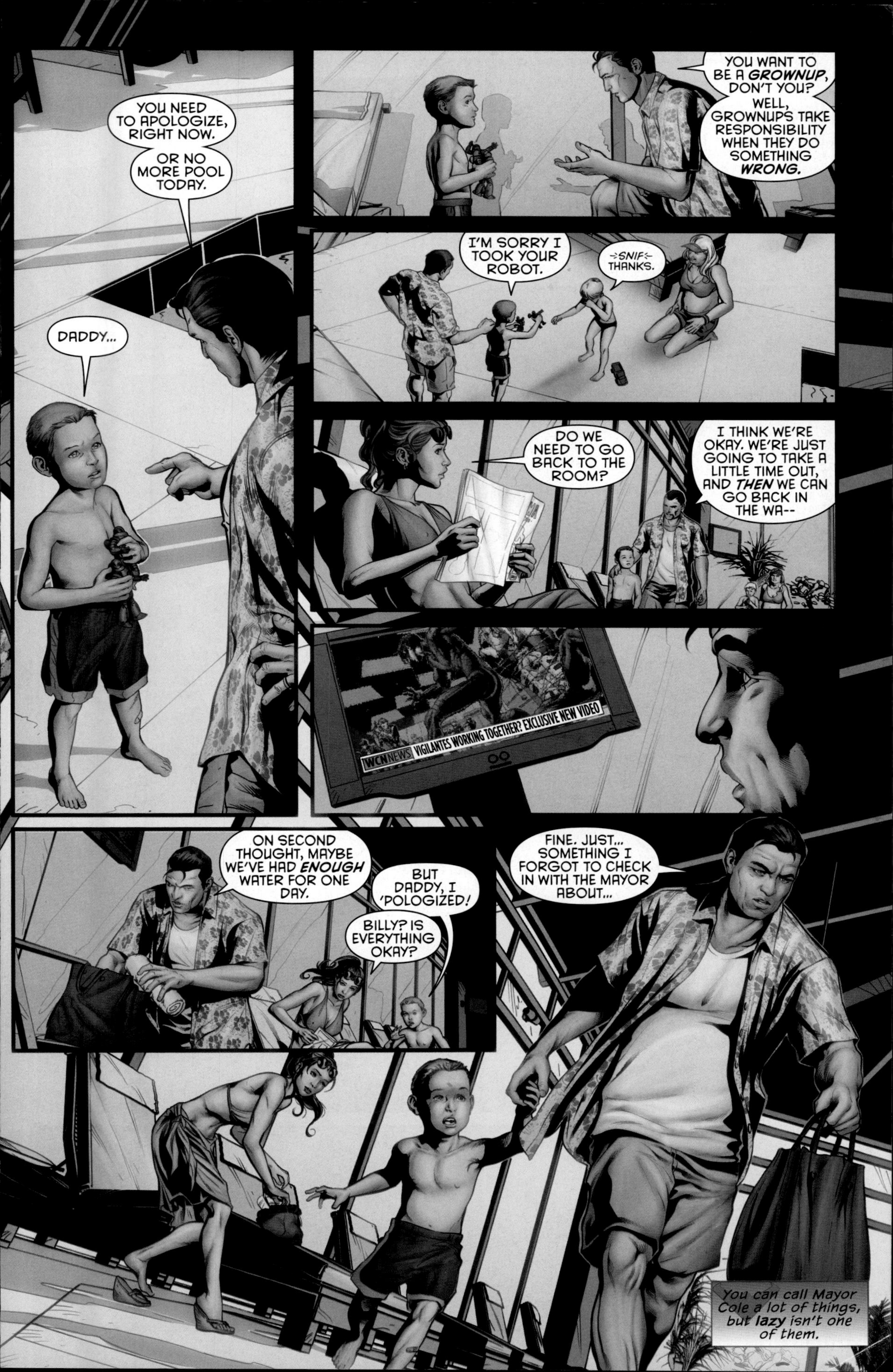
YOU NEED TO APOLOGIZE, RIGHT NOW.
OR NO MORE POOL TODAY.
DADDY...
YOU WANT TO BE A *GROWNUP*, DON'T YOU? WELL, GROWNUPS TAKE RESPONSIBILITY WHEN THEY DO SOMETHING *WRONG.*
I'M SORRY I TOOK YOUR ROBOT.
SNIF THANKS.
DO WE NEED TO GO BACK TO THE ROOM?
I THINK WE'RE OKAY. WE'RE JUST GOING TO TAKE A LITTLE TIME OUT, AND *THEN* WE CAN GO BACK IN THE WA--
WCN NEWS VIGILANTES WORKING TOGETHER? EXCLUSIVE NEW VIDEO
ON SECOND THOUGHT, MAYBE WE'VE HAD *ENOUGH* WATER FOR ONE DAY.
BUT DADDY, I 'POLOGIZED!
BILLY? IS EVERYTHING OKAY?
FINE. JUST... SOMETHING I FORGOT TO CHECK IN WITH THE MAYOR ABOUT...
*You can call Mayor Cole a lot of things, but **lazy** isn't one of them.*

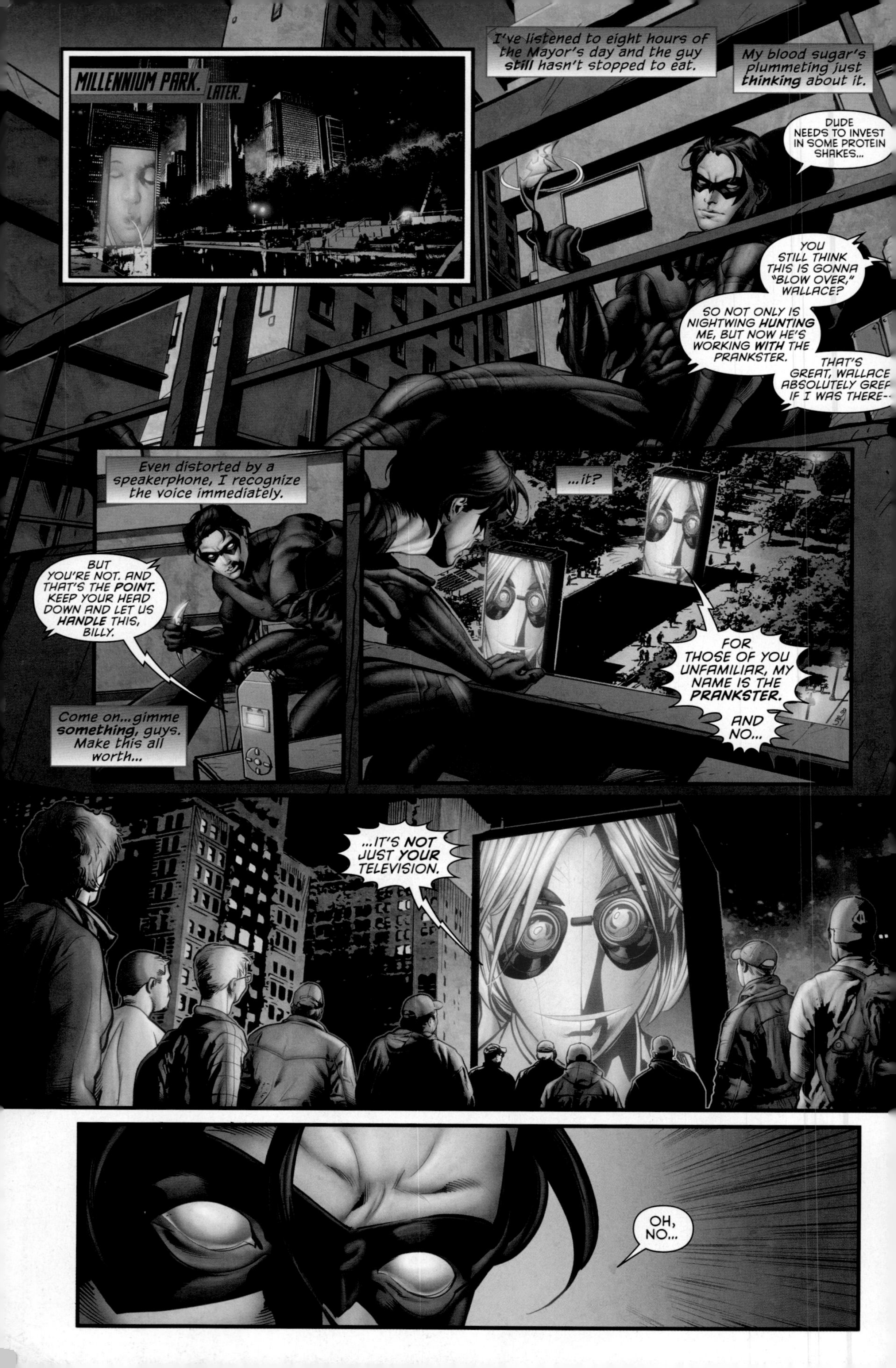
MILLENNIUM PARK. LATER.
I've listened to eight hours of the Mayor's day and the guy still hasn't stopped to eat.
My blood sugar's plummeting just thinking about it.
DUDE NEEDS TO INVEST IN SOME PROTEIN SHAKES...
YOU STILL THINK THIS IS GONNA "BLOW OVER," WALLACE?
SO NOT ONLY IS NIGHTWING HUNTING ME, BUT NOW HE'S WORKING WITH THE PRANKSTER.
THAT'S GREAT, WALLACE. ABSOLUTELY GREAT. IF I WAS THERE--
Even distorted by a speakerphone, I recognize the voice immediately.
BUT YOU'RE NOT. AND THAT'S THE POINT. KEEP YOUR HEAD DOWN AND LET US HANDLE THIS, BILLY.
Come on...gimme something, guys. Make this all worth...
...it?
FOR THOSE OF YOU UNFAMILIAR, MY NAME IS THE PRANKSTER.
AND NO...
...IT'S NOT JUST YOUR TELEVISION.
OH, NO...

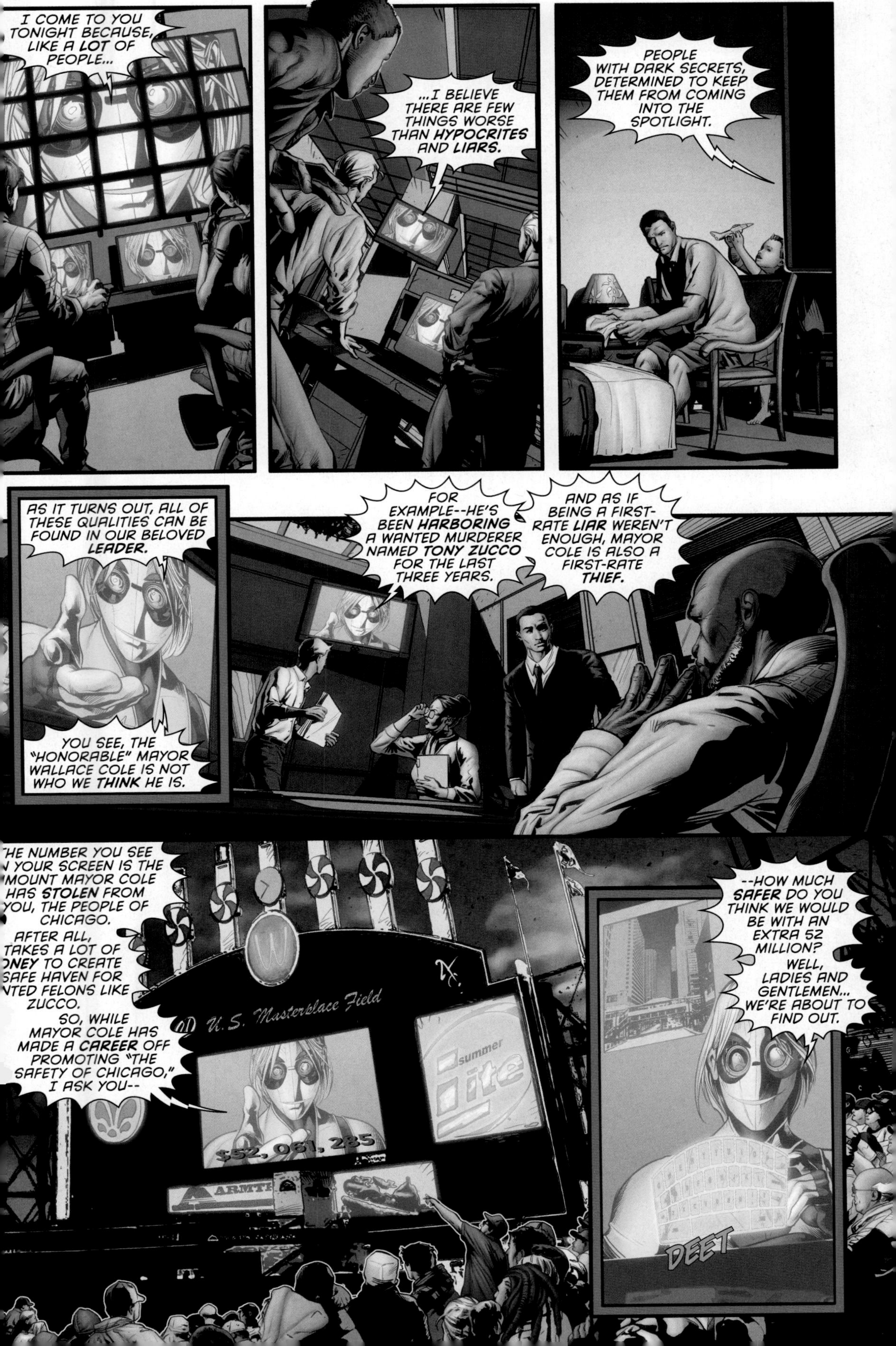
I COME TO YOU TONIGHT BECAUSE, LIKE A LOT OF PEOPLE...
...I BELIEVE THERE ARE FEW THINGS WORSE THAN HYPOCRITES AND LIARS.
PEOPLE WITH DARK SECRETS, DETERMINED TO KEEP THEM FROM COMING INTO THE SPOTLIGHT.
AS IT TURNS OUT, ALL OF THESE QUALITIES CAN BE FOUND IN OUR BELOVED LEADER.
YOU SEE, THE "HONORABLE" MAYOR WALLACE COLE IS NOT WHO WE THINK HE IS.
FOR EXAMPLE--HE'S BEEN HARBORING A WANTED MURDERER NAMED TONY ZUCCO FOR THE LAST THREE YEARS.
AND AS IF BEING A FIRST-RATE LIAR WEREN'T ENOUGH, MAYOR COLE IS ALSO A FIRST-RATE THIEF.
HE NUMBER YOU SEE N YOUR SCREEN IS THE MOUNT MAYOR COLE HAS STOLEN FROM YOU, THE PEOPLE OF CHICAGO.
AFTER ALL, TAKES A LOT OF ONEY TO CREATE SAFE HAVEN FOR NTED FELONS LIKE ZUCCO.
SO, WHILE MAYOR COLE HAS MADE A CAREER OFF PROMOTING "THE SAFETY OF CHICAGO," I ASK YOU--
U.S. Masterplace Field
summer lite
$52,061,285
ARMT
--HOW MUCH SAFER DO YOU THINK WE WOULD BE WITH AN EXTRA 52 MILLION?
WELL, LADIES AND GENTLEMEN... WE'RE ABOUT TO FIND OUT.
DEET

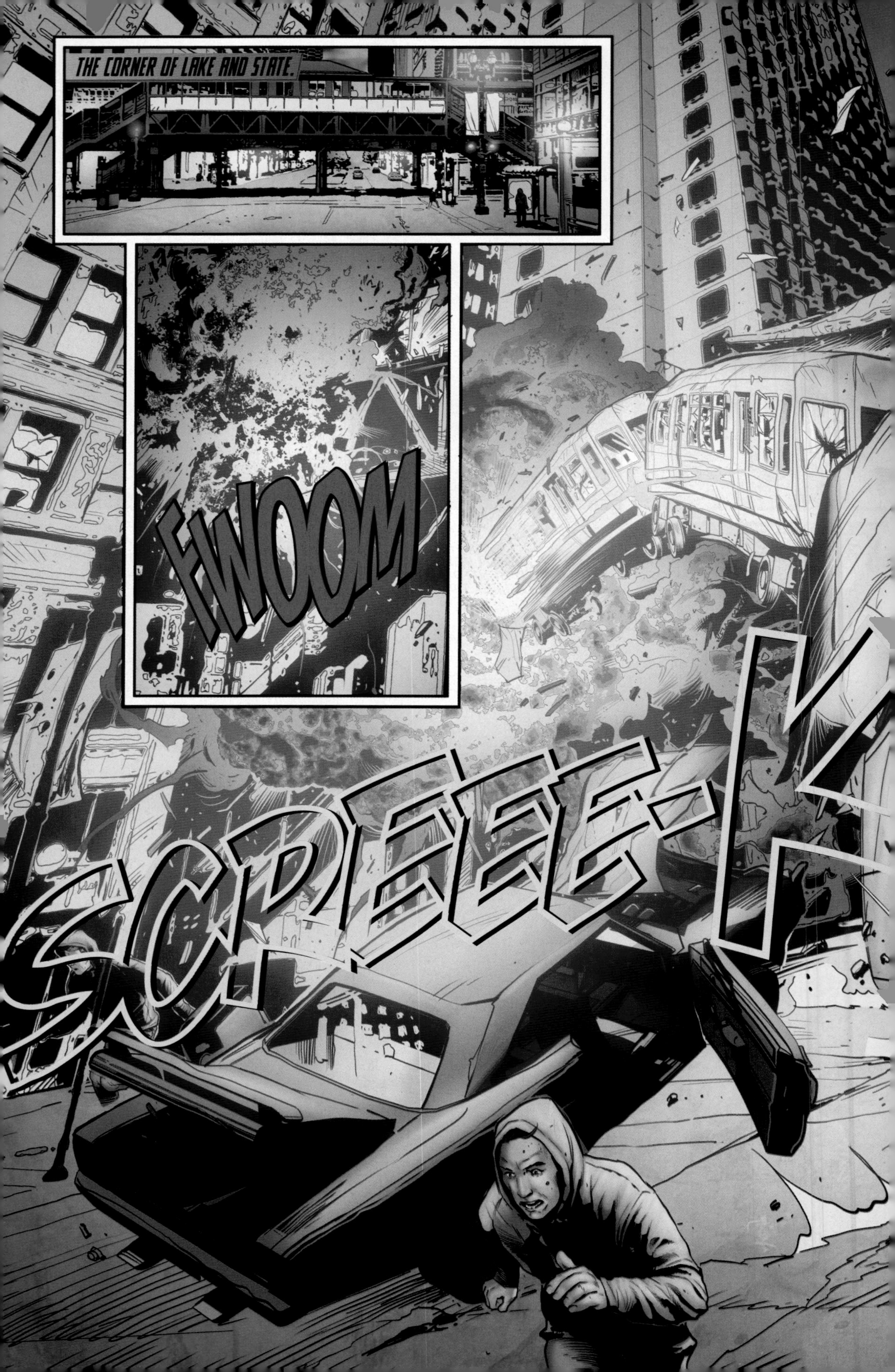
THE CORNER OF LAKE AND STATE.
FWOOM
SCREEE-K

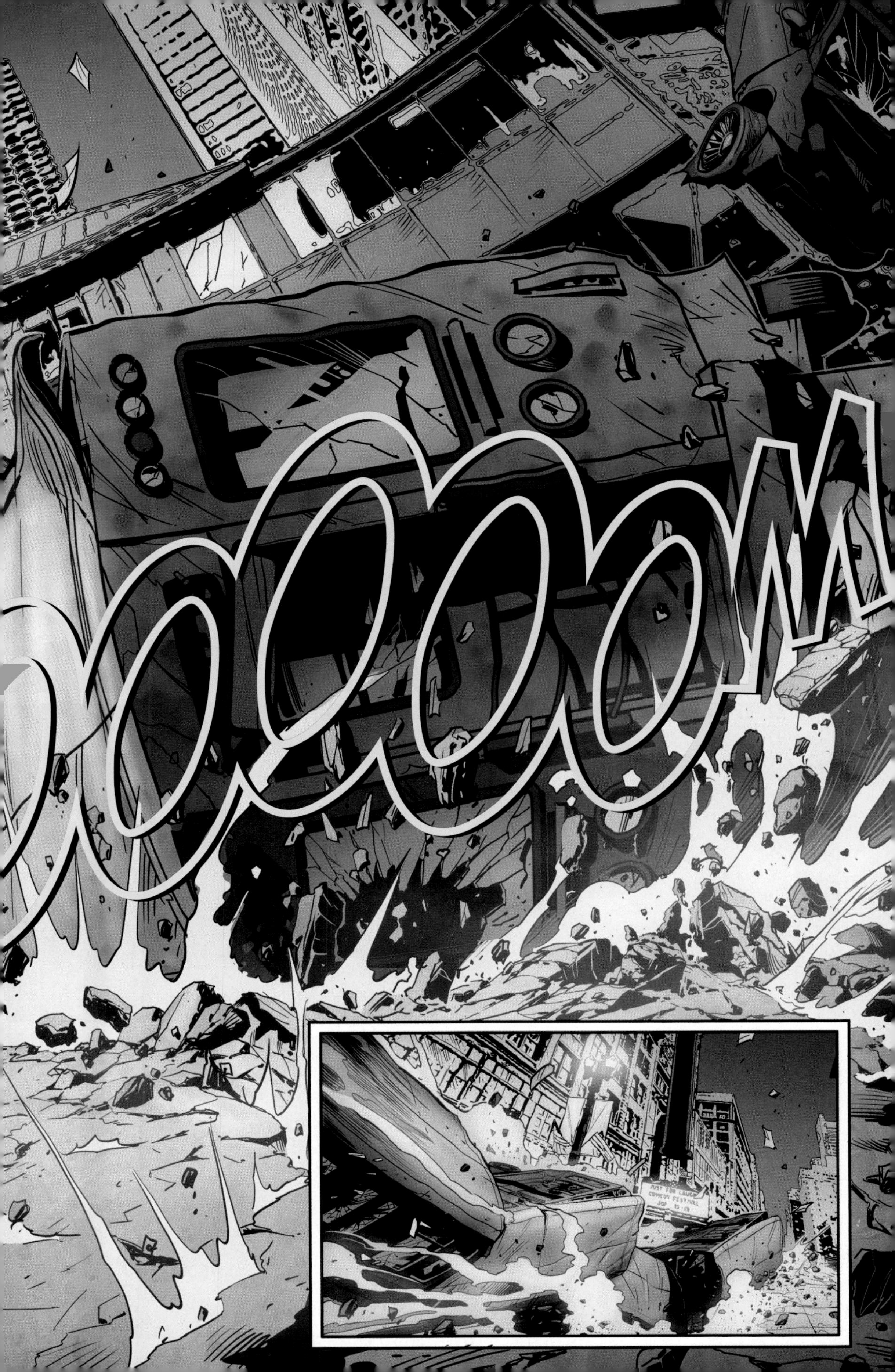
OOOOOOM

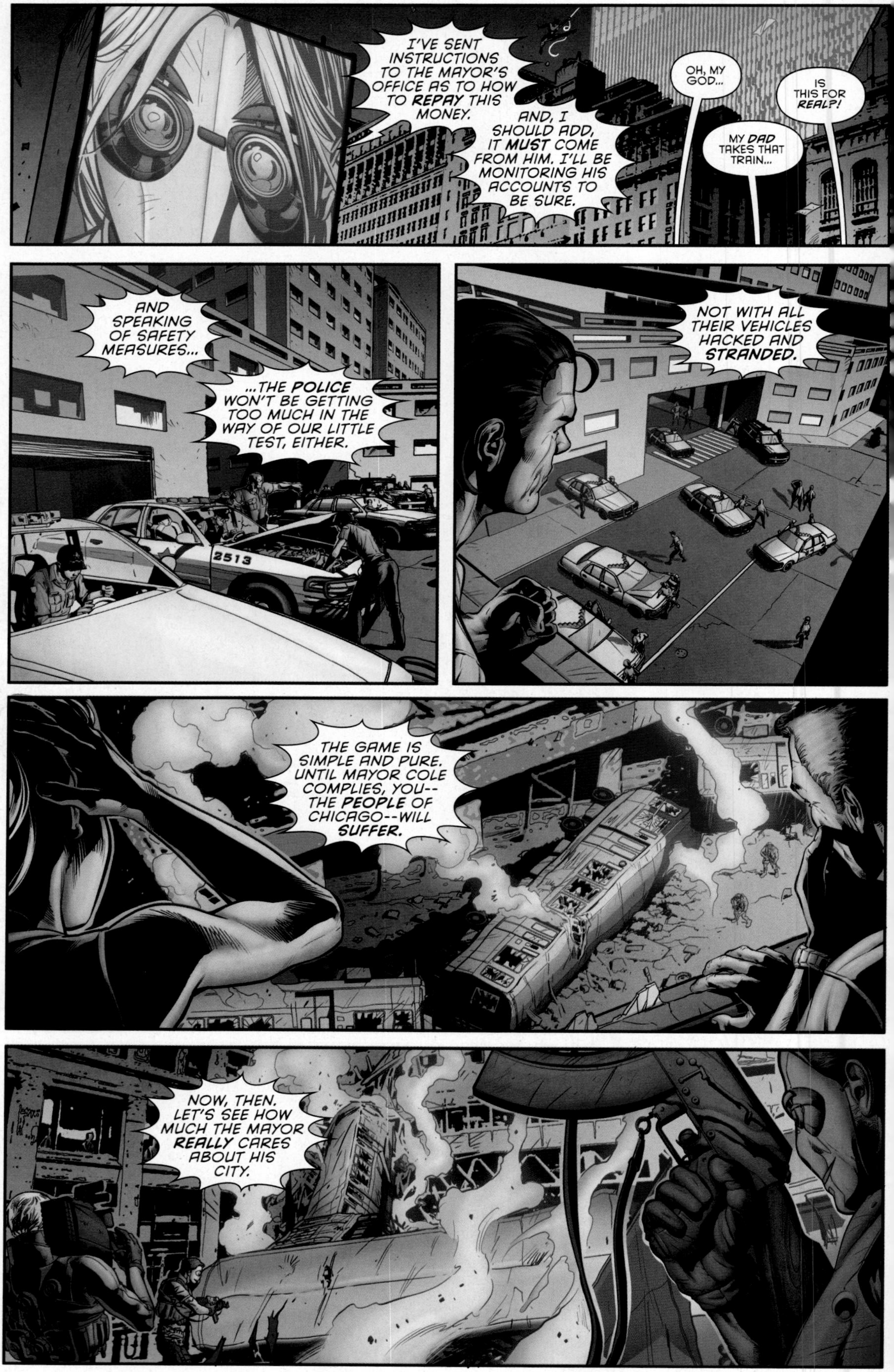
I'VE SENT INSTRUCTIONS TO THE MAYOR'S OFFICE AS TO HOW TO REPAY THIS MONEY.
AND, I SHOULD ADD, IT MUST COME FROM HIM. I'LL BE MONITORING HIS ACCOUNTS TO BE SURE.
OH, MY GOD...
MY DAD TAKES THAT TRAIN...
IS THIS FOR REAL?!
AND SPEAKING OF SAFETY MEASURES...
...THE POLICE WON'T BE GETTING TOO MUCH IN THE WAY OF OUR LITTLE TEST, EITHER.
2513
NOT WITH ALL THEIR VEHICLES HACKED AND STRANDED.
THE GAME IS SIMPLE AND PURE. UNTIL MAYOR COLE COMPLIES, YOU--THE PEOPLE OF CHICAGO--WILL SUFFER.
NOW, THEN. LET'S SEE HOW MUCH THE MAYOR REALLY CARES ABOUT HIS CITY.

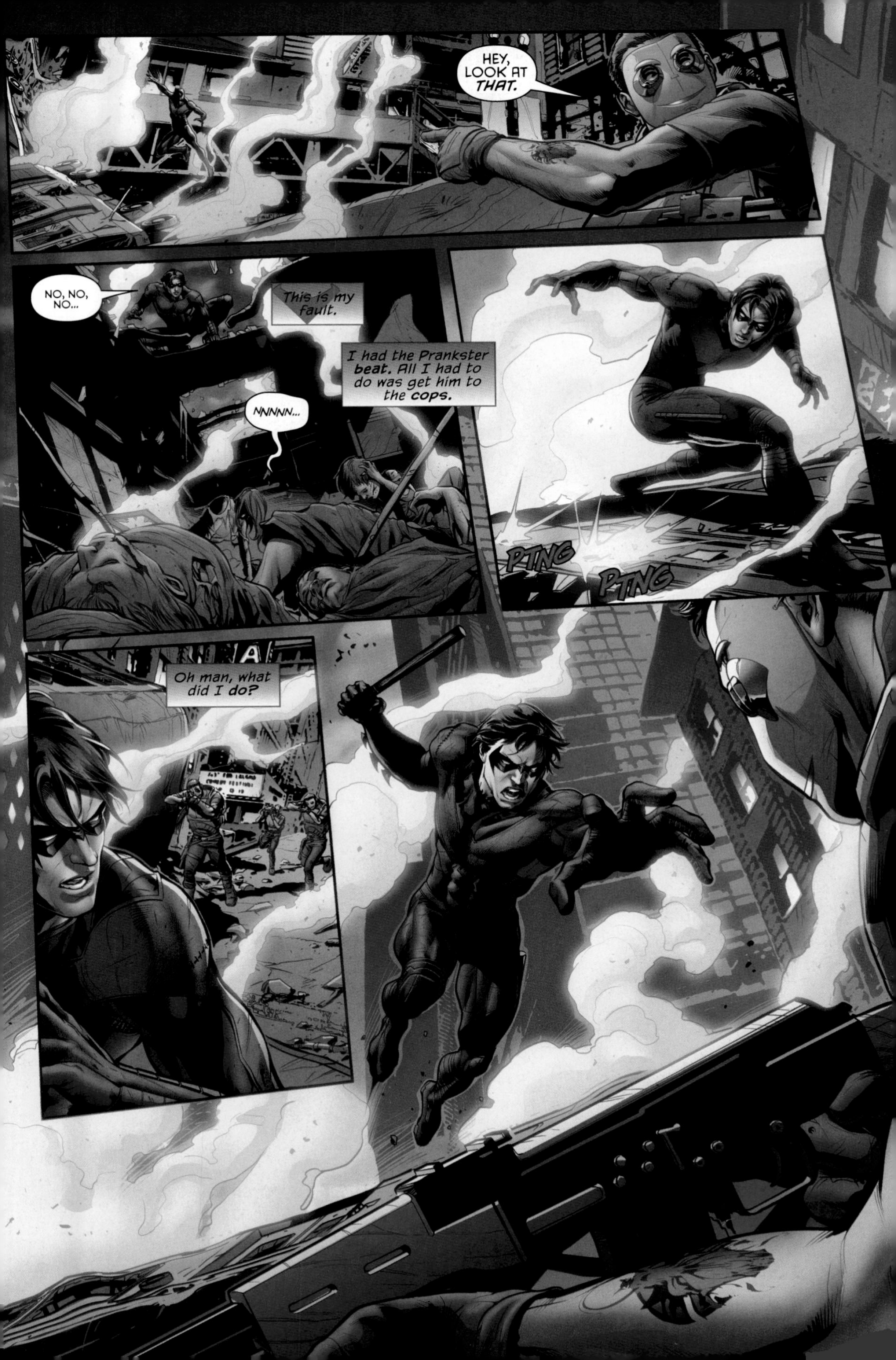
HEY, LOOK AT THAT.
NO, NO, NO...
This is my fault.
I had the Prankster beat. All I had to do was get him to the cops.
NNNNN...
PTNG
PTNG
Oh man, what did I do?

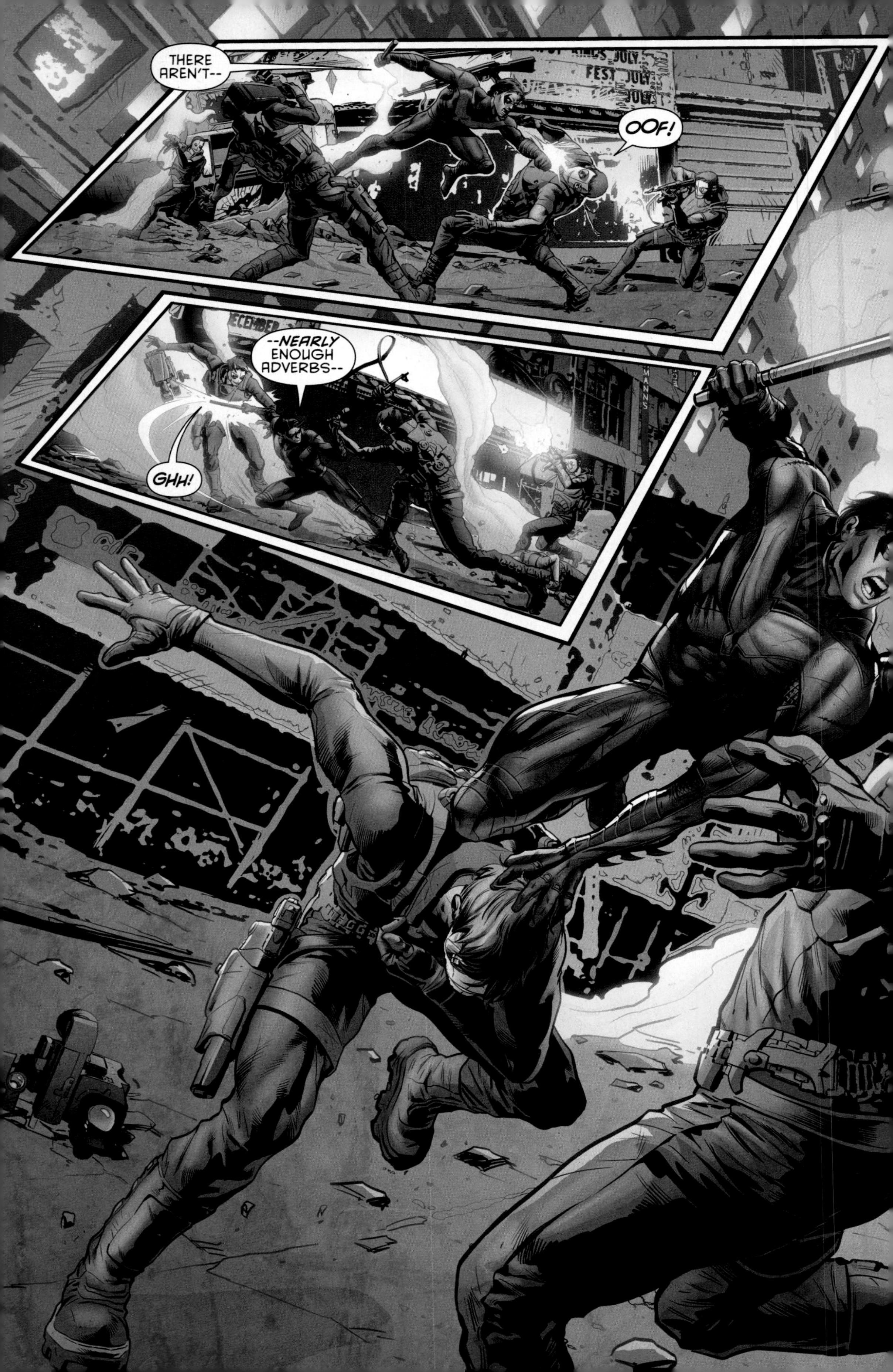
THERE AREN'T--
OOF!
--NEARLY ENOUGH ADVERBS--
GHH!

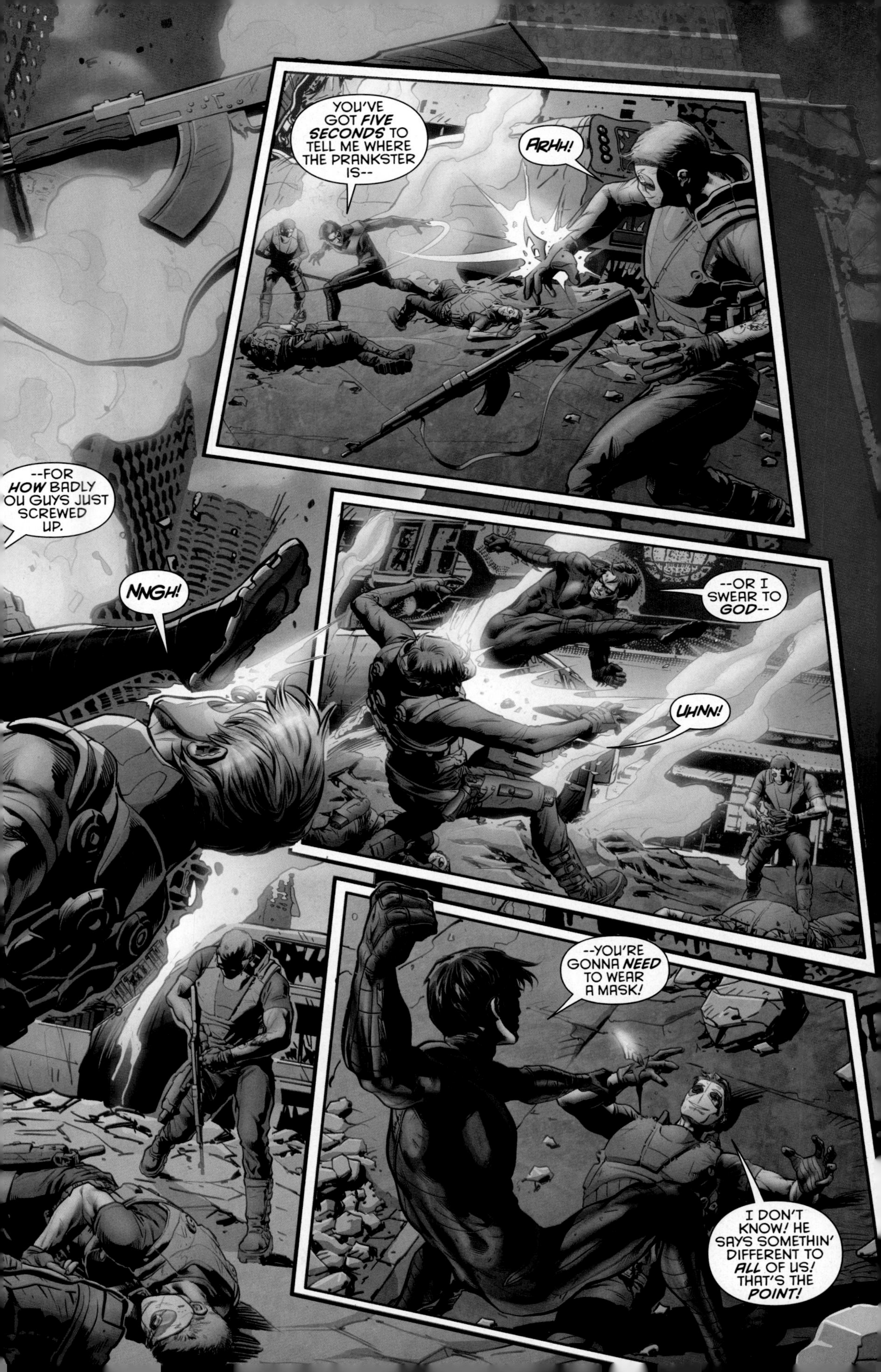
YOU'VE GOT FIVE SECONDS TO TELL ME WHERE THE PRANKSTER IS--
ARHH!
--OR I SWEAR TO GOD--
UHNN!
--FOR HOW BADLY OU GUYS JUST SCREWED UP.
NNGH!
--YOU'RE GONNA NEED TO WEAR A MASK!
I DON'T KNOW! HE SAYS SOMETHIN' DIFFERENT TO ALL OF US! THAT'S THE POINT!

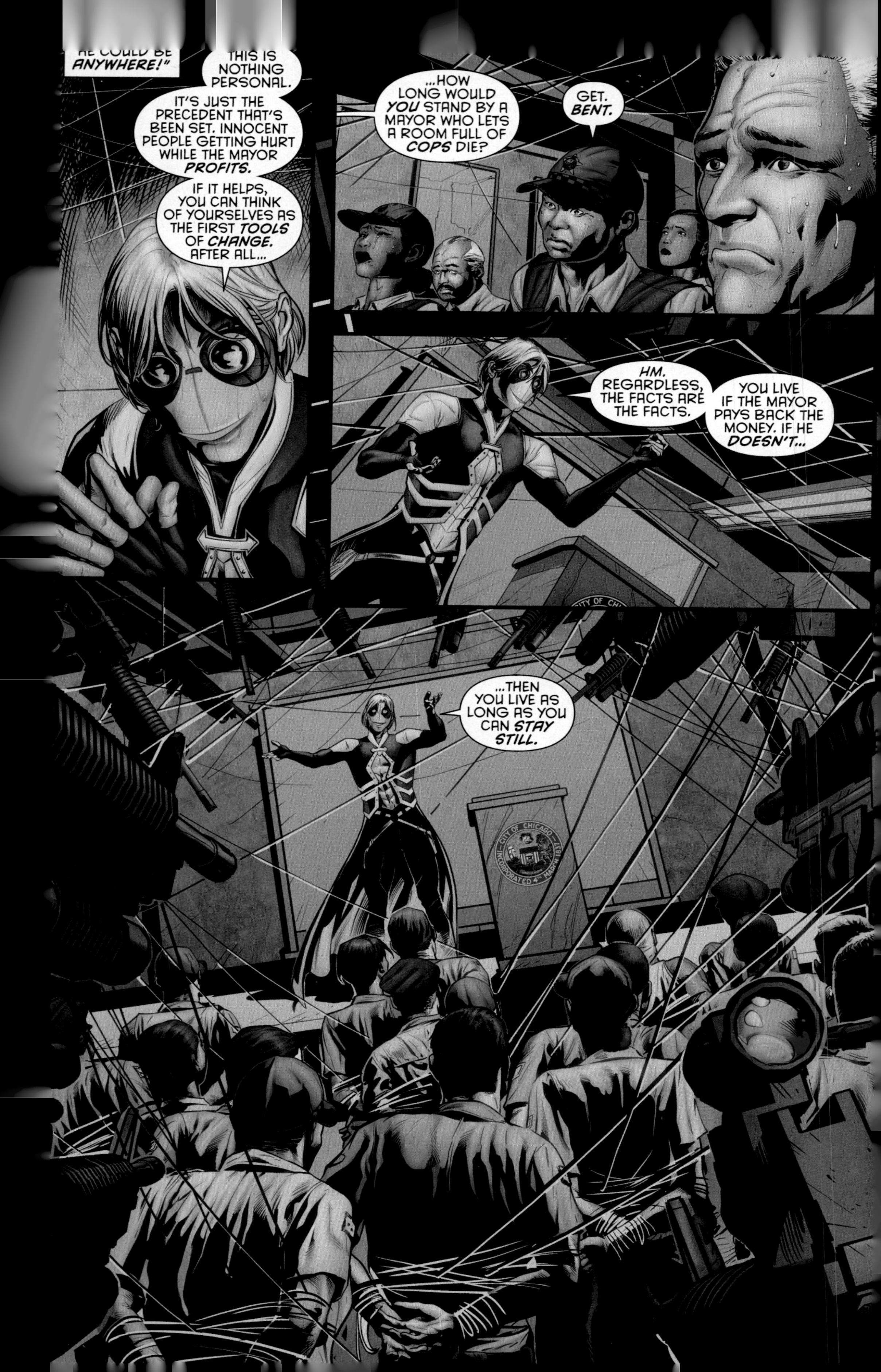
HE COULD BE ANYWHERE!"
THIS IS NOTHING PERSONAL.
IT'S JUST THE PRECEDENT THAT'S BEEN SET. INNOCENT PEOPLE GETTING HURT WHILE THE MAYOR PROFITS.
IF IT HELPS, YOU CAN THINK OF YOURSELVES AS THE FIRST TOOLS OF CHANGE. AFTER ALL...
...HOW LONG WOULD YOU STAND BY A MAYOR WHO LETS A ROOM FULL OF COPS DIE?
GET. BENT.
HM. REGARDLESS, THE FACTS ARE THE FACTS.
YOU LIVE IF THE MAYOR PAYS BACK THE MONEY. IF HE DOESN'T...
...THEN YOU LIVE AS LONG AS YOU CAN STAY STILL.
CITY OF CHICAGO
INCORPORATED 4TH MARCH 1837

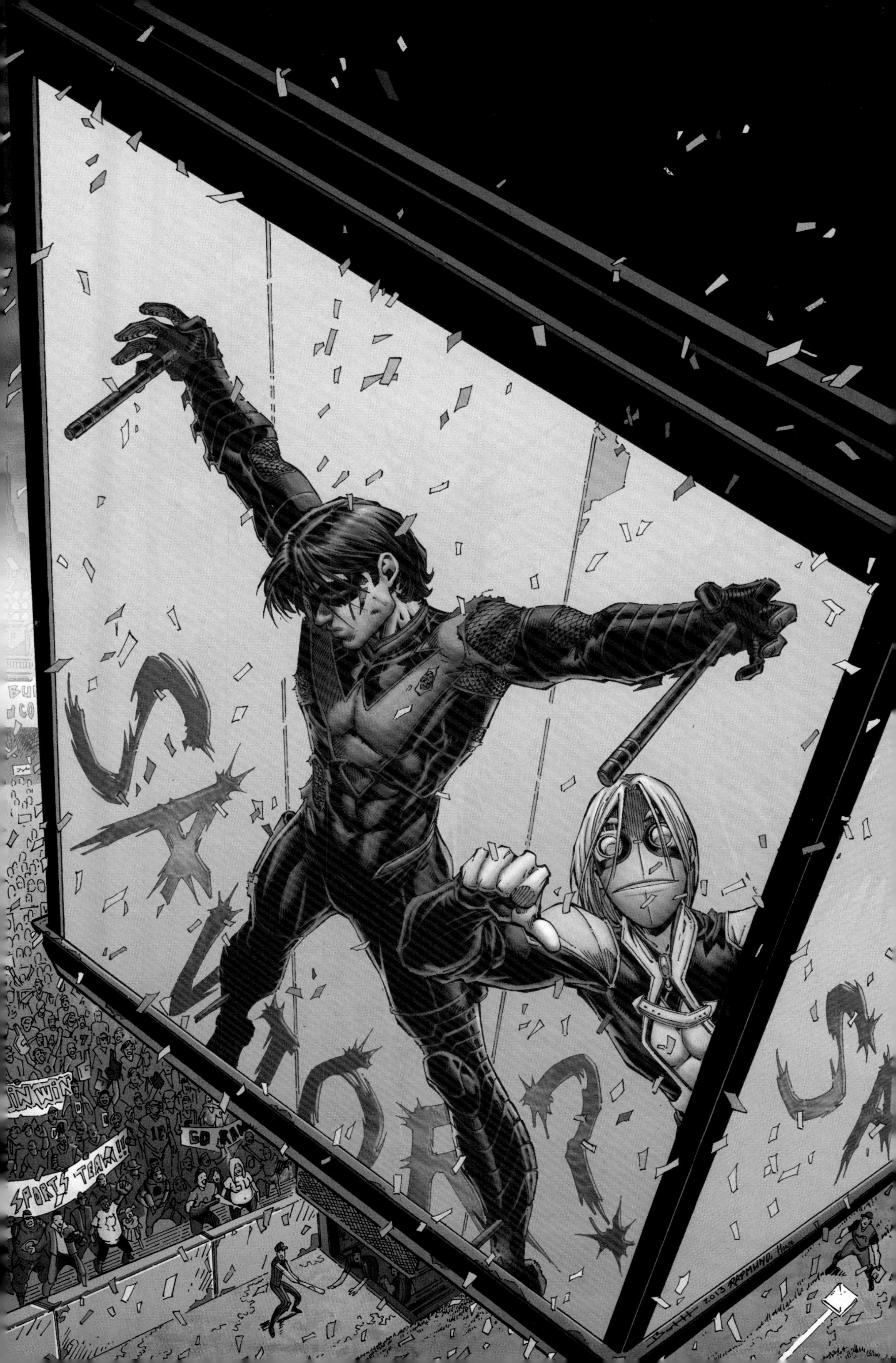
SPORTS TEAM!!

WORLD TURNED UPSIDE DOWN

KYLE HIGGINS writer **WILL CONRAD** artist cover art by **BRETT BOOTH, NORM RAPMUND & ANDREW DALHOUSE**

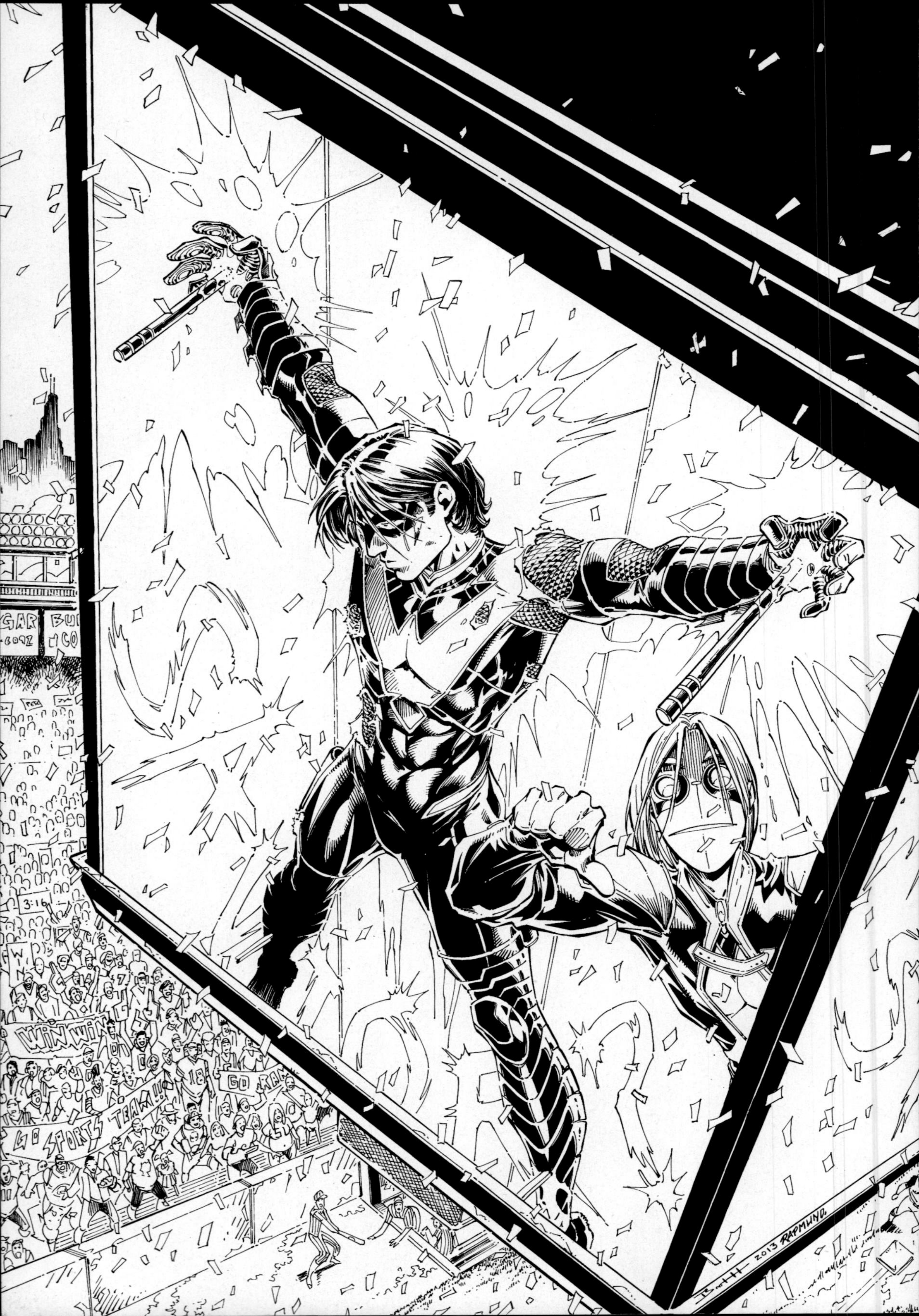
3:16
WIN WIN
GO RAM
GO SPORTS TEAM!!!
2013 RAPMUND

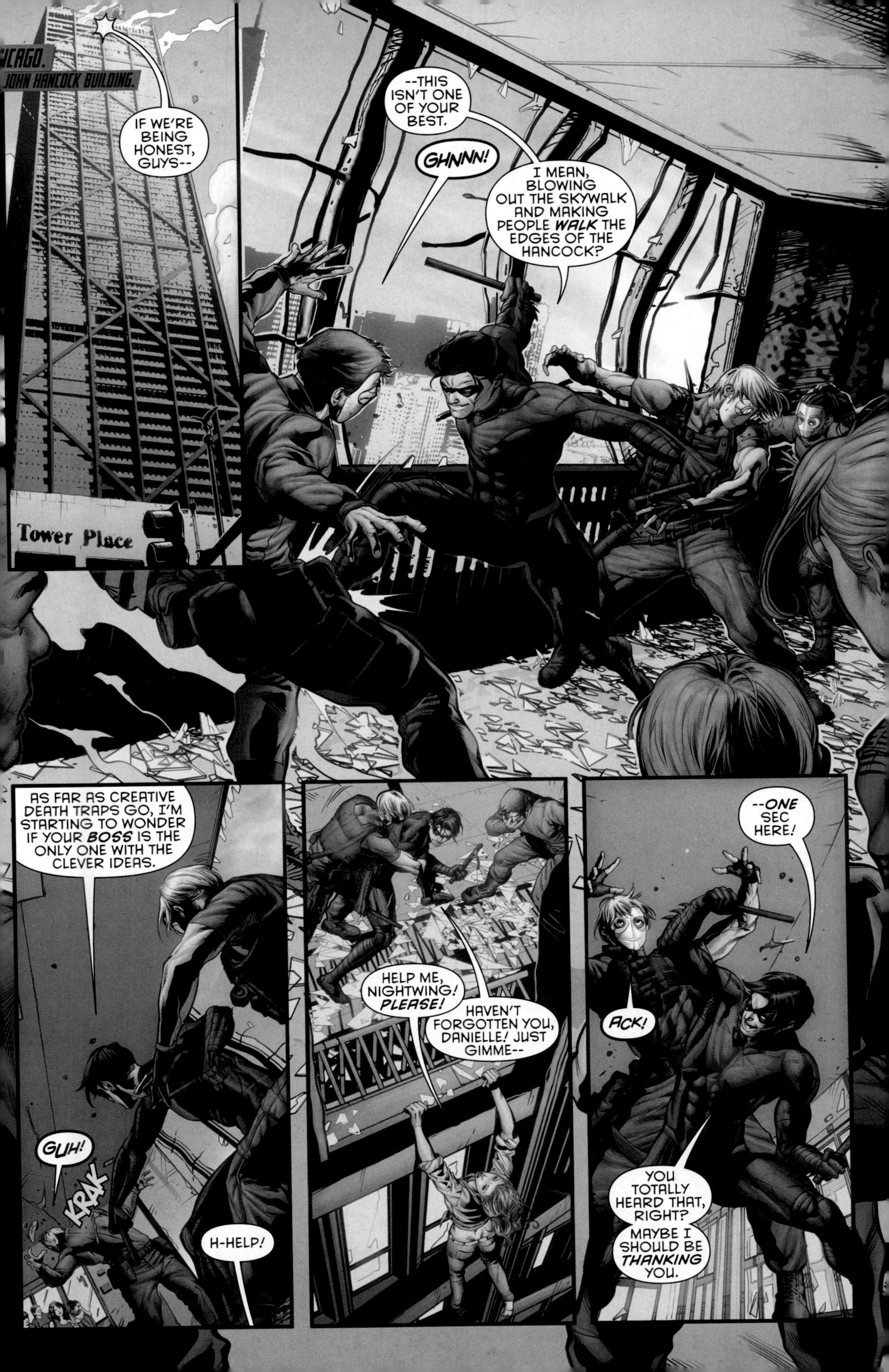

...CAGO.
JOHN HANCOCK BUILDING.
IF WE'RE BEING HONEST, GUYS--
--THIS ISN'T ONE OF YOUR BEST.
GHNNN!
I MEAN, BLOWING OUT THE SKYWALK AND MAKING PEOPLE WALK THE EDGES OF THE HANCOCK?
Tower Place
AS FAR AS CREATIVE DEATH TRAPS GO, I'M STARTING TO WONDER IF YOUR BOSS IS THE ONLY ONE WITH THE CLEVER IDEAS.
GUH!
KRAK
H-HELP!
HELP ME, NIGHTWING! PLEASE!
HAVEN'T FORGOTTEN YOU, DANIELLE! JUST GIMME--
--ONE SEC HERE!
ACK!
YOU TOTALLY HEARD THAT, RIGHT?
MAYBE I SHOULD BE THANKING YOU.

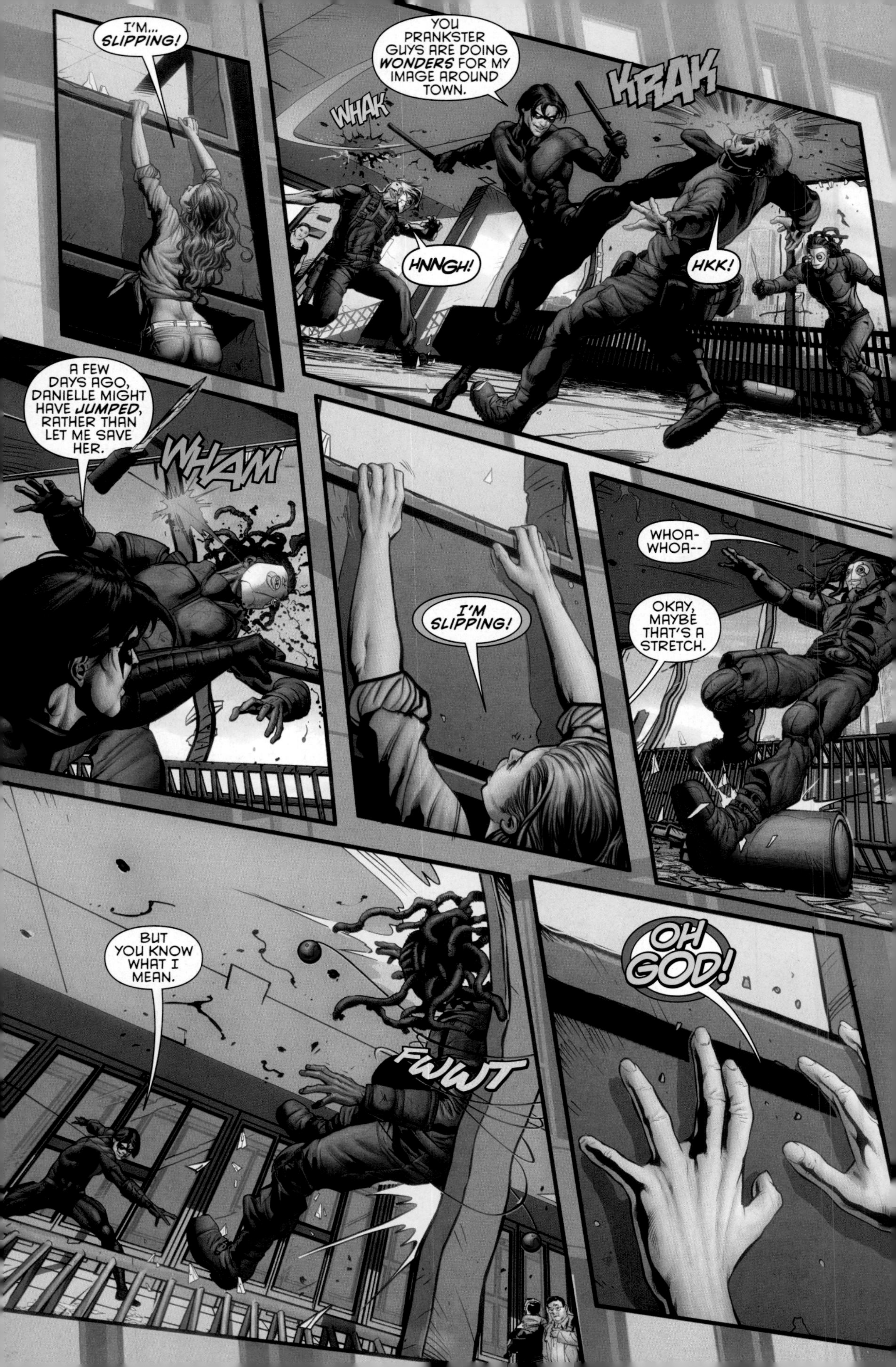
I'M... SLIPPING!
YOU PRANKSTER GUYS ARE DOING WONDERS FOR MY IMAGE AROUND TOWN.
KRAK
WHAK
HNNGH!
HKK!
A FEW DAYS AGO, DANIELLE MIGHT HAVE JUMPED, RATHER THAN LET ME SAVE HER.
WHAM
I'M SLIPPING!
WHOA-WHOA--
OKAY, MAYBE THAT'S A STRETCH.
BUT YOU KNOW WHAT I MEAN.
FWWT
OH GOD!

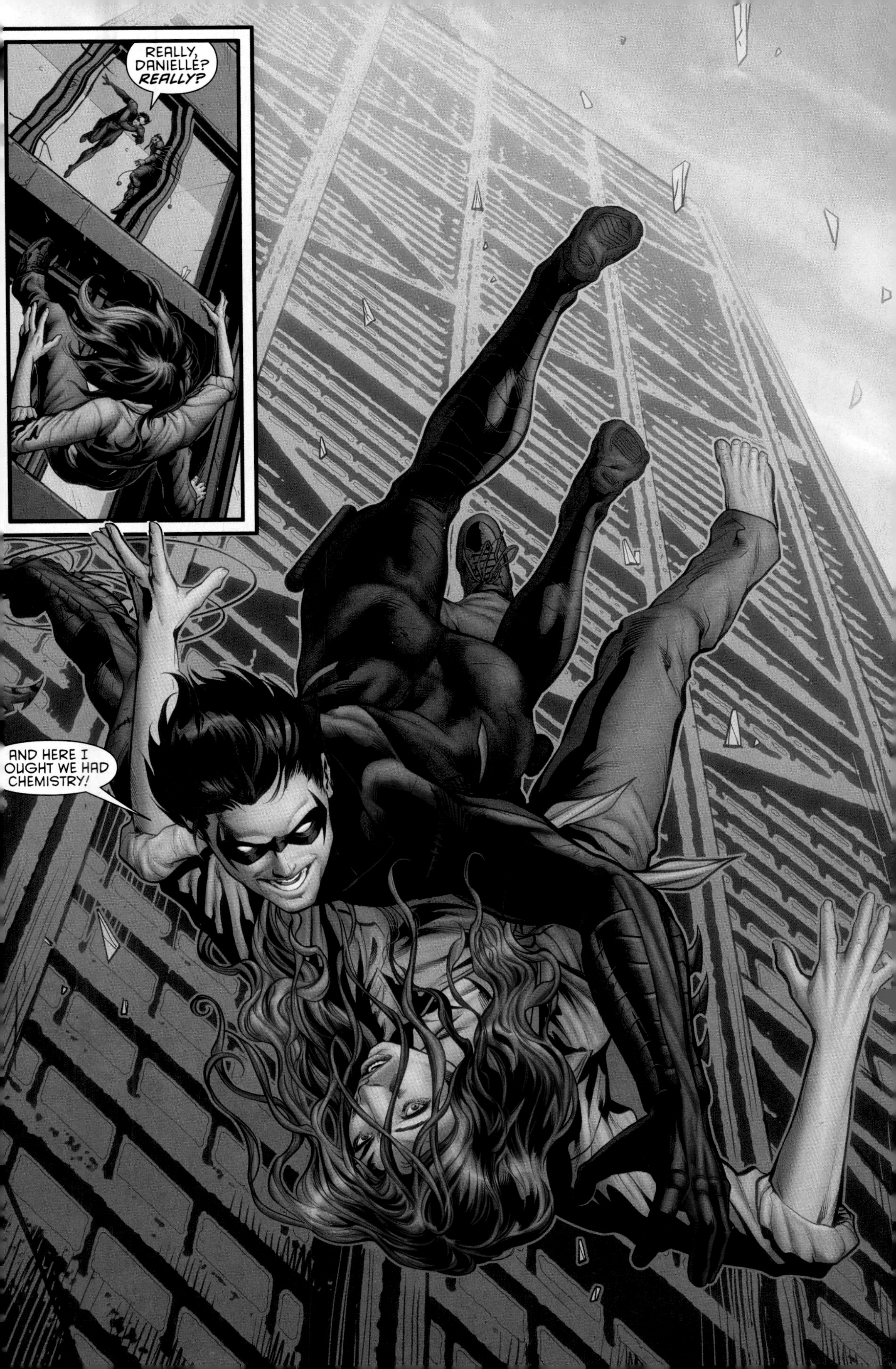
REALLY, DANIELLE? REALLY?
AND HERE I OUGHT WE HAD CHEMISTRY!

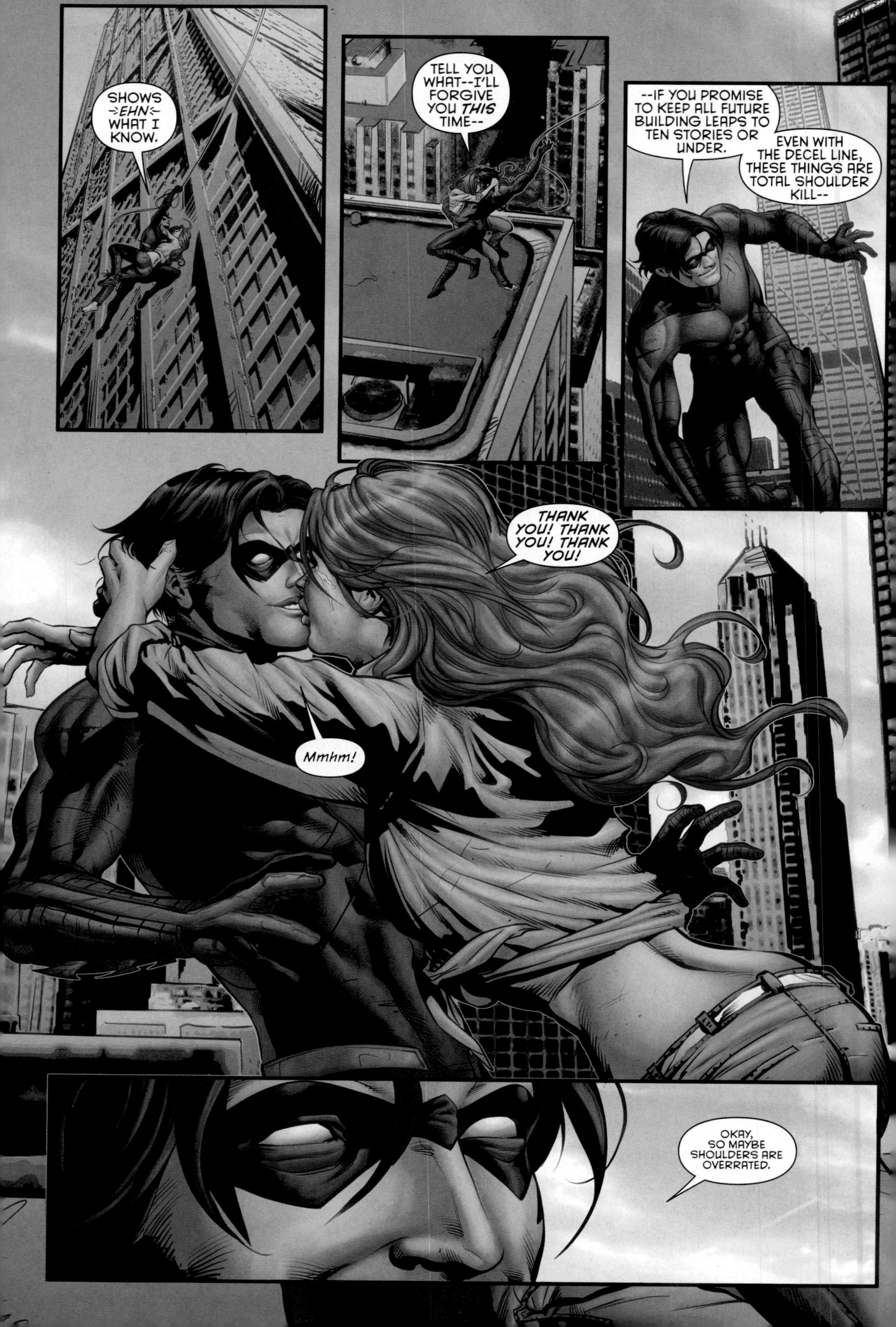
SHOWS -EHN- WHAT I KNOW.
TELL YOU WHAT--I'LL FORGIVE YOU THIS TIME--
--IF YOU PROMISE TO KEEP ALL FUTURE BUILDING LEAPS TO TEN STORIES OR UNDER.
EVEN WITH THE DECEL LINE, THESE THINGS ARE TOTAL SHOULDER KILL--
THANK YOU! THANK YOU! THANK YOU!
Mmhm!
OKAY, SO MAYBE SHOULDERS ARE OVERRATED.

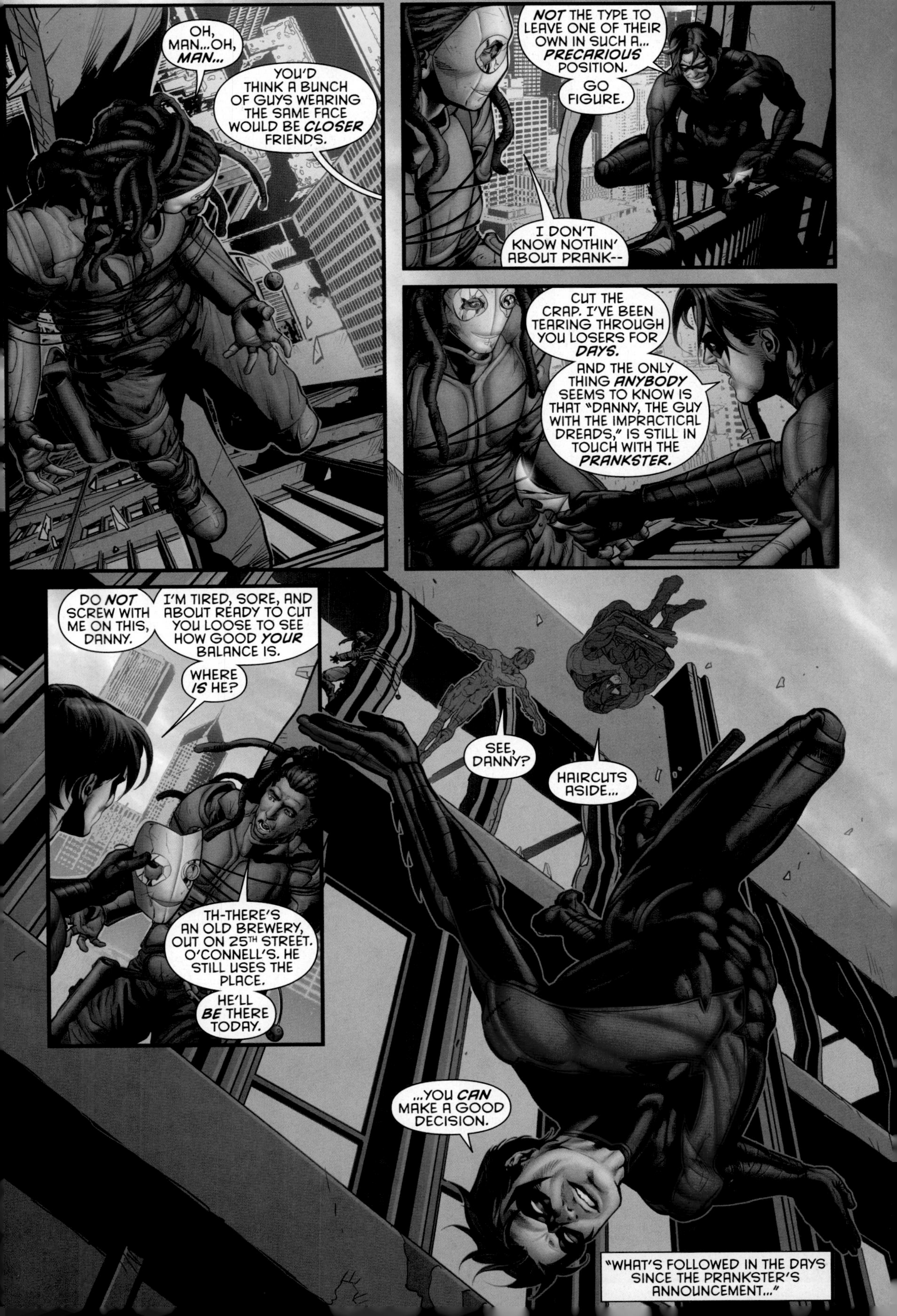

OH, MAN...OH, MAN...
YOU'D THINK A BUNCH OF GUYS WEARING THE SAME FACE WOULD BE CLOSER FRIENDS.
NOT THE TYPE TO LEAVE ONE OF THEIR OWN IN SUCH A... PRECARIOUS POSITION.
GO FIGURE.
I DON'T KNOW NOTHIN' ABOUT PRANK--
CUT THE CRAP. I'VE BEEN TEARING THROUGH YOU LOSERS FOR DAYS.
AND THE ONLY THING ANYBODY SEEMS TO KNOW IS THAT "DANNY, THE GUY WITH THE IMPRACTICAL DREADS," IS STILL IN TOUCH WITH THE PRANKSTER.
DO NOT SCREW WITH ME ON THIS, DANNY.
I'M TIRED, SORE, AND ABOUT READY TO CUT YOU LOOSE TO SEE HOW GOOD YOUR BALANCE IS.
WHERE IS HE?
TH-THERE'S AN OLD BREWERY, OUT ON 25TH STREET. O'CONNELL'S. HE STILL USES THE PLACE.
HE'LL BE THERE TODAY.
SEE, DANNY?
HAIRCUTS ASIDE...
...YOU CAN MAKE A GOOD DECISION.
"WHAT'S FOLLOWED IN THE DAYS SINCE THE PRANKSTER'S ANNOUNCEMENT..."

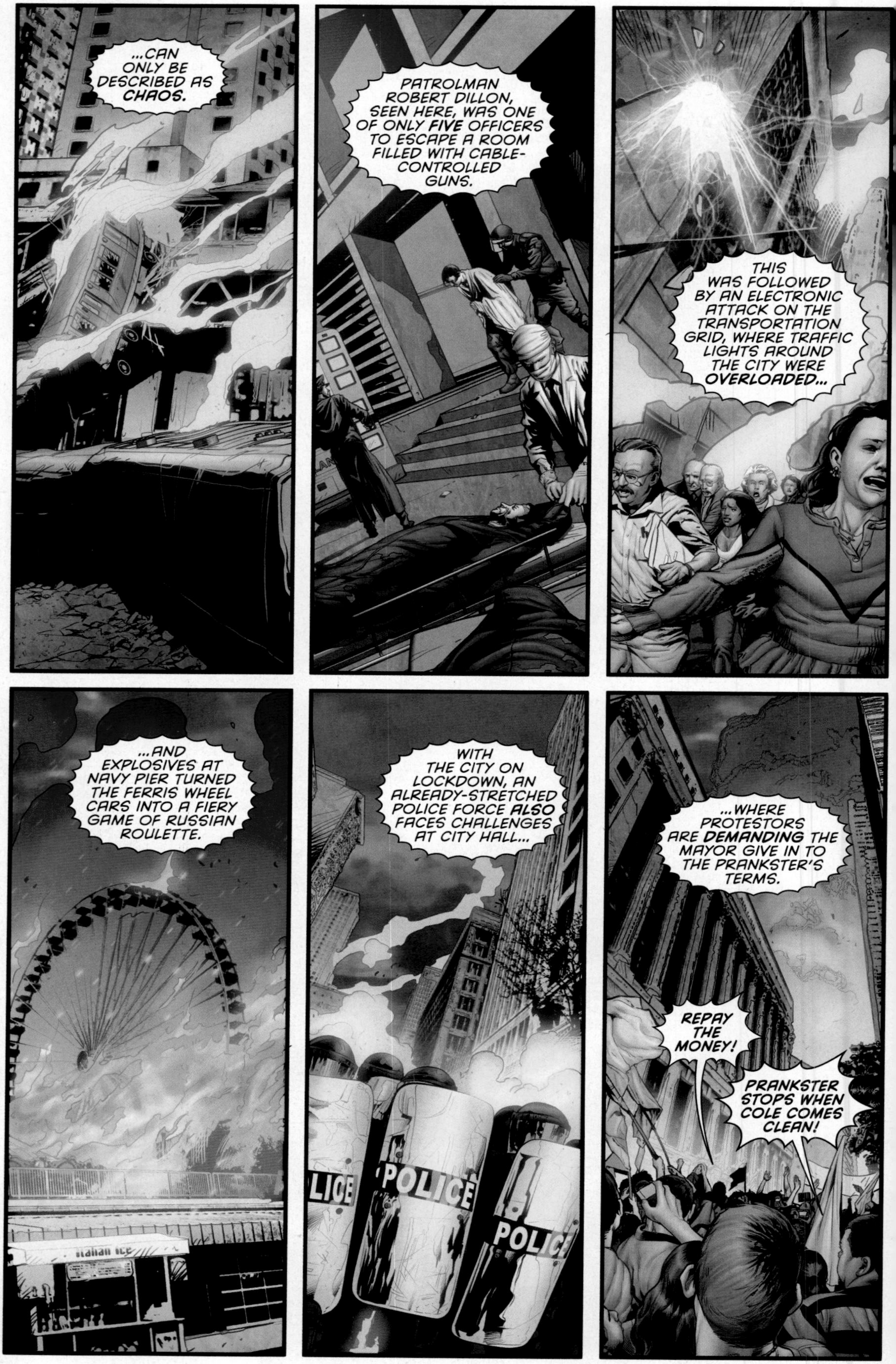
...CAN ONLY BE DESCRIBED AS CHAOS.
PATROLMAN ROBERT DILLON, SEEN HERE, WAS ONE OF ONLY FIVE OFFICERS TO ESCAPE A ROOM FILLED WITH CABLE-CONTROLLED GUNS.
THIS WAS FOLLOWED BY AN ELECTRONIC ATTACK ON THE TRANSPORTATION GRID, WHERE TRAFFIC LIGHTS AROUND THE CITY WERE OVERLOADED...
...AND EXPLOSIVES AT NAVY PIER TURNED THE FERRIS WHEEL CARS INTO A FIERY GAME OF RUSSIAN ROULETTE.
Italian Ice
WITH THE CITY ON LOCKDOWN, AN ALREADY-STRETCHED POLICE FORCE ALSO FACES CHALLENGES AT CITY HALL...
LICE
POLICE
POLICE
...WHERE PROTESTORS ARE DEMANDING THE MAYOR GIVE IN TO THE PRANKSTER'S TERMS.
REPAY THE MONEY!
PRANKSTER STOPS WHEN COLE COMES CLEAN!

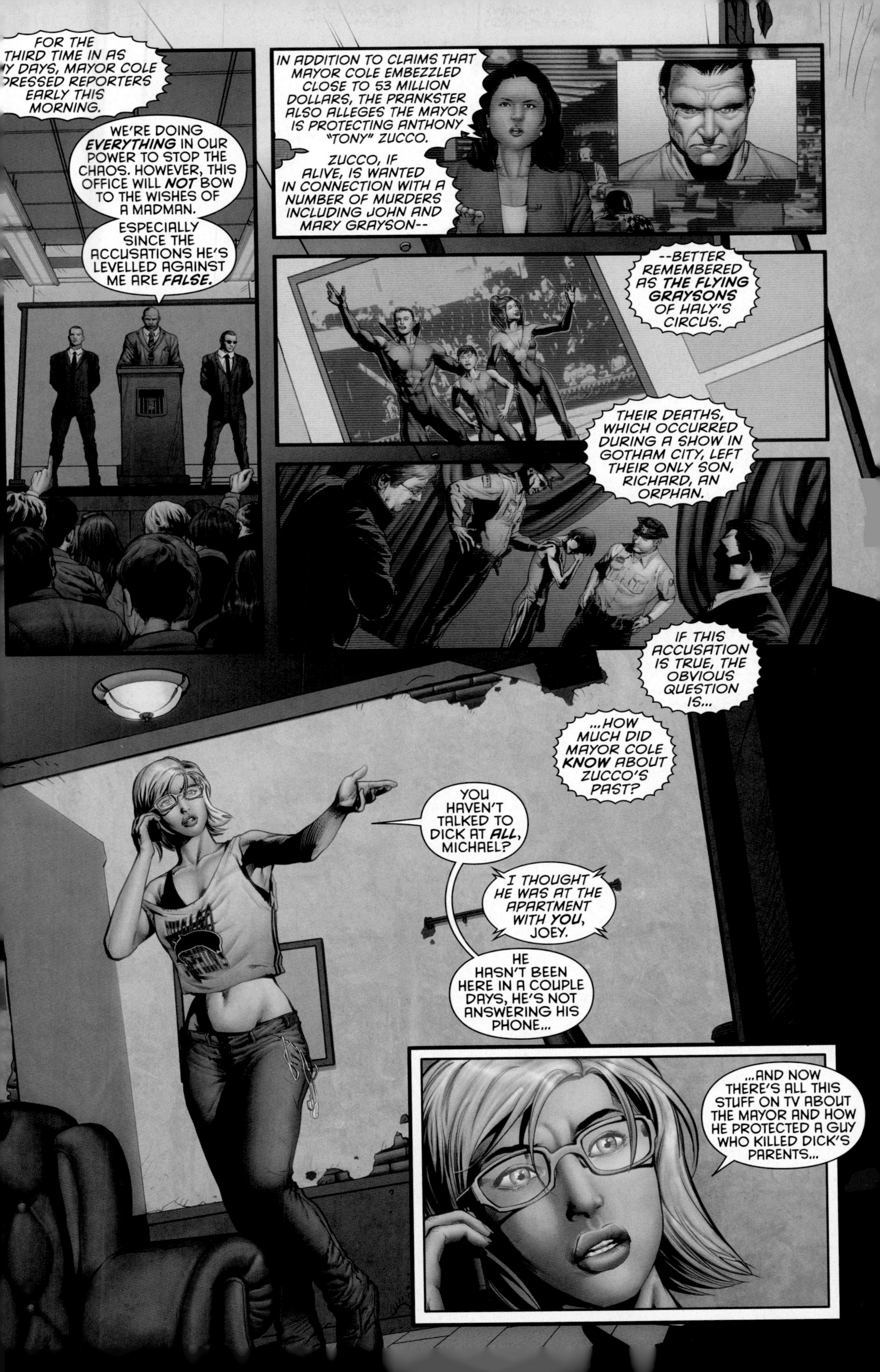
FOR THE THIRD TIME IN AS
Y DAYS, MAYOR COLE
DRESSED REPORTERS EARLY THIS MORNING.
WE'RE DOING EVERYTHING IN OUR POWER TO STOP THE CHAOS. HOWEVER, THIS OFFICE WILL NOT BOW TO THE WISHES OF A MADMAN.
ESPECIALLY SINCE THE ACCUSATIONS HE'S LEVELLED AGAINST ME ARE FALSE.
IN ADDITION TO CLAIMS THAT MAYOR COLE EMBEZZLED CLOSE TO 53 MILLION DOLLARS, THE PRANKSTER ALSO ALLEGES THE MAYOR IS PROTECTING ANTHONY "TONY" ZUCCO.
ZUCCO, IF ALIVE, IS WANTED IN CONNECTION WITH A NUMBER OF MURDERS INCLUDING JOHN AND MARY GRAYSON--
--BETTER REMEMBERED AS THE FLYING GRAYSONS OF HALY'S CIRCUS.
THEIR DEATHS, WHICH OCCURRED DURING A SHOW IN GOTHAM CITY, LEFT THEIR ONLY SON, RICHARD, AN ORPHAN.
IF THIS ACCUSATION IS TRUE, THE OBVIOUS QUESTION IS...
...HOW MUCH DID MAYOR COLE KNOW ABOUT ZUCCO'S PAST?
YOU HAVEN'T TALKED TO DICK AT ALL, MICHAEL?
I THOUGHT HE WAS AT THE APARTMENT WITH YOU, JOEY.
HE HASN'T BEEN HERE IN A COUPLE DAYS, HE'S NOT ANSWERING HIS PHONE...
...AND NOW THERE'S ALL THIS STUFF ON TV ABOUT THE MAYOR AND HOW HE PROTECTED A GUY WHO KILLED DICK'S PARENTS...

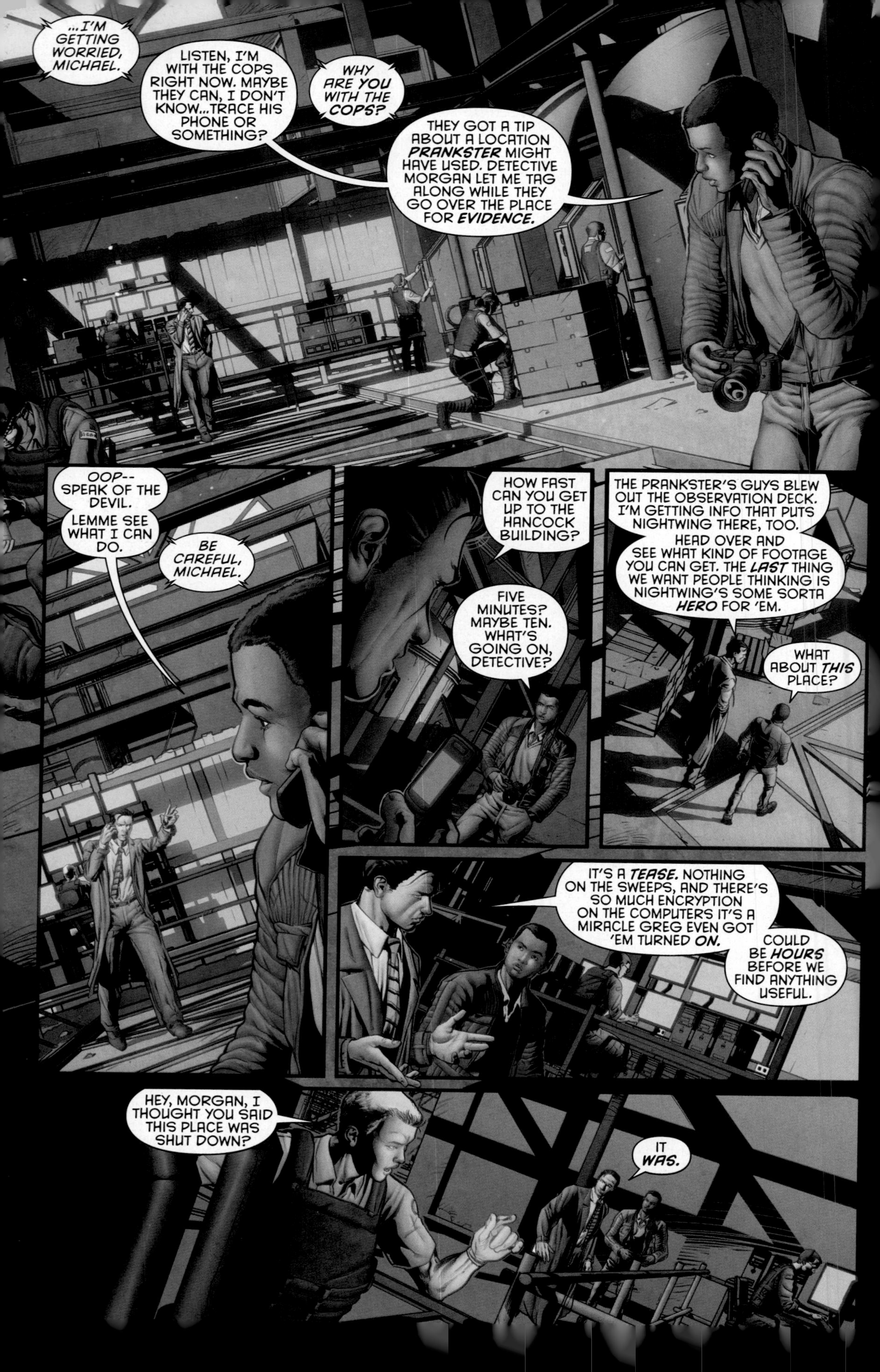
...I'M GETTING WORRIED, MICHAEL.
LISTEN, I'M WITH THE COPS RIGHT NOW. MAYBE THEY CAN, I DON'T KNOW...TRACE HIS PHONE OR SOMETHING?
WHY ARE YOU WITH THE COPS?
THEY GOT A TIP ABOUT A LOCATION PRANKSTER MIGHT HAVE USED. DETECTIVE MORGAN LET ME TAG ALONG WHILE THEY GO OVER THE PLACE FOR EVIDENCE.
OOP-- SPEAK OF THE DEVIL.
LEMME SEE WHAT I CAN DO.
BE CAREFUL, MICHAEL.
HOW FAST CAN YOU GET UP TO THE HANCOCK BUILDING?
FIVE MINUTES? MAYBE TEN. WHAT'S GOING ON, DETECTIVE?
THE PRANKSTER'S GUYS BLEW OUT THE OBSERVATION DECK. I'M GETTING INFO THAT PUTS NIGHTWING THERE, TOO.
HEAD OVER AND SEE WHAT KIND OF FOOTAGE YOU CAN GET. THE LAST THING WE WANT PEOPLE THINKING IS NIGHTWING'S SOME SORTA HERO FOR 'EM.
WHAT ABOUT THIS PLACE?
IT'S A TEASE. NOTHING ON THE SWEEPS, AND THERE'S SO MUCH ENCRYPTION ON THE COMPUTERS IT'S A MIRACLE GREG EVEN GOT 'EM TURNED ON.
COULD BE HOURS BEFORE WE FIND ANYTHING USEFUL.
HEY, MORGAN, I THOUGHT YOU SAID THIS PLACE WAS SHUT DOWN?
IT WAS.

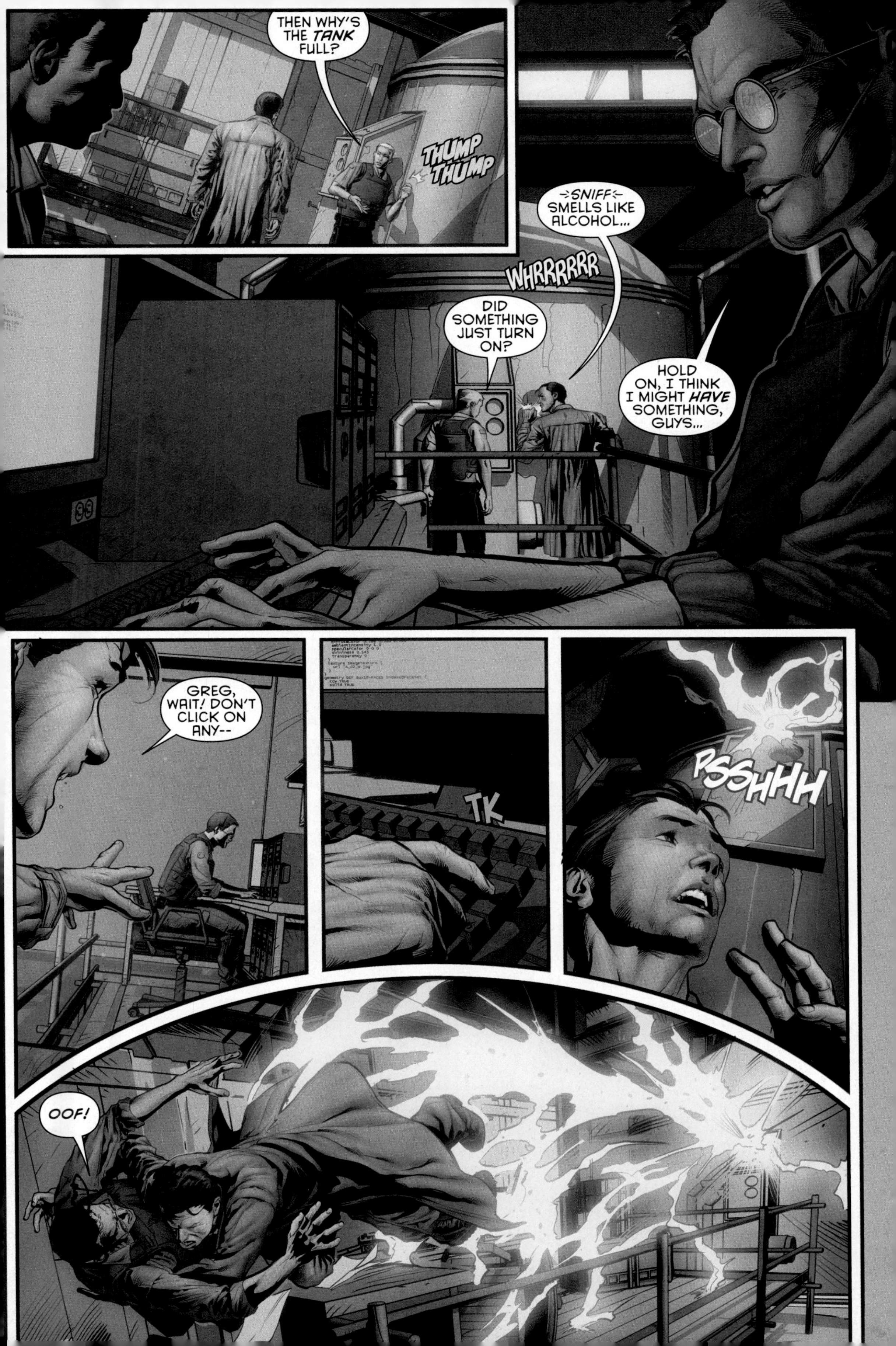
THEN WHY'S THE *TANK* FULL?
THUMP THUMP
-SNIFF- SMELLS LIKE ALCOHOL...
WHRRRRRR
DID SOMETHING JUST TURN ON?
HOLD ON, I THINK I MIGHT *HAVE* SOMETHING, GUYS...
GREG, WAIT! DON'T CLICK ON ANY--
TK
PSSHHH
OOF!

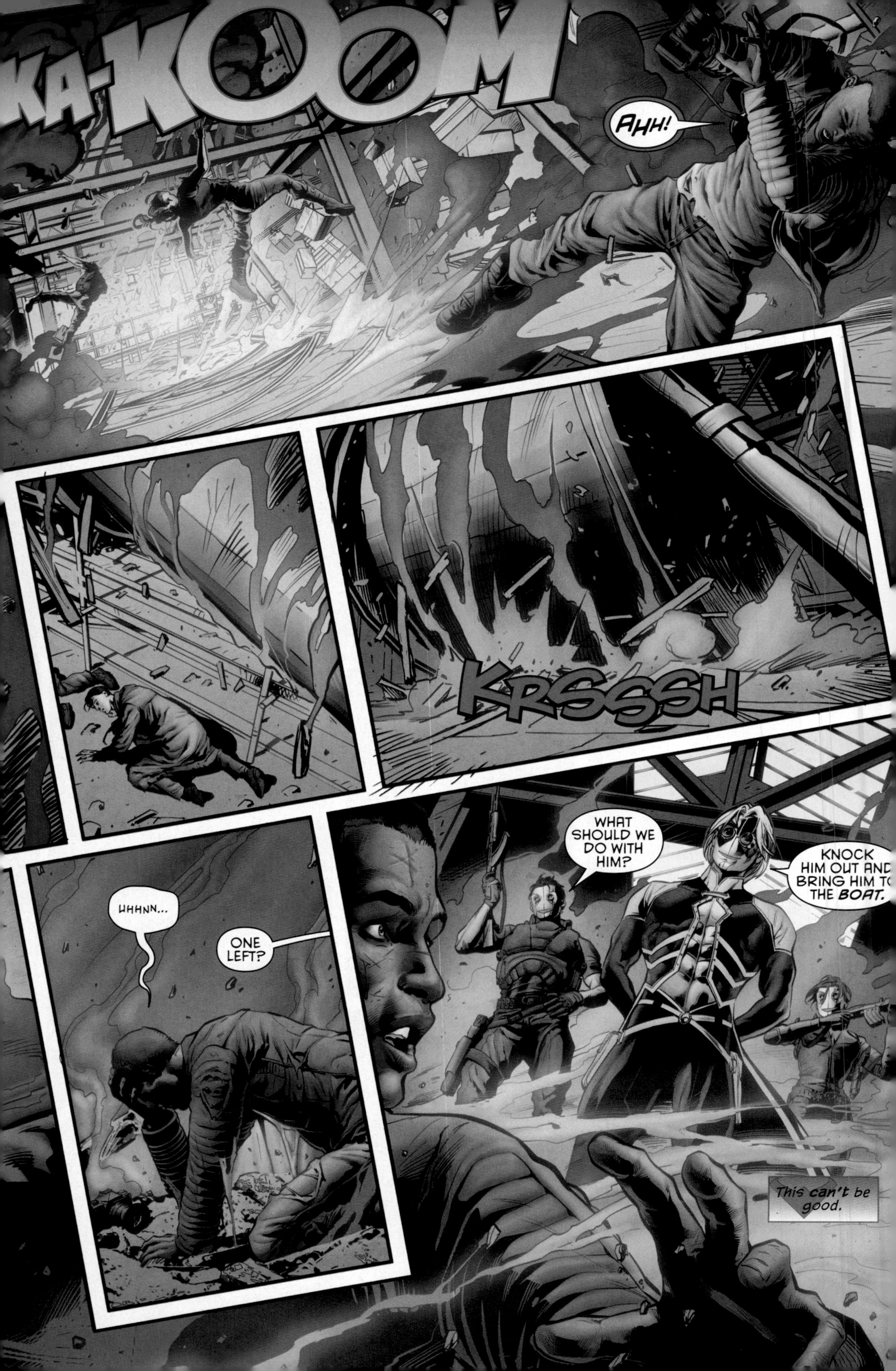
KA-KOOM
AHH!
KRSSSSH
UHHNN...
ONE LEFT?
WHAT SHOULD WE DO WITH HIM?
KNOCK HIM OUT AND BRING HIM TO THE BOAT.
This can't be good.

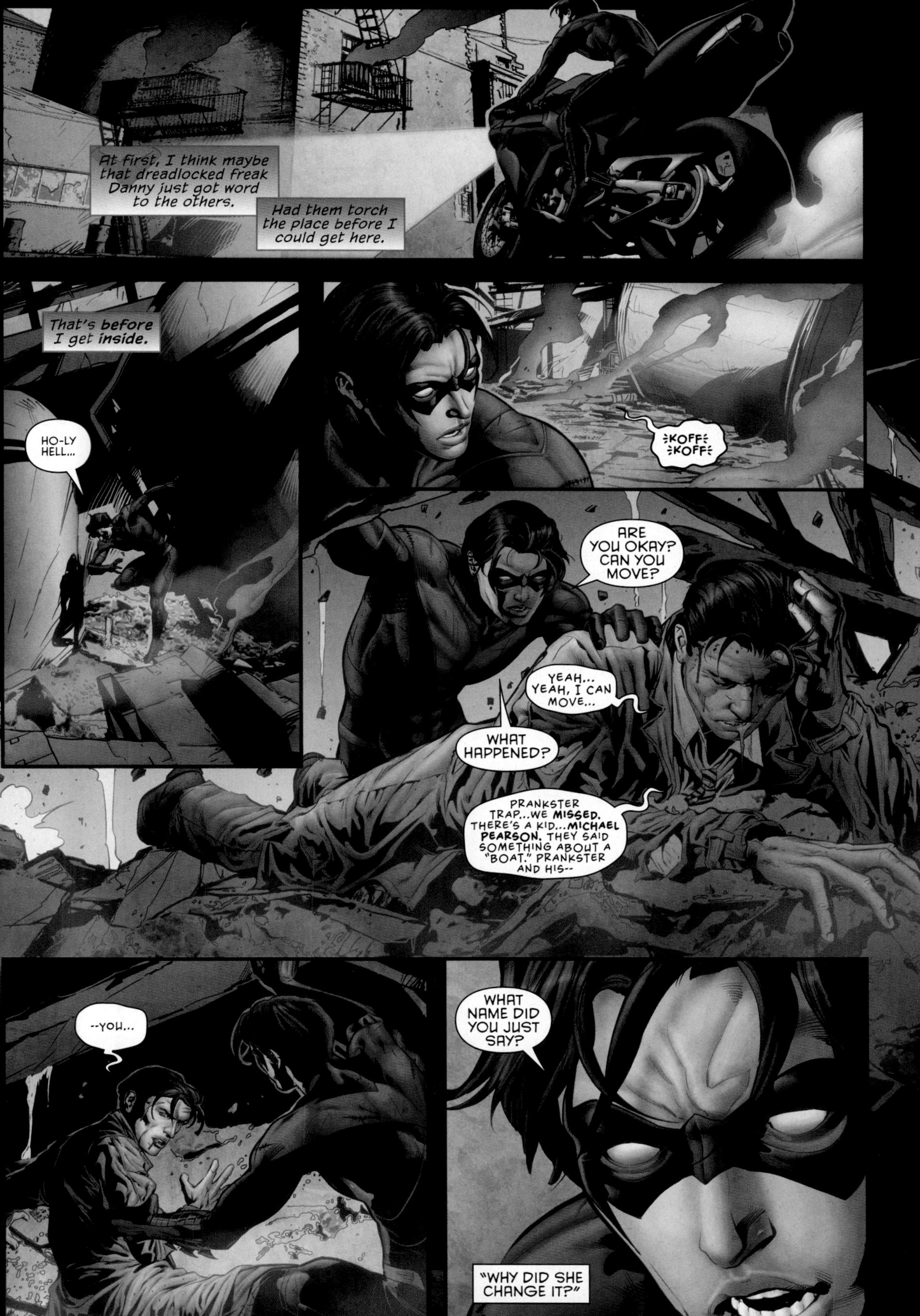
At first, I think maybe that dreadlocked freak Danny just got word to the others.
Had them torch the place before I could get here.
That's before I get inside.
HO-LY HELL...
KOFF KOFF
ARE YOU OKAY? CAN YOU MOVE?
YEAH... YEAH, I CAN MOVE...
WHAT HAPPENED?
PRANKSTER TRAP...WE MISSED. THERE'S A KID...MICHAEL PEARSON. THEY SAID SOMETHING ABOUT A "BOAT." PRANKSTER AND HIS--
--YOU...
WHAT NAME DID YOU JUST SAY?
"WHY DID SHE CHANGE IT?"

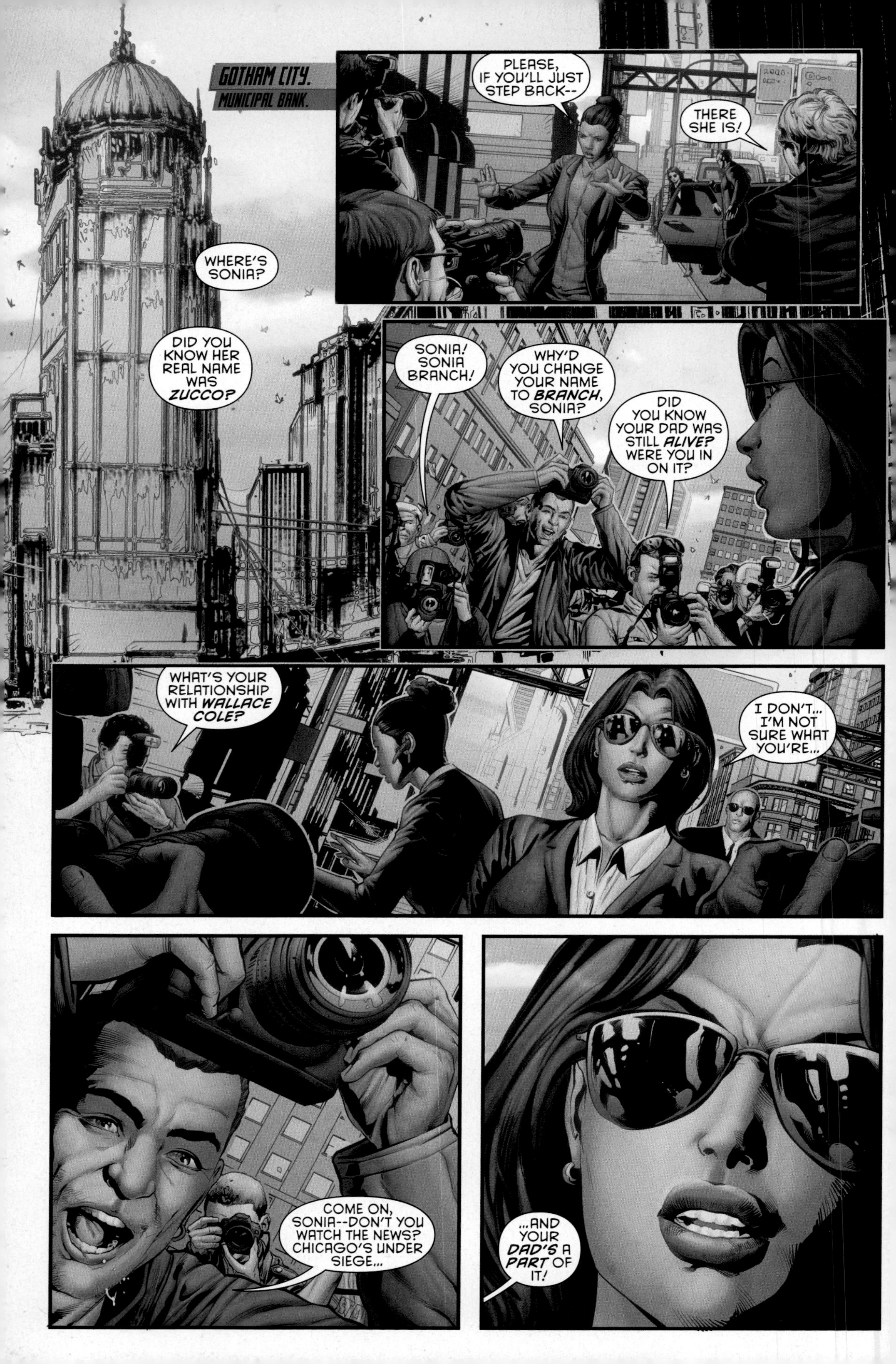
GOTHAM CITY.
MUNICIPAL BANK.
PLEASE, IF YOU'LL JUST STEP BACK--
THERE SHE IS!
WHERE'S SONIA?
DID YOU KNOW HER REAL NAME WAS ZUCCO?
SONIA! SONIA BRANCH!
WHY'D YOU CHANGE YOUR NAME TO BRANCH, SONIA?
DID YOU KNOW YOUR DAD WAS STILL ALIVE? WERE YOU IN ON IT?
WHAT'S YOUR RELATIONSHIP WITH WALLACE COLE?
I DON'T... I'M NOT SURE WHAT YOU'RE...
COME ON, SONIA--DON'T YOU WATCH THE NEWS? CHICAGO'S UNDER SIEGE...
...AND YOUR DAD'S A PART OF IT!

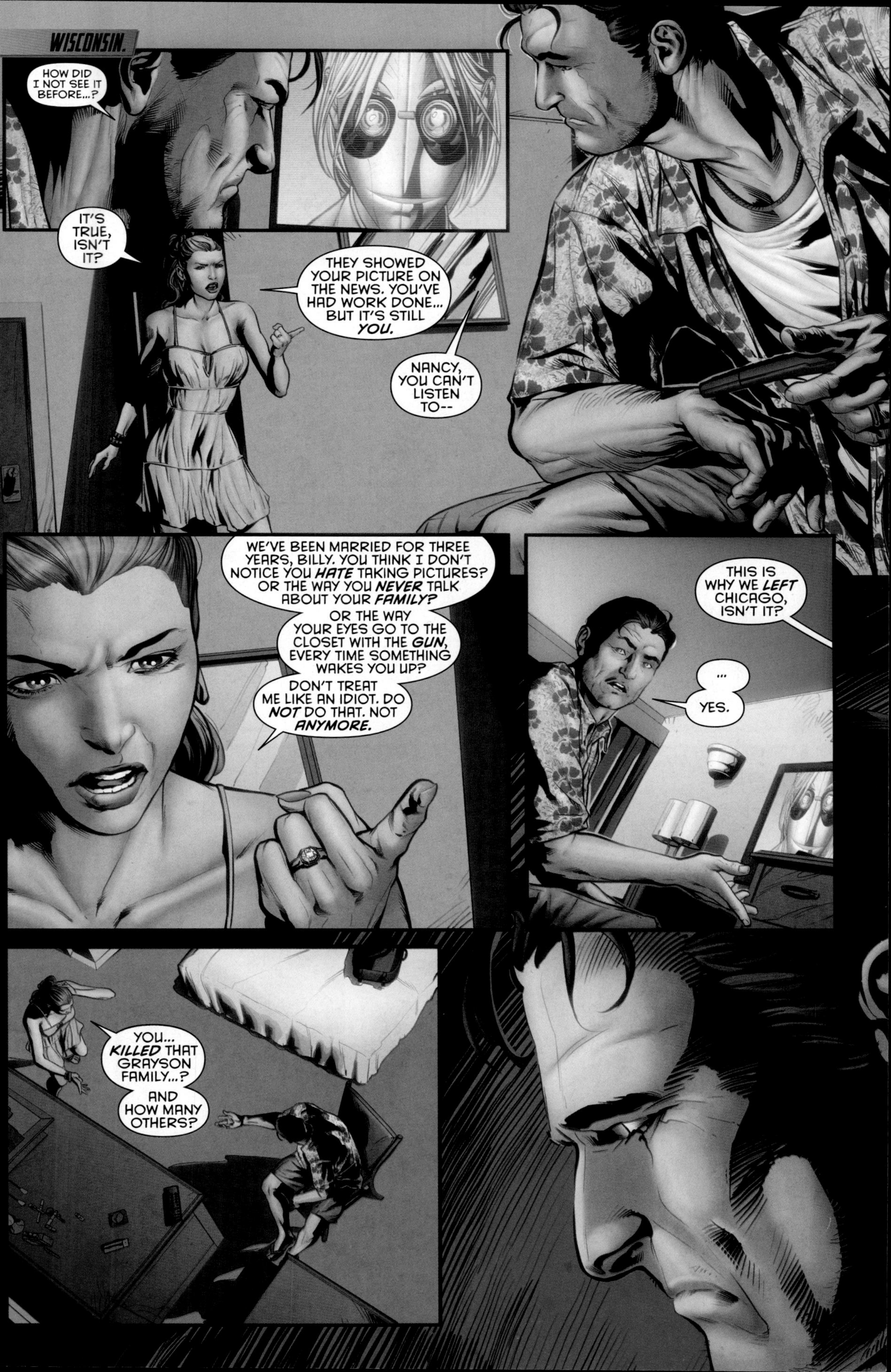
WISCONSIN.
HOW DID I NOT SEE IT BEFORE...?
IT'S TRUE, ISN'T IT?
THEY SHOWED YOUR PICTURE ON THE NEWS. YOU'VE HAD WORK DONE... BUT IT'S STILL YOU.
NANCY, YOU CAN'T LISTEN TO--
WE'VE BEEN MARRIED FOR THREE YEARS, BILLY. YOU THINK I DON'T NOTICE YOU HATE TAKING PICTURES? OR THE WAY YOU NEVER TALK ABOUT YOUR FAMILY?
OR THE WAY YOUR EYES GO TO THE CLOSET WITH THE GUN, EVERY TIME SOMETHING WAKES YOU UP?
DON'T TREAT ME LIKE AN IDIOT. DO NOT DO THAT. NOT ANYMORE.
THIS IS WHY WE LEFT CHICAGO, ISN'T IT?
...
YES.
YOU... KILLED THAT GRAYSON FAMILY...?
AND HOW MANY OTHERS?

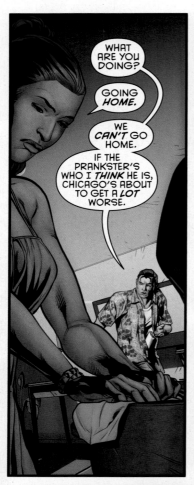

WHAT ARE YOU DOING?

GOING *HOME.*

WE *CAN'T* GO HOME.

IF THE PRANKSTER'S WHO I *THINK* HE IS, CHICAGO'S ABOUT TO GET A *LOT* WORSE.

AND YOU'RE *OKAY* WITH THAT?

I CAN'T RISK REACHING OUT AGAIN, NANCY. WE'RE IN THE *CLEAR.* IF I GO BACK, OR EVEN *CALL...*

I DON'T KNOW *WHAT* MIGHT HAPPEN.

THIS NIGHTWING GUY HAS BEEN HUNTING ME FOR *YEARS.* AND NOW WITH THE WHOLE CITY KNOWING WHO I AM--

SO YOU'RE WILLING TO LET PEOPLE *DIE* BECAUSE GOING BACK MEANS FACING WHAT YOU *DID?* THE IRONY'S SO ON THE NOSE, IT'S *LAUGHABLE.*

WHAT ARE YOU TALKING ABOUT?

YOU'VE BEEN GIVING SPEECHES TO OUR SON ALL WEEK ABOUT GROWNUPS "TAKING RESPONSIBILITY FOR THEIR ACTIONS."

YOU'RE A GOOD LIAR, BILLY. I'LL GIVE *THAT* MUCH.

THE SAD PART IS...

...ONE DAY BRIAN'S GOING TO FIGURE IT OUT, TOO.

WOW!

YOU'RE *GIVING* HIM TO ME?! BUT HE'S YOUR *FAVORITE!*

I KNOW. BUT IT'S OKAY, I *ALREADY* PLAYED WITH HIM A LOT. AND 'SIDES, I NEVER SHOULDA TAKEN YOUR *ROBOT.*

WOW... T'ANKS, BRIAN.

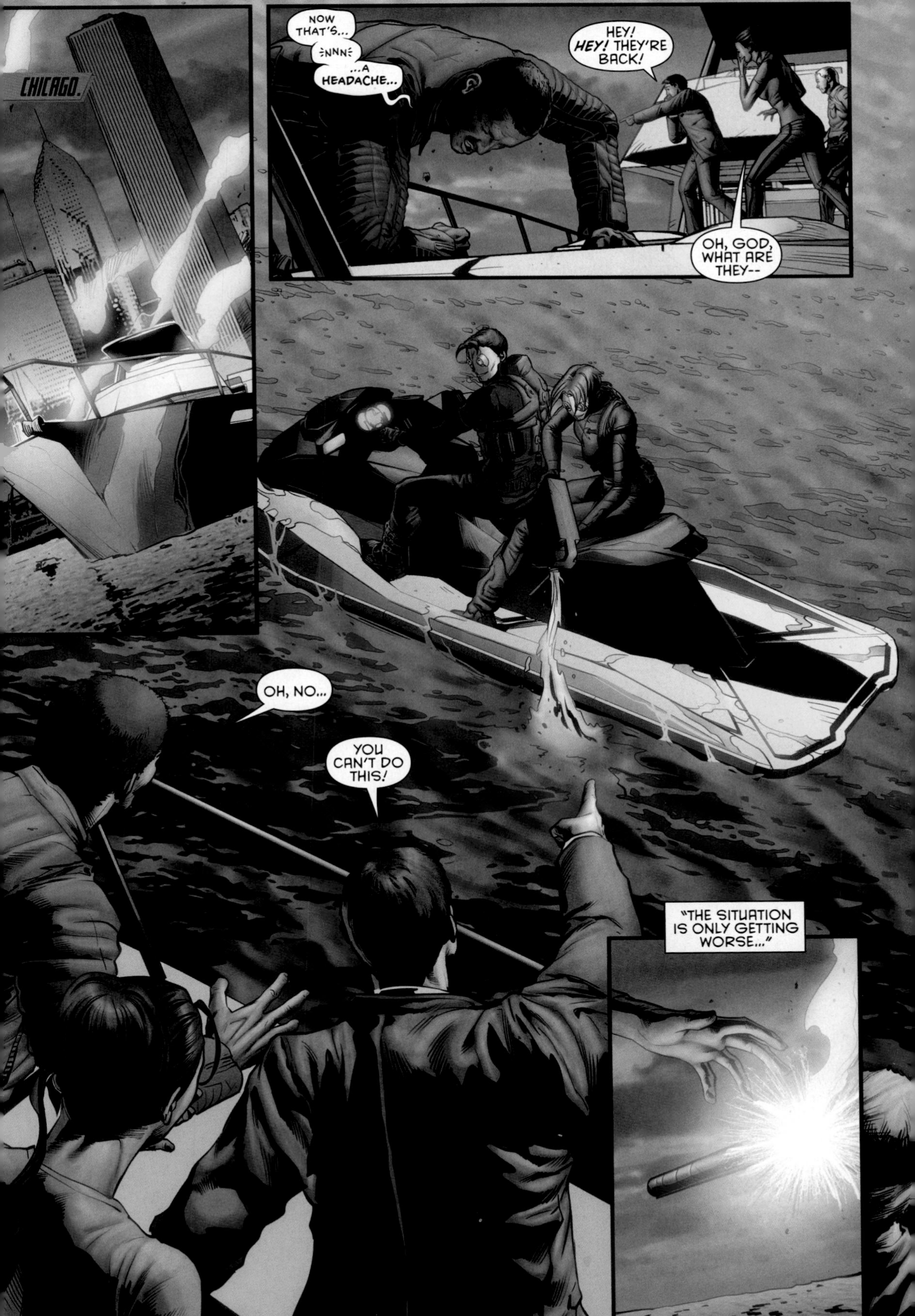
CHICAGO.
NOW THAT'S...
NNN
...A HEADACHE...
HEY! HEY! THEY'RE BACK!
OH, GOD, WHAT ARE THEY--
OH, NO...
YOU CAN'T DO THIS!
"THE SITUATION IS ONLY GETTING WORSE..."

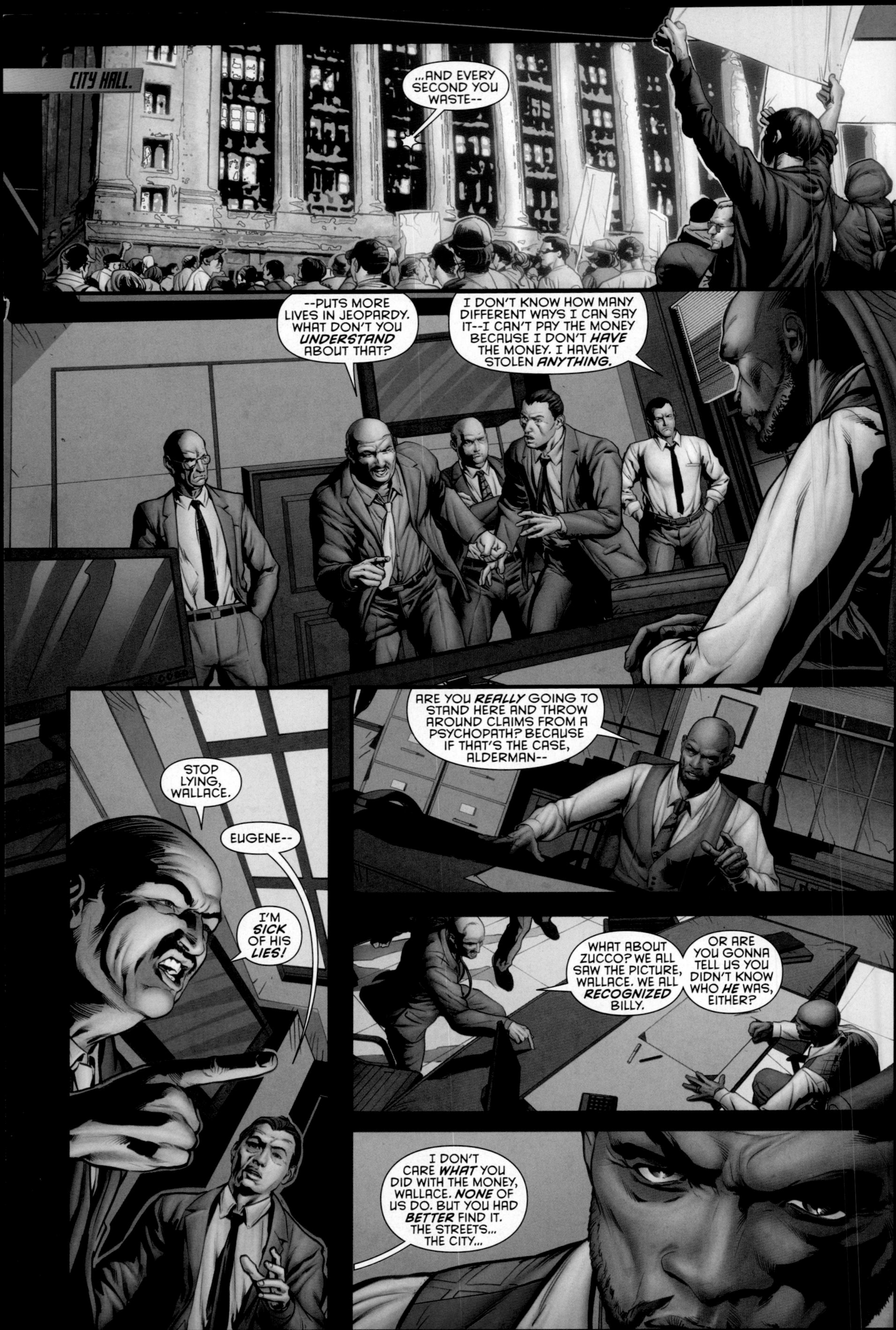
CITY HALL.
...AND EVERY SECOND YOU WASTE--
--PUTS MORE LIVES IN JEOPARDY. WHAT DON'T YOU UNDERSTAND ABOUT THAT?
I DON'T KNOW HOW MANY DIFFERENT WAYS I CAN SAY IT--I CAN'T PAY THE MONEY BECAUSE I DON'T HAVE THE MONEY. I HAVEN'T STOLEN ANYTHING.
STOP LYING, WALLACE.
EUGENE--
I'M SICK OF HIS LIES!
ARE YOU REALLY GOING TO STAND HERE AND THROW AROUND CLAIMS FROM A PSYCHOPATH? BECAUSE IF THAT'S THE CASE, ALDERMAN--
WHAT ABOUT ZUCCO? WE ALL SAW THE PICTURE, WALLACE. WE ALL RECOGNIZED BILLY.
OR ARE YOU GONNA TELL US YOU DIDN'T KNOW WHO HE WAS, EITHER?
I DON'T CARE WHAT YOU DID WITH THE MONEY, WALLACE. NONE OF US DO. BUT YOU HAD BETTER FIND IT. THE STREETS... THE CITY...

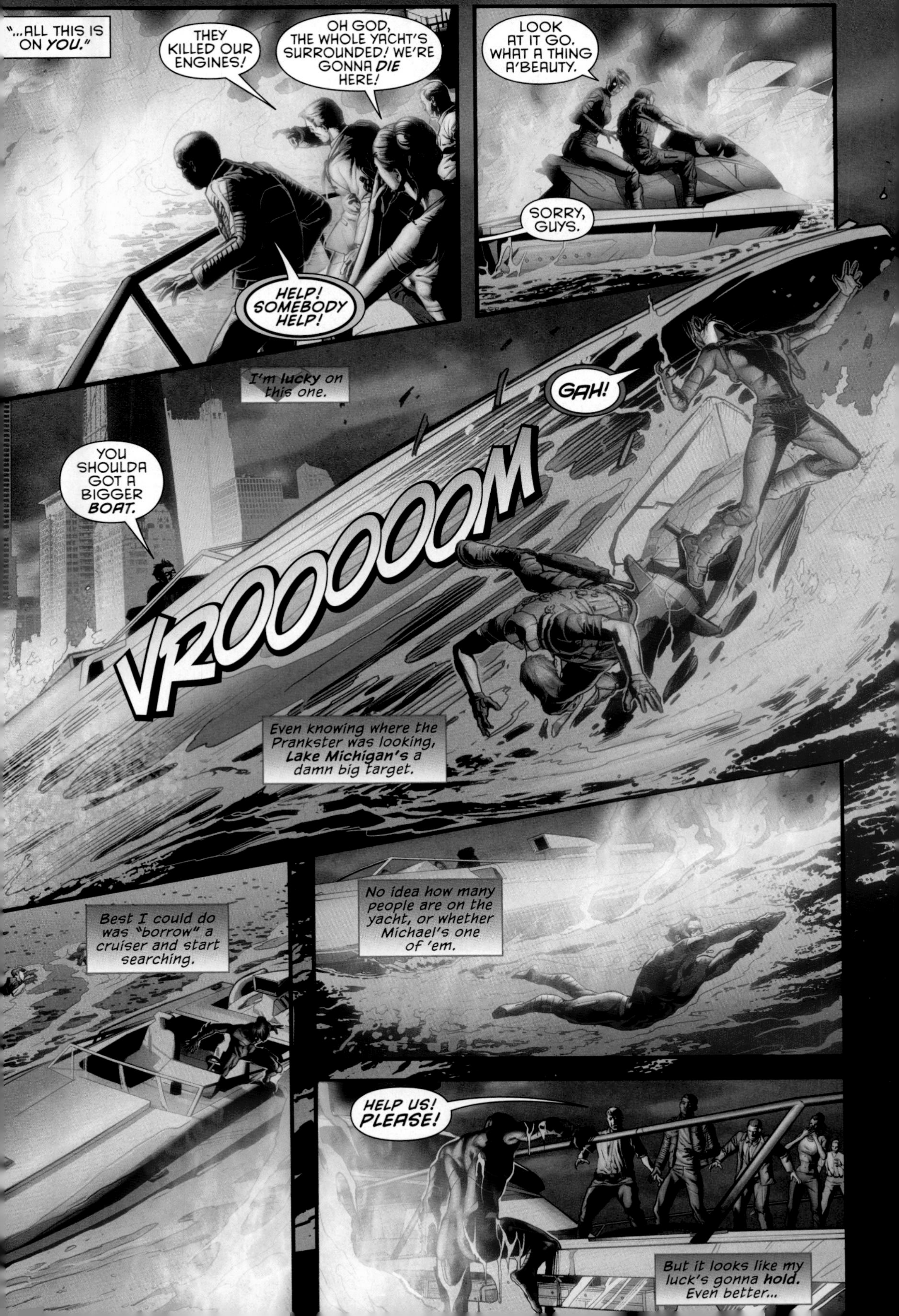
"...ALL THIS IS ON *YOU.*"
THEY KILLED OUR ENGINES!
OH GOD, THE WHOLE YACHT'S SURROUNDED! WE'RE GONNA *DIE* HERE!
HELP! SOMEBODY HELP!
LOOK AT IT GO. WHAT A THING A'BEAUTY.
SORRY, GUYS.
I'm **lucky** on this one.
GAH!
YOU SHOULDA GOT A BIGGER *BOAT.*
VROOOOOOM
Even knowing where the Prankster was looking, **Lake Michigan's** a damn big target.
Best I could do was "borrow" a cruiser and start searching.
No idea how many people are on the yacht, or whether Michael's one of 'em.
HELP US! PLEASE!
But it looks like my luck's gonna **hold.** Even better...

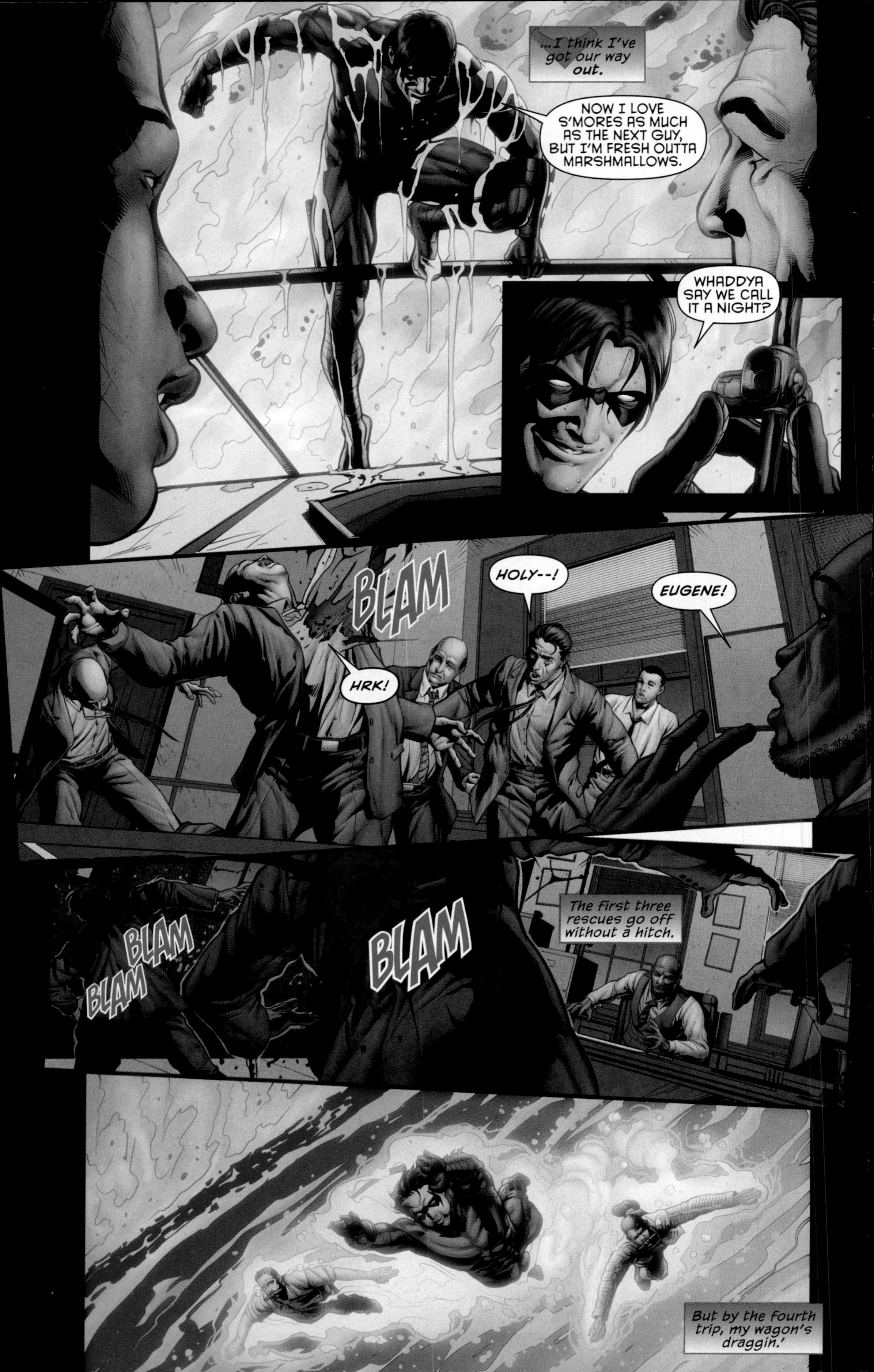
...I think I've got our way out.
NOW I LOVE S'MORES AS MUCH AS THE NEXT GUY, BUT I'M FRESH OUTTA MARSHMALLOWS.
WHADDYA SAY WE CALL IT A NIGHT?
BLAM
HOLY--!
EUGENE!
HRK!
BLAM
BLAM
BLAM
The first three rescues go off without a hitch.
But by the fourth trip, my wagon's draggin.'

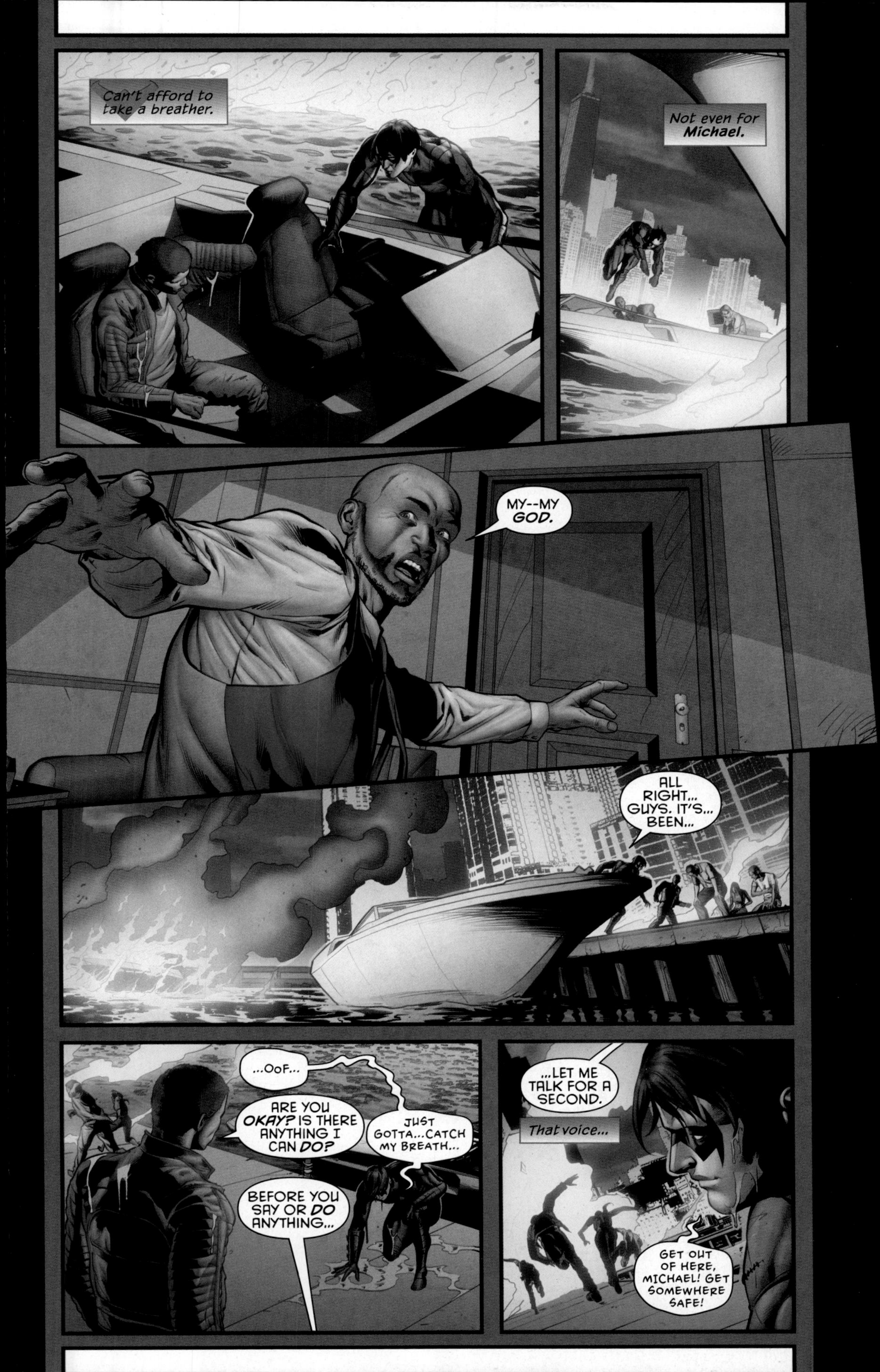
Can't afford to take a breather.
Not even for Michael.
MY--MY GOD.
ALL RIGHT... GUYS. IT'S... BEEN...
...OOF...
ARE YOU OKAY? IS THERE ANYTHING I CAN DO?
JUST GOTTA...CATCH MY BREATH...
BEFORE YOU SAY OR DO ANYTHING...
...LET ME TALK FOR A SECOND.
That voice...
GET OUT OF HERE, MICHAEL! GET SOMEWHERE SAFE!

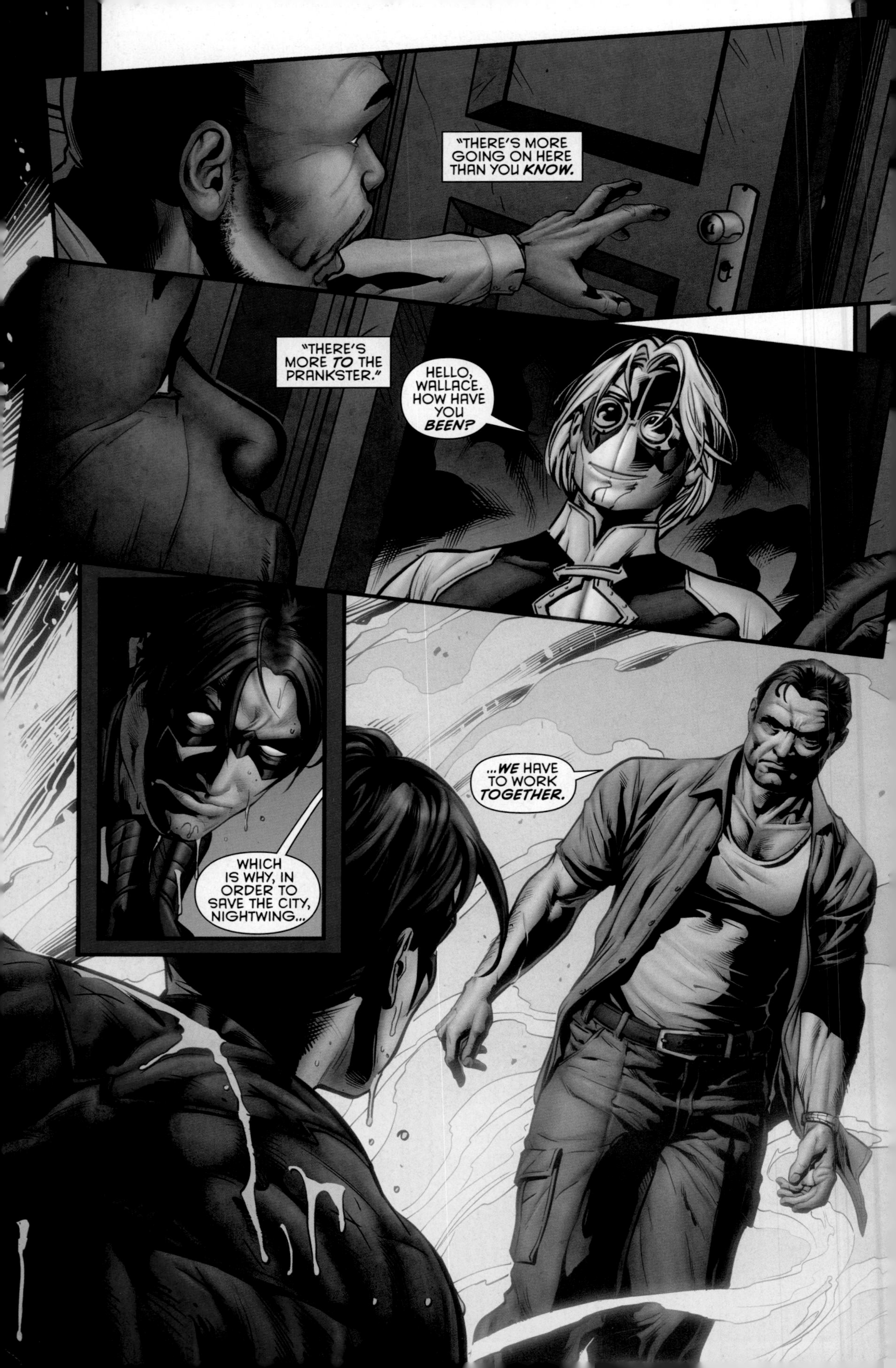
"THERE'S MORE GOING ON HERE THAN YOU *KNOW*.
"THERE'S MORE *TO* THE PRANKSTER."
HELLO, WALLACE. HOW HAVE YOU *BEEN*?
WHICH IS WHY, IN ORDER TO SAVE THE CITY, NIGHTWING...
...*WE* HAVE TO WORK *TOGETHER*.

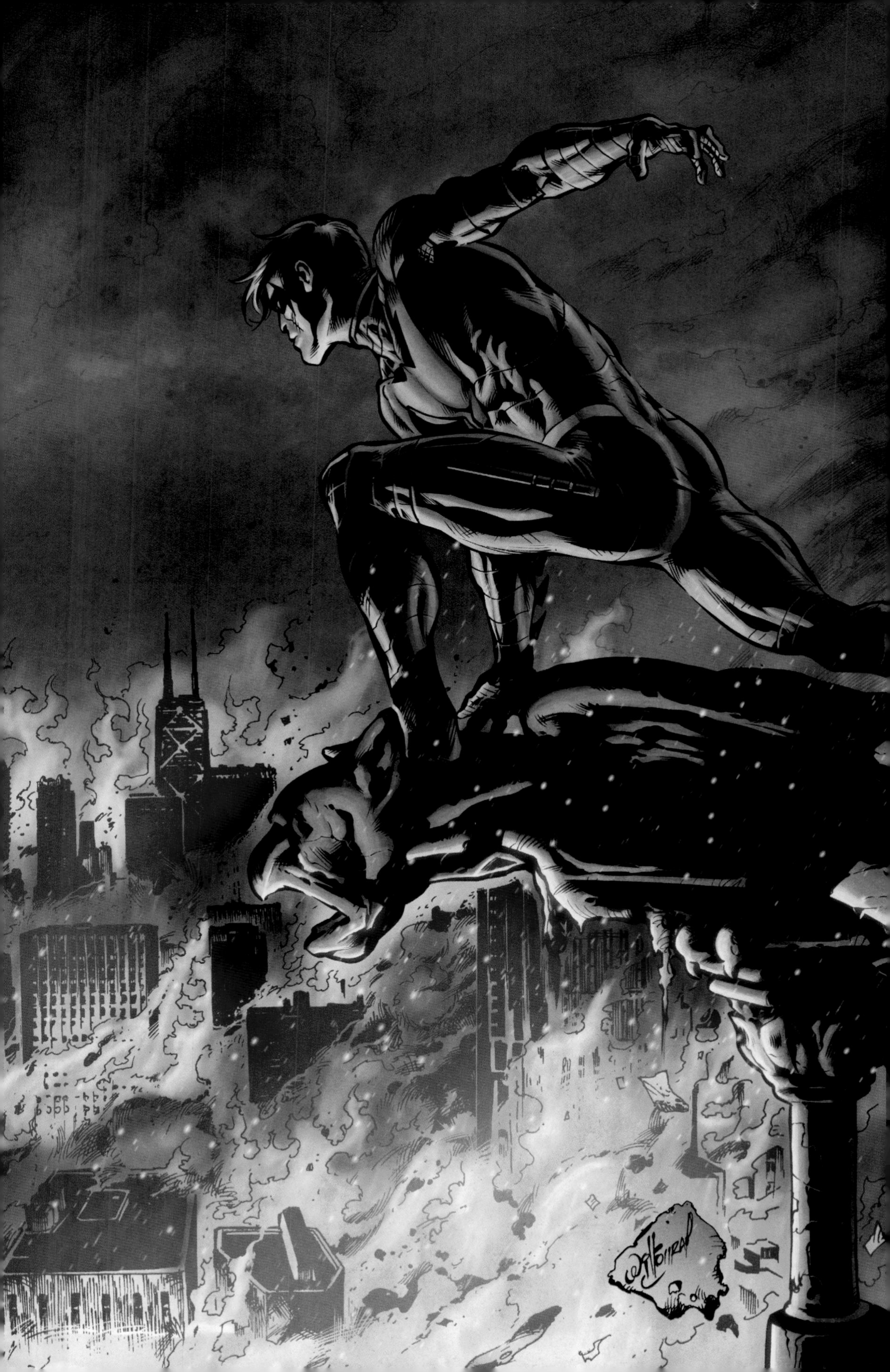

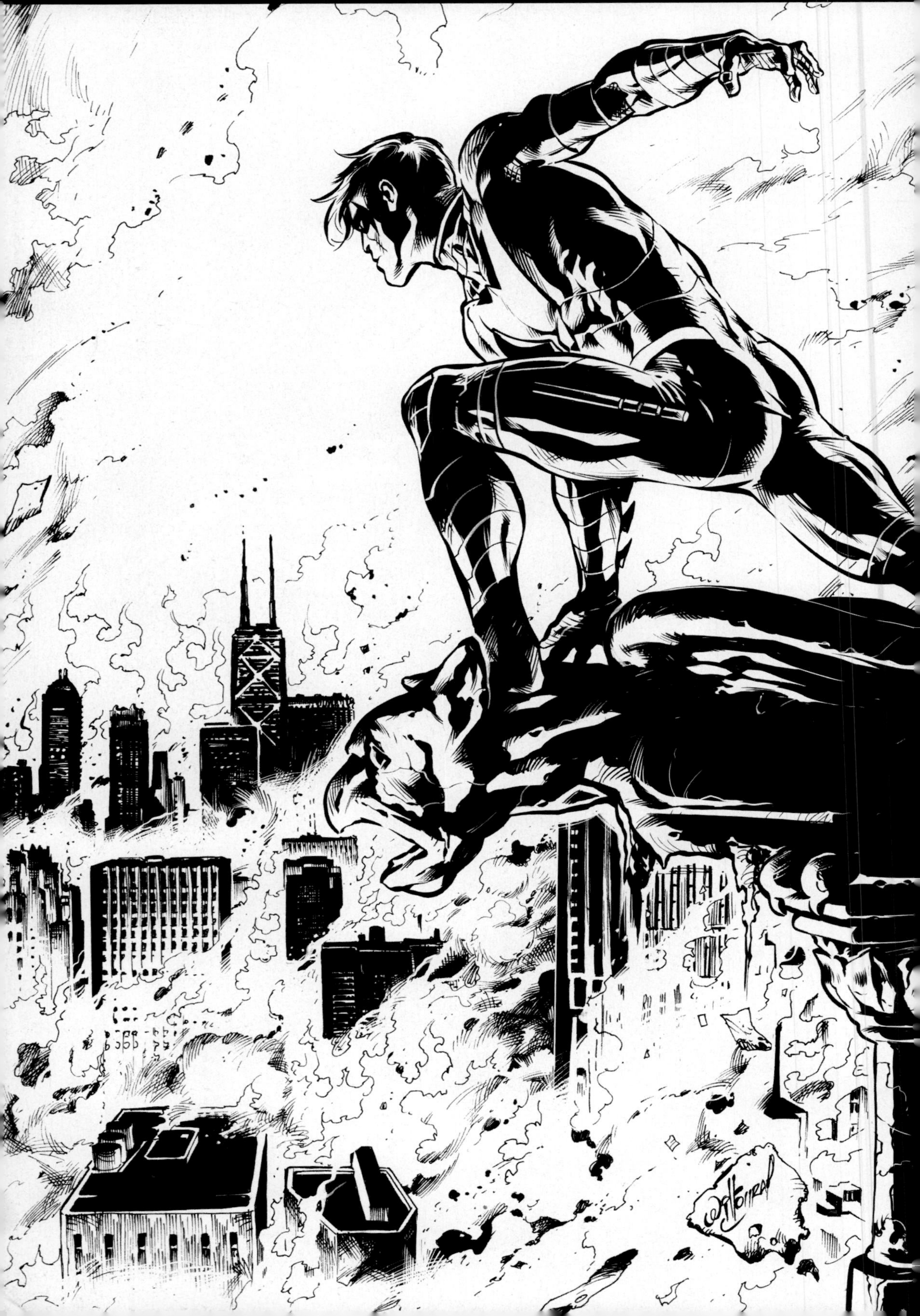

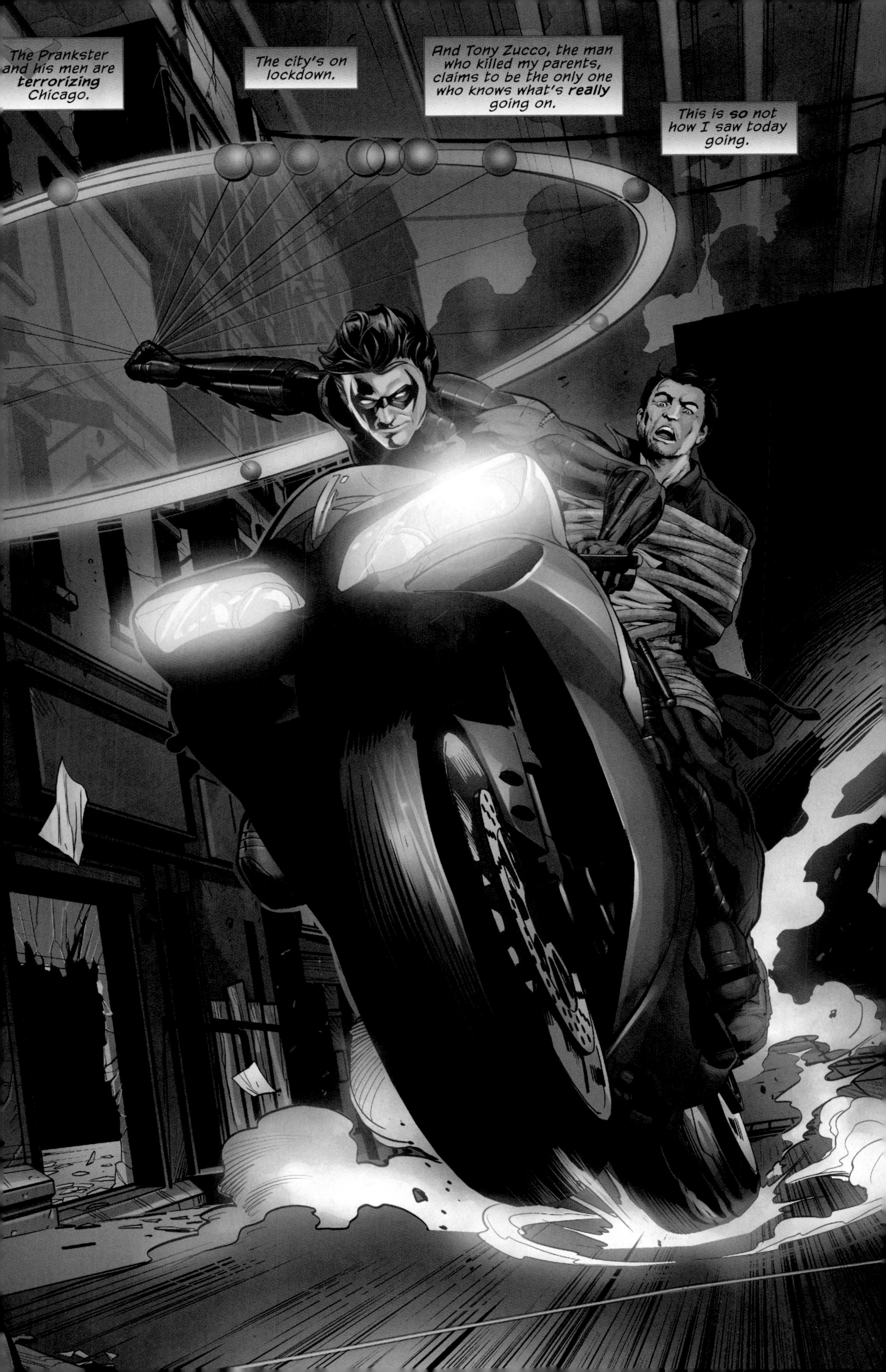
The Prankster and his men are terrorizing Chicago.
The city's on lockdown.
And Tony Zucco, the man who killed my parents, claims to be the only one who knows what's really going on.
This is so not how I saw today going.

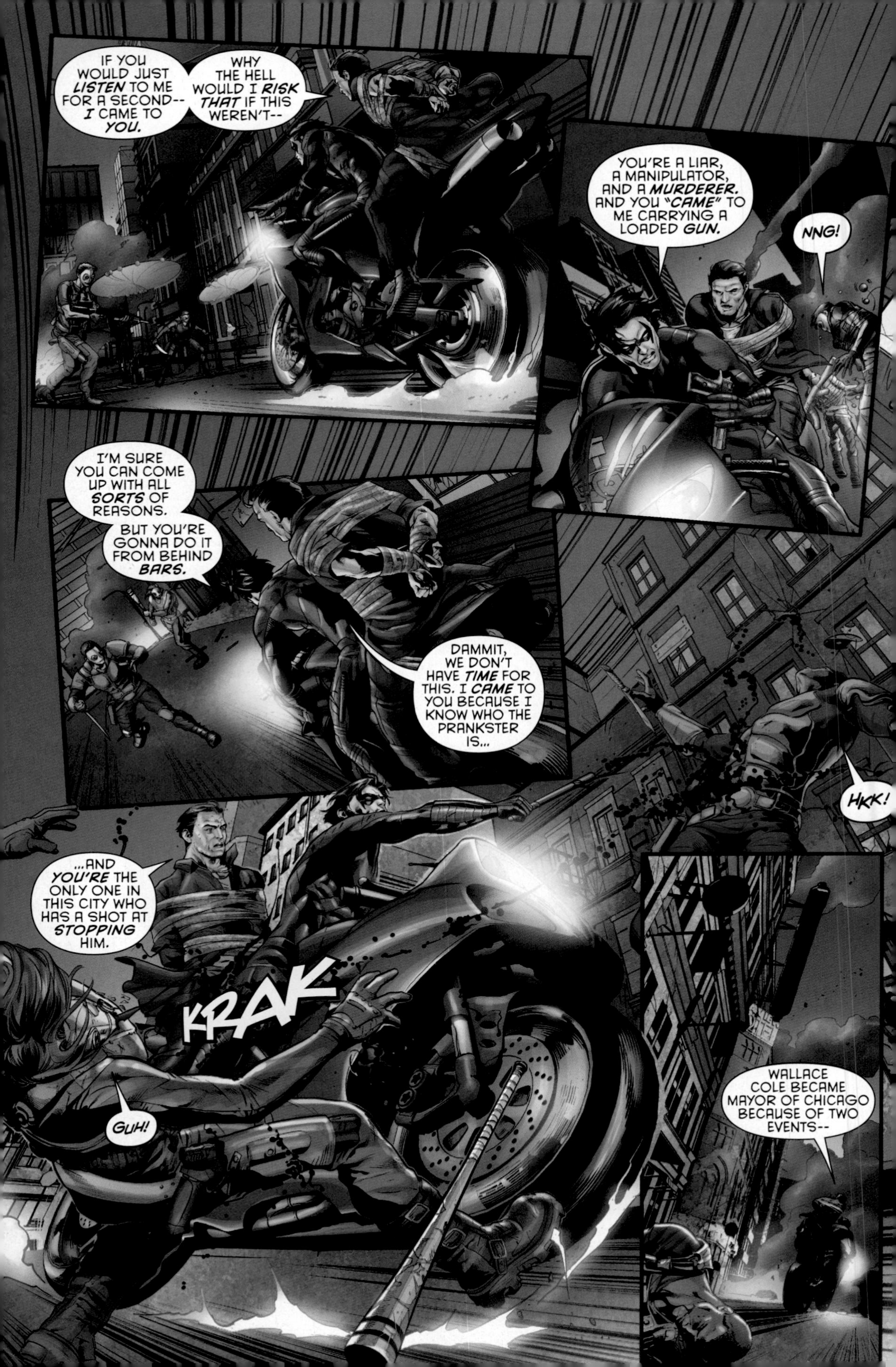
IF YOU WOULD JUST LISTEN TO ME FOR A SECOND-- I CAME TO YOU.
WHY THE HELL WOULD I RISK THAT IF THIS WEREN'T--
YOU'RE A LIAR, A MANIPULATOR, AND A MURDERER. AND YOU "CAME" TO ME CARRYING A LOADED GUN.
NNG!
I'M SURE YOU CAN COME UP WITH ALL SORTS OF REASONS.
BUT YOU'RE GONNA DO IT FROM BEHIND BARS.
DAMMIT, WE DON'T HAVE TIME FOR THIS. I CAME TO YOU BECAUSE I KNOW WHO THE PRANKSTER IS...
HKK!
...AND YOU'RE THE ONLY ONE IN THIS CITY WHO HAS A SHOT AT STOPPING HIM.
KRAK
GUH!
WALLACE COLE BECAME MAYOR OF CHICAGO BECAUSE OF TWO EVENTS--

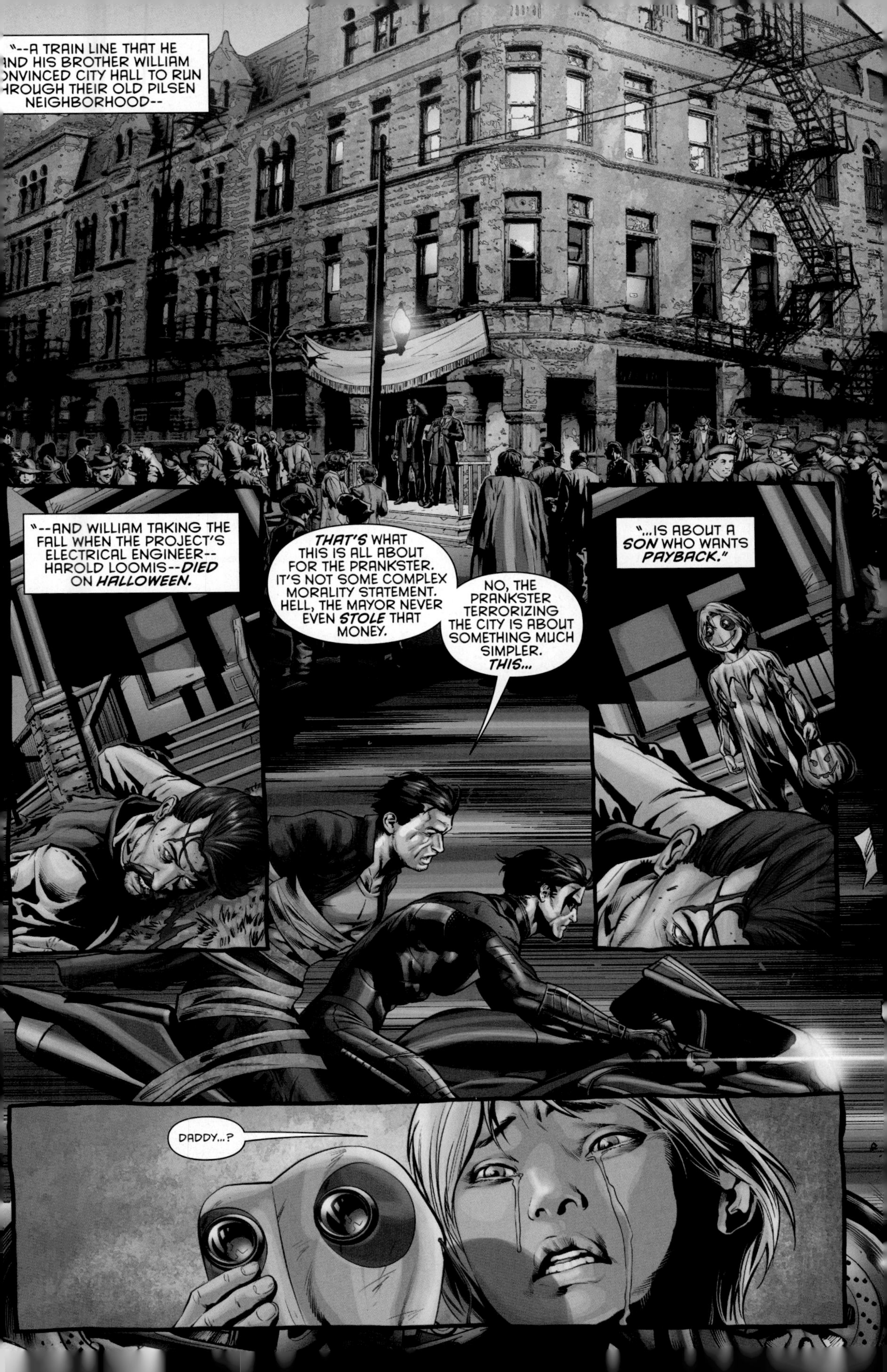
"--A TRAIN LINE THAT HE AND HIS BROTHER WILLIAM CONVINCED CITY HALL TO RUN THROUGH THEIR OLD PILSEN NEIGHBORHOOD--
"--AND WILLIAM TAKING THE FALL WHEN THE PROJECT'S ELECTRICAL ENGINEER--HAROLD LOOMIS--DIED ON HALLOWEEN.
THAT'S WHAT THIS IS ALL ABOUT FOR THE PRANKSTER. IT'S NOT SOME COMPLEX MORALITY STATEMENT. HELL, THE MAYOR NEVER EVEN STOLE THAT MONEY.
NO, THE PRANKSTER TERRORIZING THE CITY IS ABOUT SOMETHING MUCH SIMPLER. THIS...
"...IS ABOUT A SON WHO WANTS PAYBACK."
DADDY...?

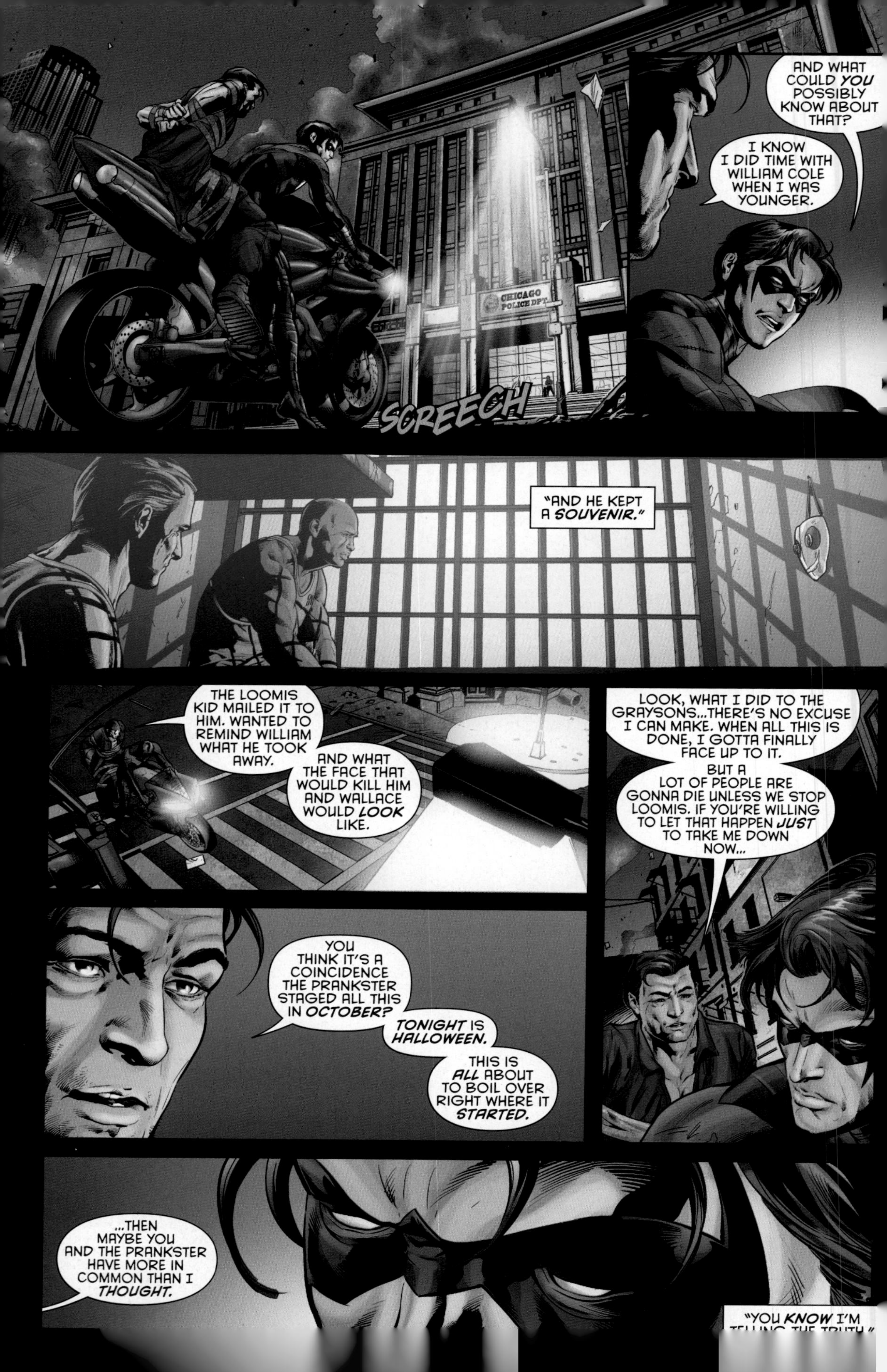
CHICAGO POLICE DPT.
SCREECH
AND WHAT COULD YOU POSSIBLY KNOW ABOUT THAT?
I KNOW I DID TIME WITH WILLIAM COLE WHEN I WAS YOUNGER.
“AND HE KEPT A SOUVENIR.”
THE LOOMIS KID MAILED IT TO HIM. WANTED TO REMIND WILLIAM WHAT HE TOOK AWAY.
AND WHAT THE FACE THAT WOULD KILL HIM AND WALLACE WOULD LOOK LIKE.
LOOK, WHAT I DID TO THE GRAYSONS...THERE'S NO EXCUSE I CAN MAKE. WHEN ALL THIS IS DONE, I GOTTA FINALLY FACE UP TO IT.
BUT A LOT OF PEOPLE ARE GONNA DIE UNLESS WE STOP LOOMIS. IF YOU'RE WILLING TO LET THAT HAPPEN JUST TO TAKE ME DOWN NOW...
YOU THINK IT'S A COINCIDENCE THE PRANKSTER STAGED ALL THIS IN OCTOBER?
TONIGHT IS HALLOWEEN.
THIS IS ALL ABOUT TO BOIL OVER RIGHT WHERE IT STARTED.
...THEN MAYBE YOU AND THE PRANKSTER HAVE MORE IN COMMON THAN I THOUGHT.
“YOU KNOW I'M

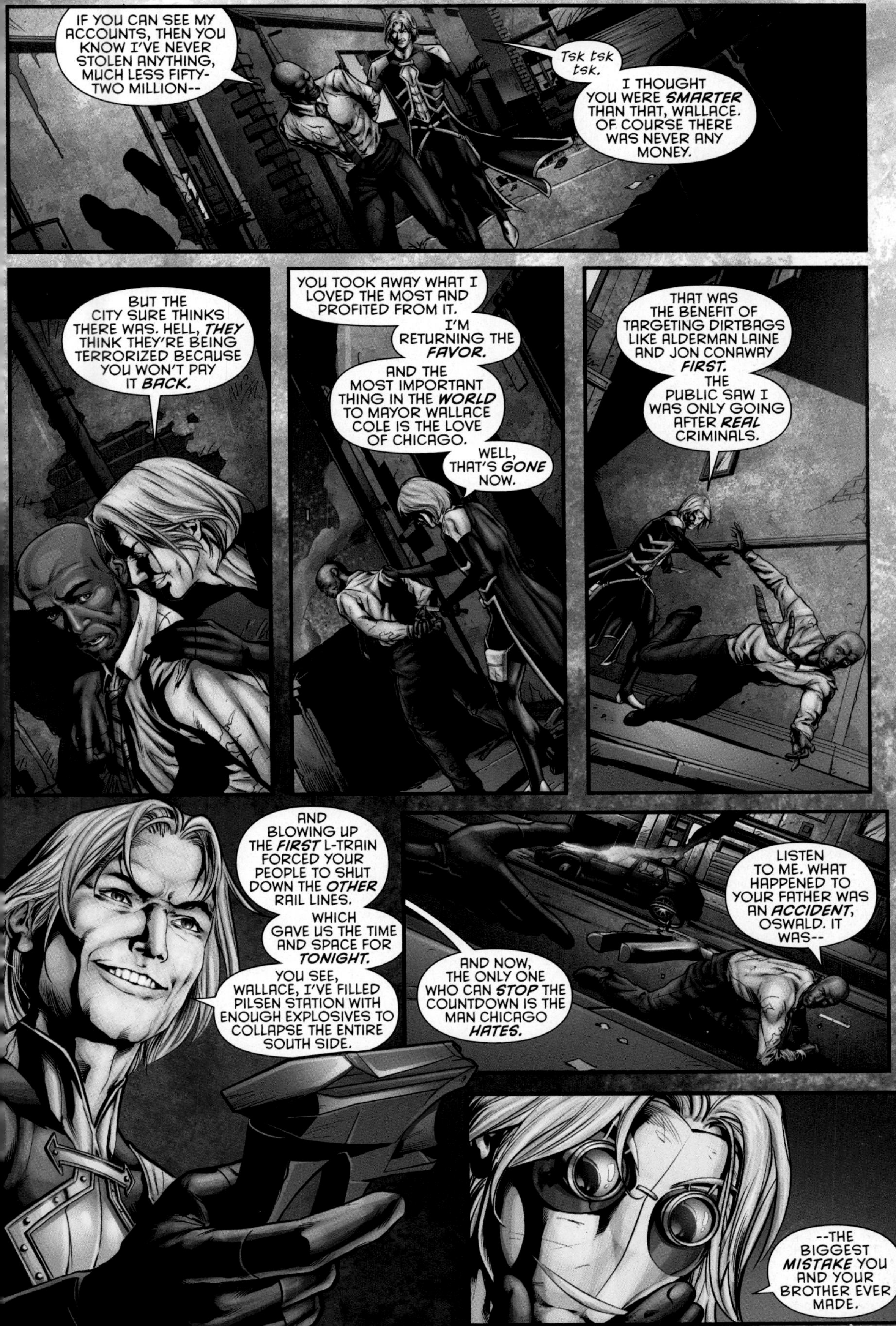
IF YOU CAN SEE MY ACCOUNTS, THEN YOU KNOW I'VE NEVER STOLEN ANYTHING, MUCH LESS FIFTY-TWO MILLION--
Tsk tsk tsk.
I THOUGHT YOU WERE SMARTER THAN THAT, WALLACE. OF COURSE THERE WAS NEVER ANY MONEY.
BUT THE CITY SURE THINKS THERE WAS. HELL, THEY THINK THEY'RE BEING TERRORIZED BECAUSE YOU WON'T PAY IT BACK.
YOU TOOK AWAY WHAT I LOVED THE MOST AND PROFITED FROM IT.
I'M RETURNING THE FAVOR.
AND THE MOST IMPORTANT THING IN THE WORLD TO MAYOR WALLACE COLE IS THE LOVE OF CHICAGO.
WELL, THAT'S GONE NOW.
THAT WAS THE BENEFIT OF TARGETING DIRTBAGS LIKE ALDERMAN LAINE AND JON CONAWAY FIRST.
THE PUBLIC SAW I WAS ONLY GOING AFTER REAL CRIMINALS.
AND BLOWING UP THE FIRST L-TRAIN FORCED YOUR PEOPLE TO SHUT DOWN THE OTHER RAIL LINES.
WHICH GAVE US THE TIME AND SPACE FOR TONIGHT.
YOU SEE, WALLACE, I'VE FILLED PILSEN STATION WITH ENOUGH EXPLOSIVES TO COLLAPSE THE ENTIRE SOUTH SIDE.
AND NOW, THE ONLY ONE WHO CAN STOP THE COUNTDOWN IS THE MAN CHICAGO HATES.
LISTEN TO ME. WHAT HAPPENED TO YOUR FATHER WAS AN ACCIDENT, OSWALD. IT WAS--
--THE BIGGEST MISTAKE YOU AND YOUR BROTHER EVER MADE.

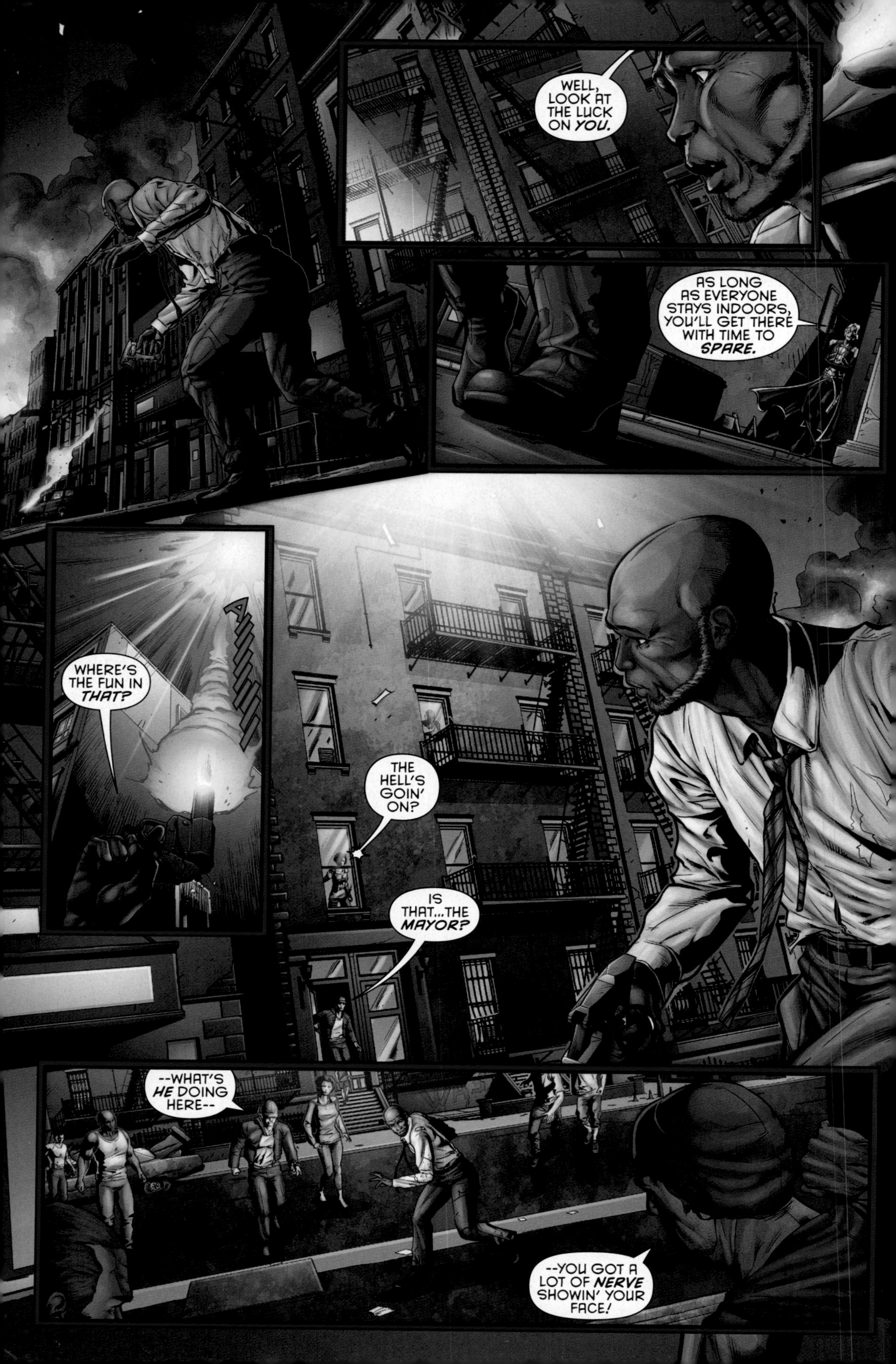
WELL, LOOK AT THE LUCK ON YOU.
AS LONG AS EVERYONE STAYS INDOORS, YOU'LL GET THERE WITH TIME TO SPARE.
WHERE'S THE FUN IN THAT?
THE HELL'S GOIN' ON?
IS THAT...THE MAYOR?
--WHAT'S HE DOING HERE--
--YOU GOT A LOT OF NERVE SHOWIN' YOUR FACE!

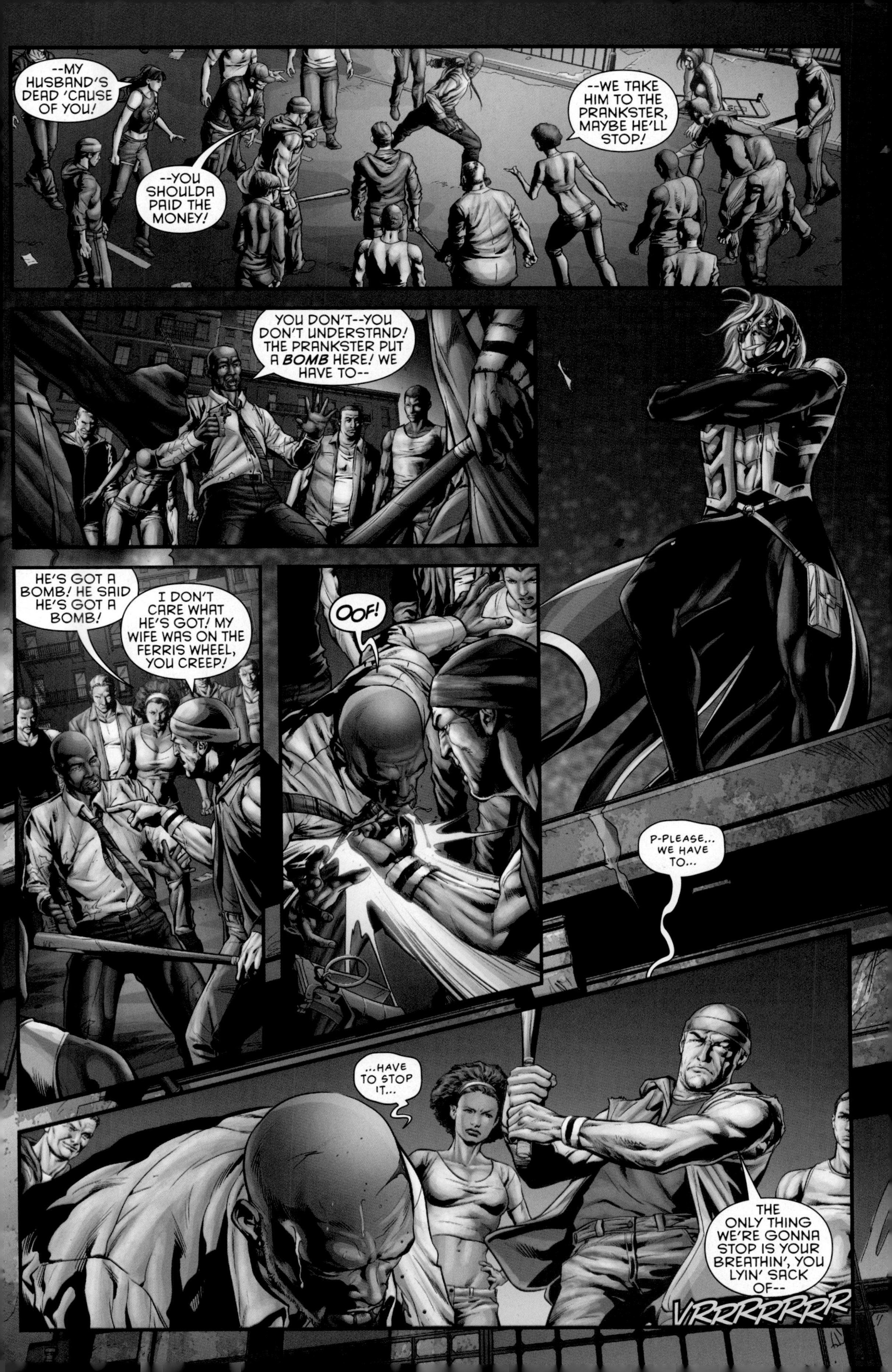
--MY HUSBAND'S DEAD 'CAUSE OF YOU!
--YOU SHOULDA PAID THE MONEY!
--WE TAKE HIM TO THE PRANKSTER, MAYBE HE'LL STOP!
YOU DON'T--YOU DON'T UNDERSTAND! THE PRANKSTER PUT A BOMB HERE! WE HAVE TO--
HE'S GOT A BOMB! HE SAID HE'S GOT A BOMB!
I DON'T CARE WHAT HE'S GOT! MY WIFE WAS ON THE FERRIS WHEEL, YOU CREEP!
OOF!
P-PLEASE... WE HAVE TO...
...HAVE TO STOP IT...
THE ONLY THING WE'RE GONNA STOP IS YOUR BREATHIN', YOU LYIN' SACK OF--
VRRRRRRRR

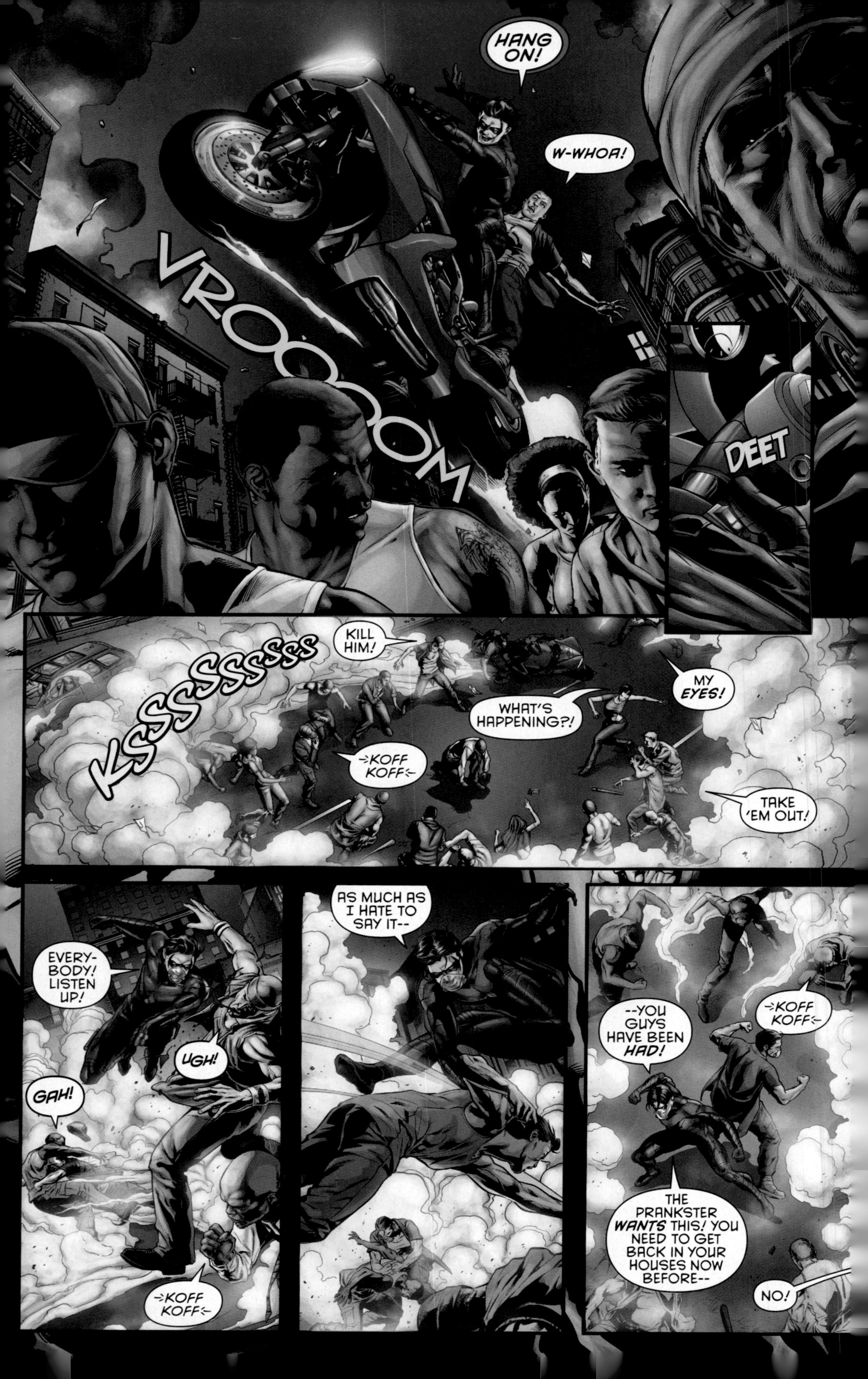
HANG ON!
W-WHOA!
VROOOOOM
DEET
KILL HIM!
KSSSSSSSS
MY EYES!
WHAT'S HAPPENING?!
-KOFF KOFF-
TAKE 'EM OUT!
EVERY-BODY! LISTEN UP!
UGH!
GAH!
-KOFF KOFF-
AS MUCH AS I HATE TO SAY IT--
--YOU GUYS HAVE BEEN HAD!
-KOFF KOFF-
THE PRANKSTER WANTS THIS! YOU NEED TO GET BACK IN YOUR HOUSES NOW BEFORE--
NO!

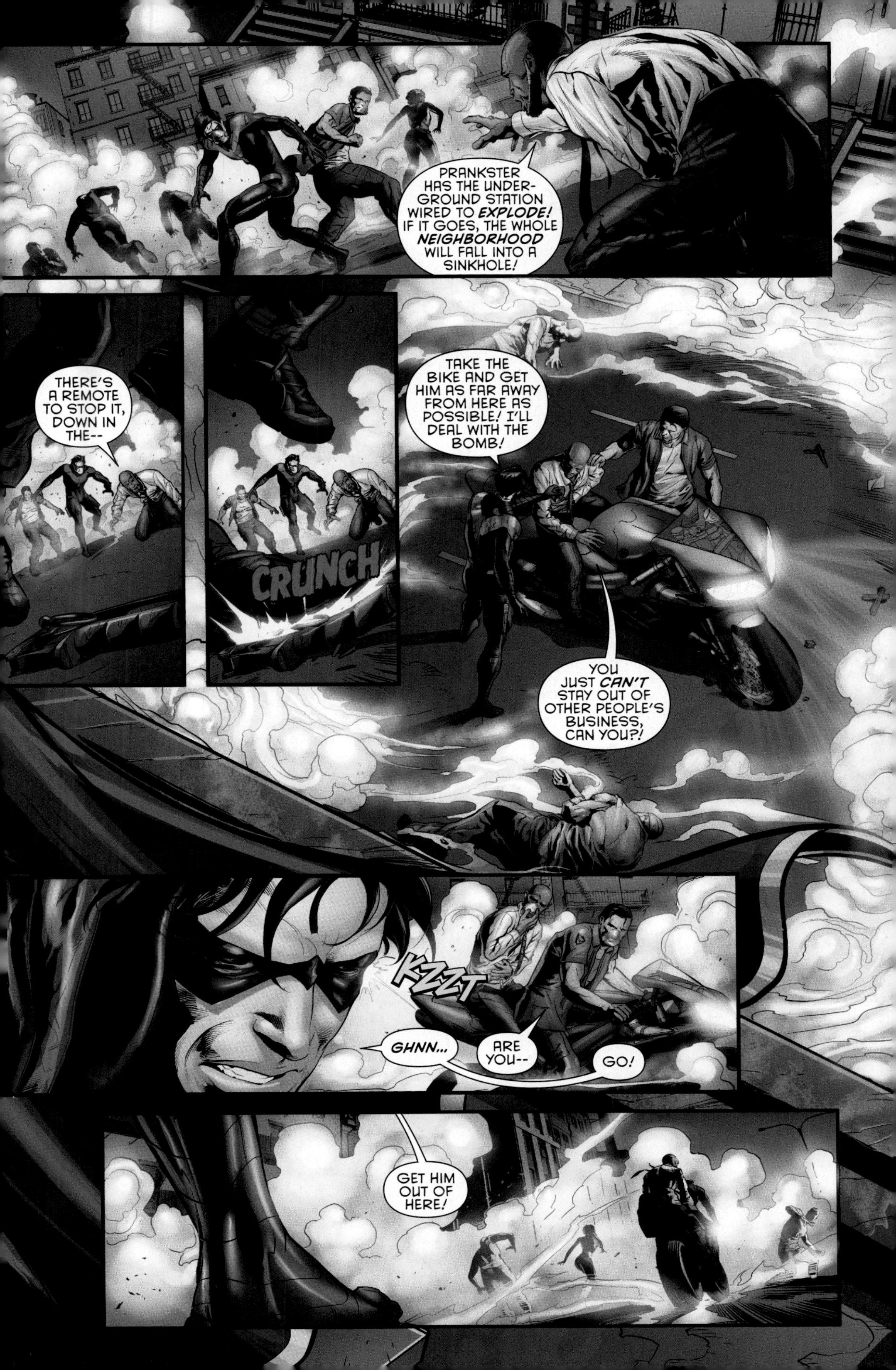
PRANKSTER HAS THE UNDERGROUND STATION WIRED TO *EXPLODE!* IF IT GOES, THE WHOLE *NEIGHBORHOOD* WILL FALL INTO A SINKHOLE!
THERE'S A REMOTE TO STOP IT, DOWN IN THE--
CRUNCH
TAKE THE BIKE AND GET HIM AS FAR AWAY FROM HERE AS POSSIBLE! I'LL DEAL WITH THE BOMB!
YOU JUST *CAN'T* STAY OUT OF OTHER PEOPLE'S BUSINESS, CAN YOU?!
KZZT
GHNN...
ARE YOU--
GO!
GET HIM OUT OF HERE!

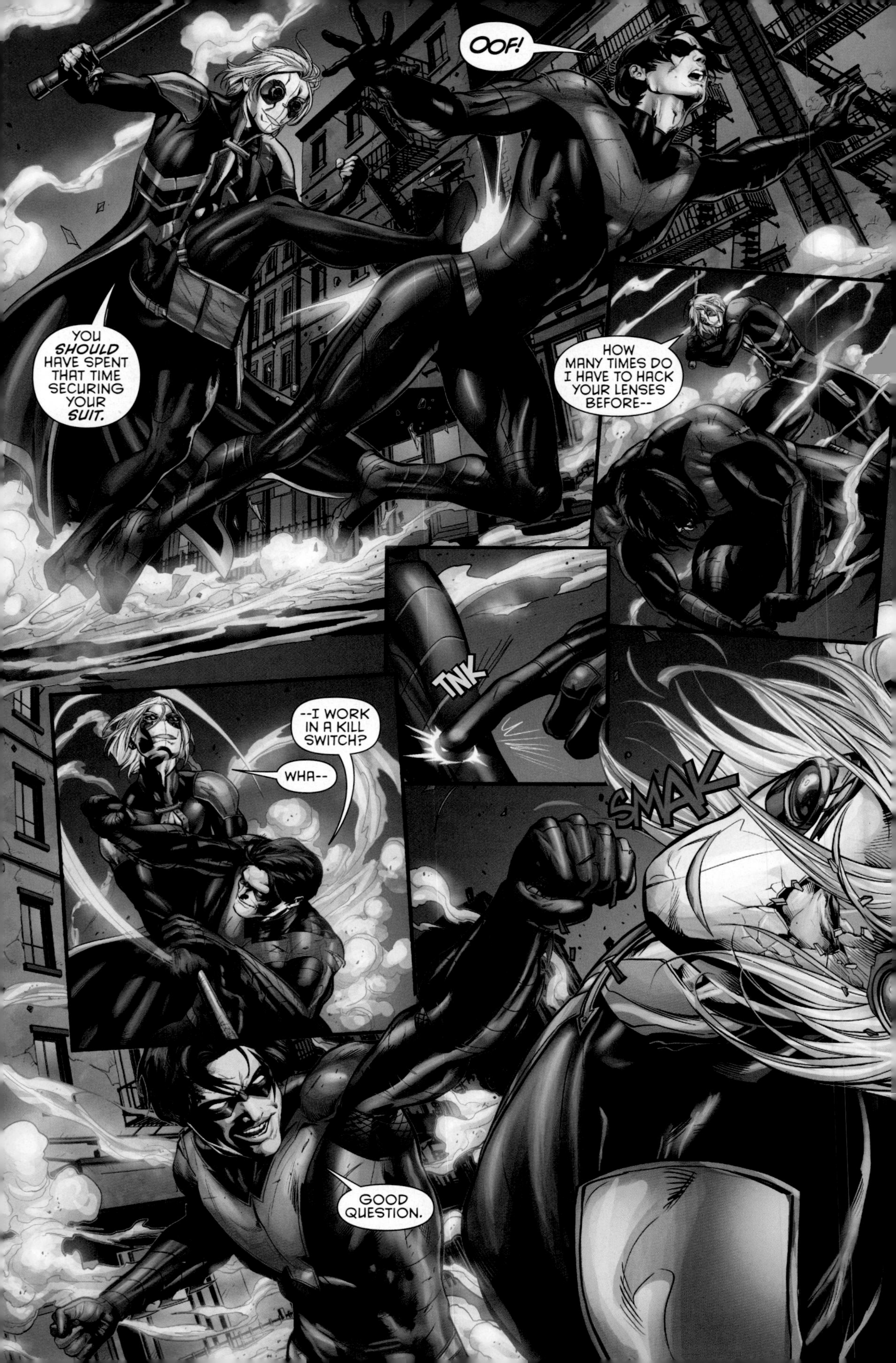
OOF!
YOU SHOULD HAVE SPENT THAT TIME SECURING YOUR SUIT.
HOW MANY TIMES DO I HAVE TO HACK YOUR LENSES BEFORE--
--I WORK IN A KILL SWITCH?
WHA--
TNK
SMAK
GOOD QUESTION.

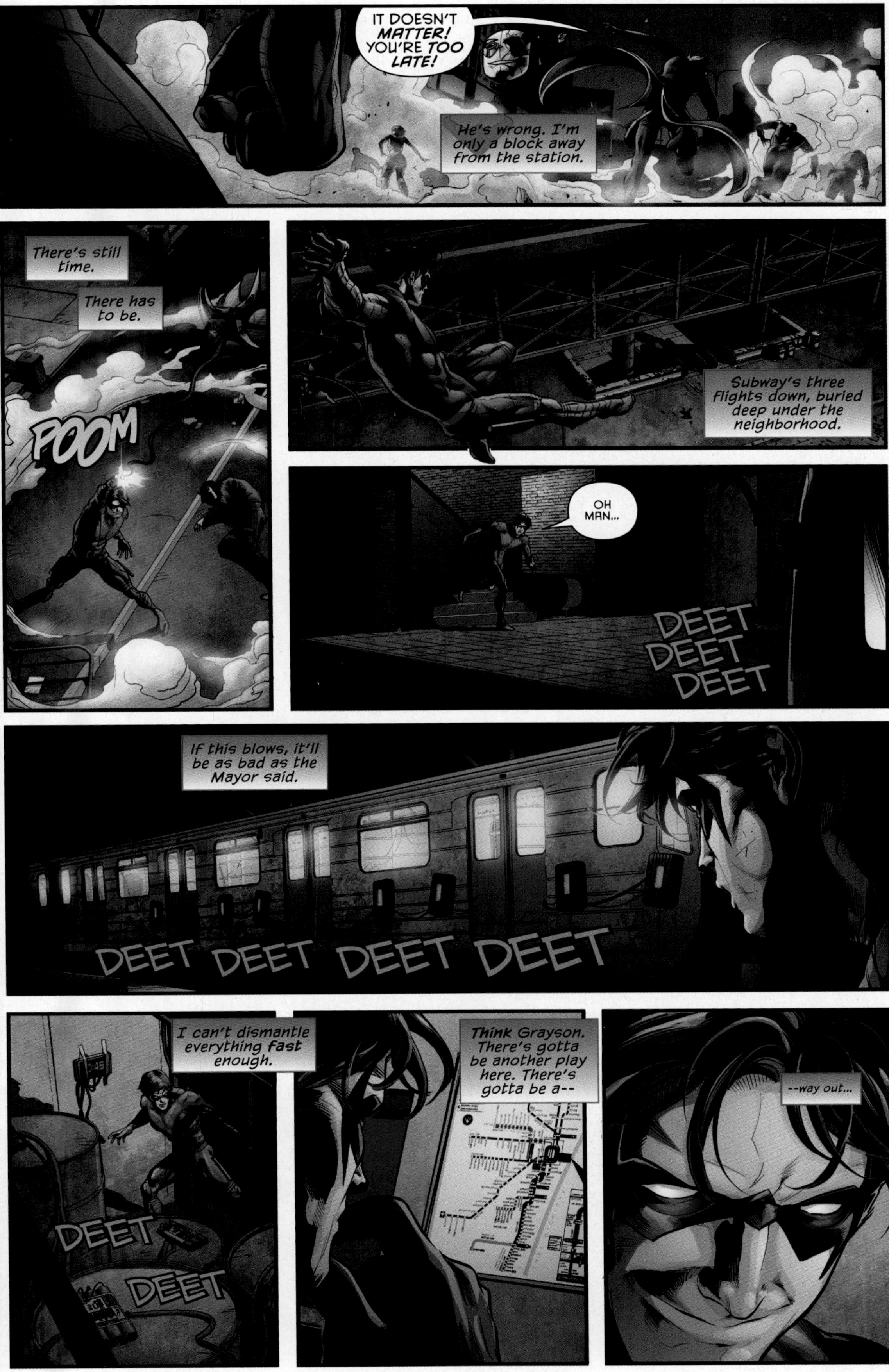
IT DOESN'T MATTER! YOU'RE TOO LATE!
He's wrong. I'm only a block away from the station.
There's still time.
There has to be.
POOM
Subway's three flights down, buried deep under the neighborhood.
OH MAN...
DEET DEET DEET
If this blows, it'll be as bad as the Mayor said.
DEET DEET DEET DEET
I can't dismantle everything fast enough.
DEET
DEET
Think Grayson. There's gotta be another play here. There's gotta be a--
--way out...

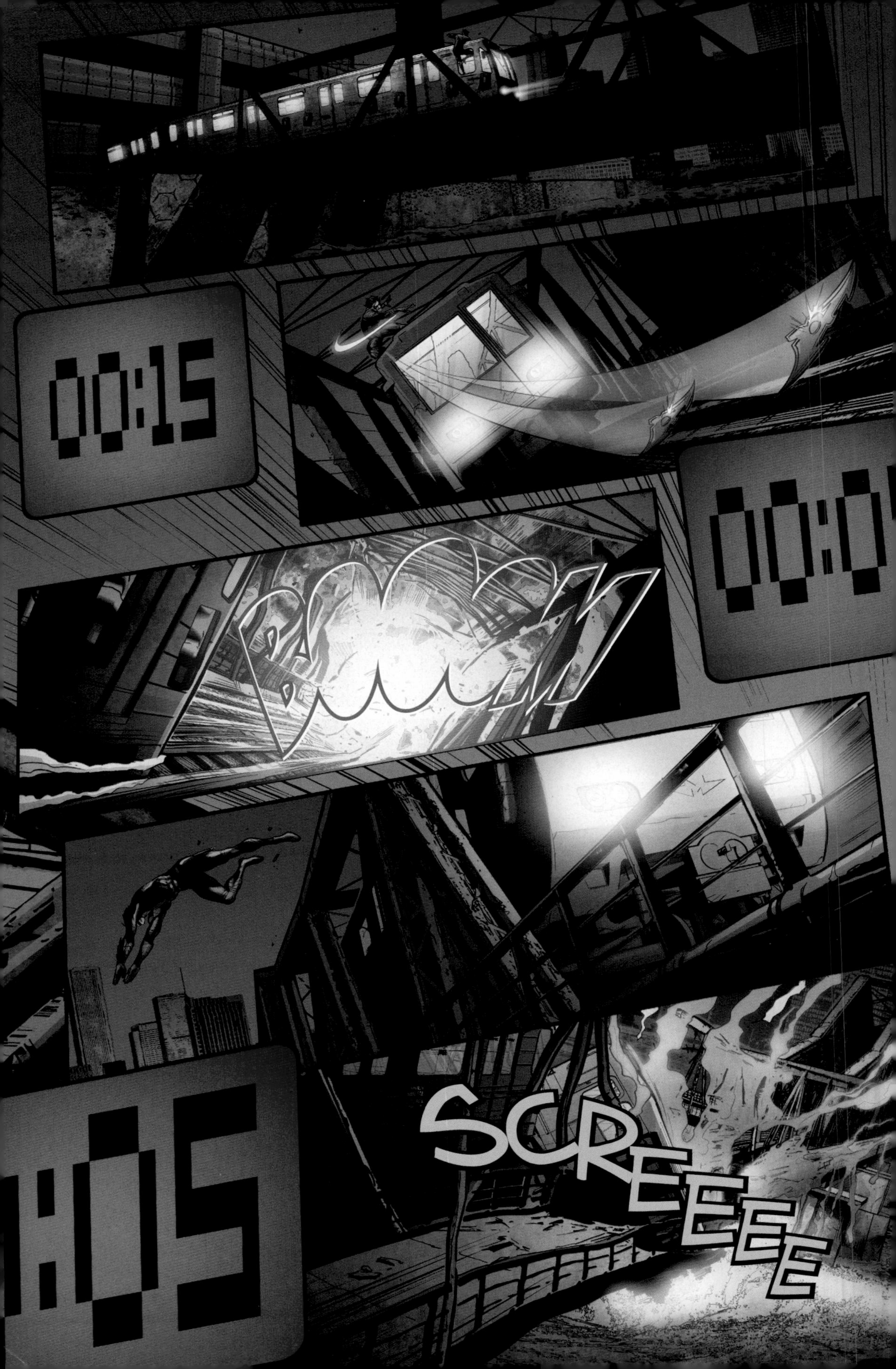
00:15
00:0
:05
SCREEEEEE

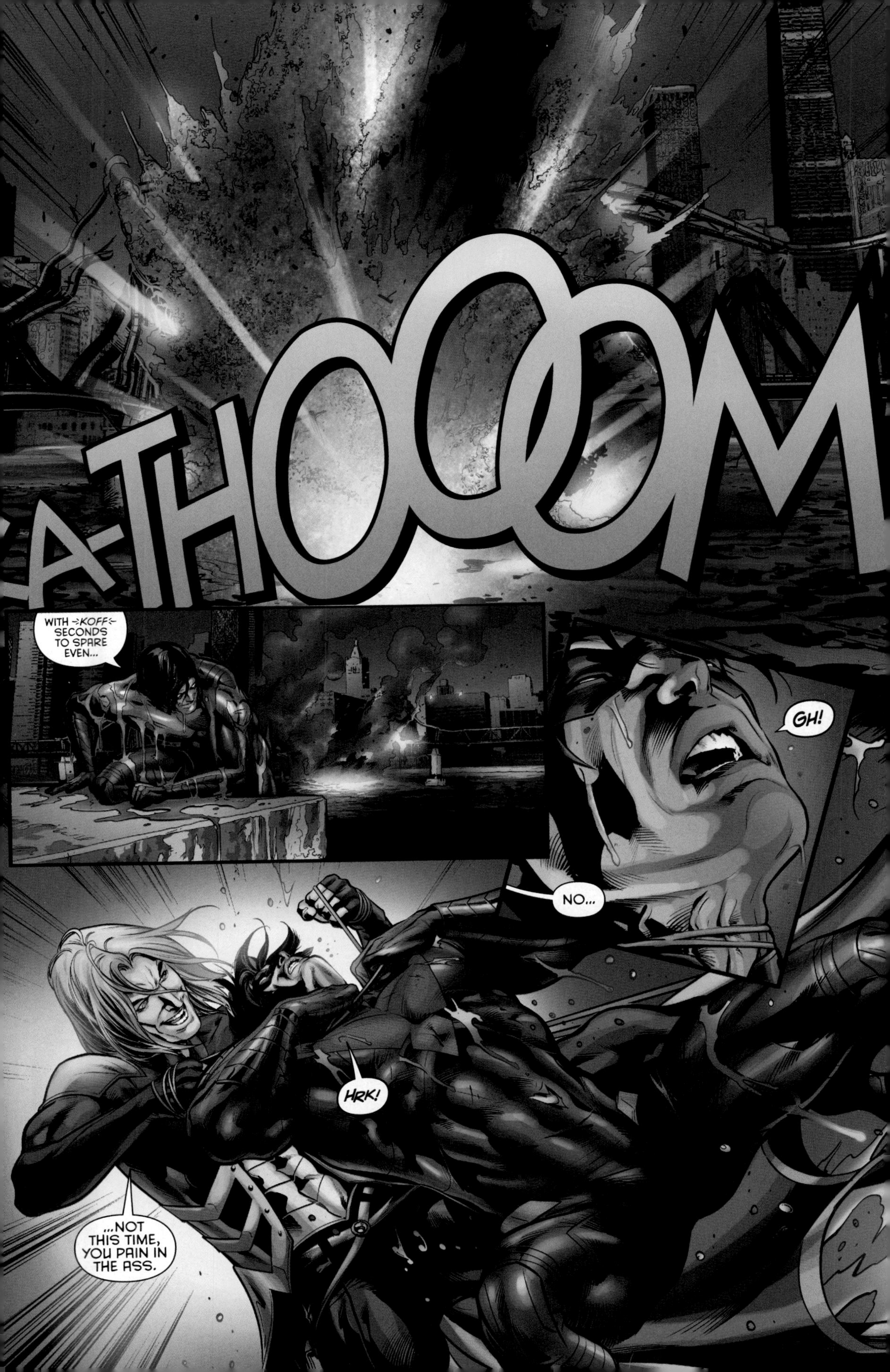
KA-THOOOOM
WITH -KOFF- SECONDS TO SPARE EVEN...
GH!
NO...
HRK!
...NOT THIS TIME, YOU PAIN IN THE ASS.

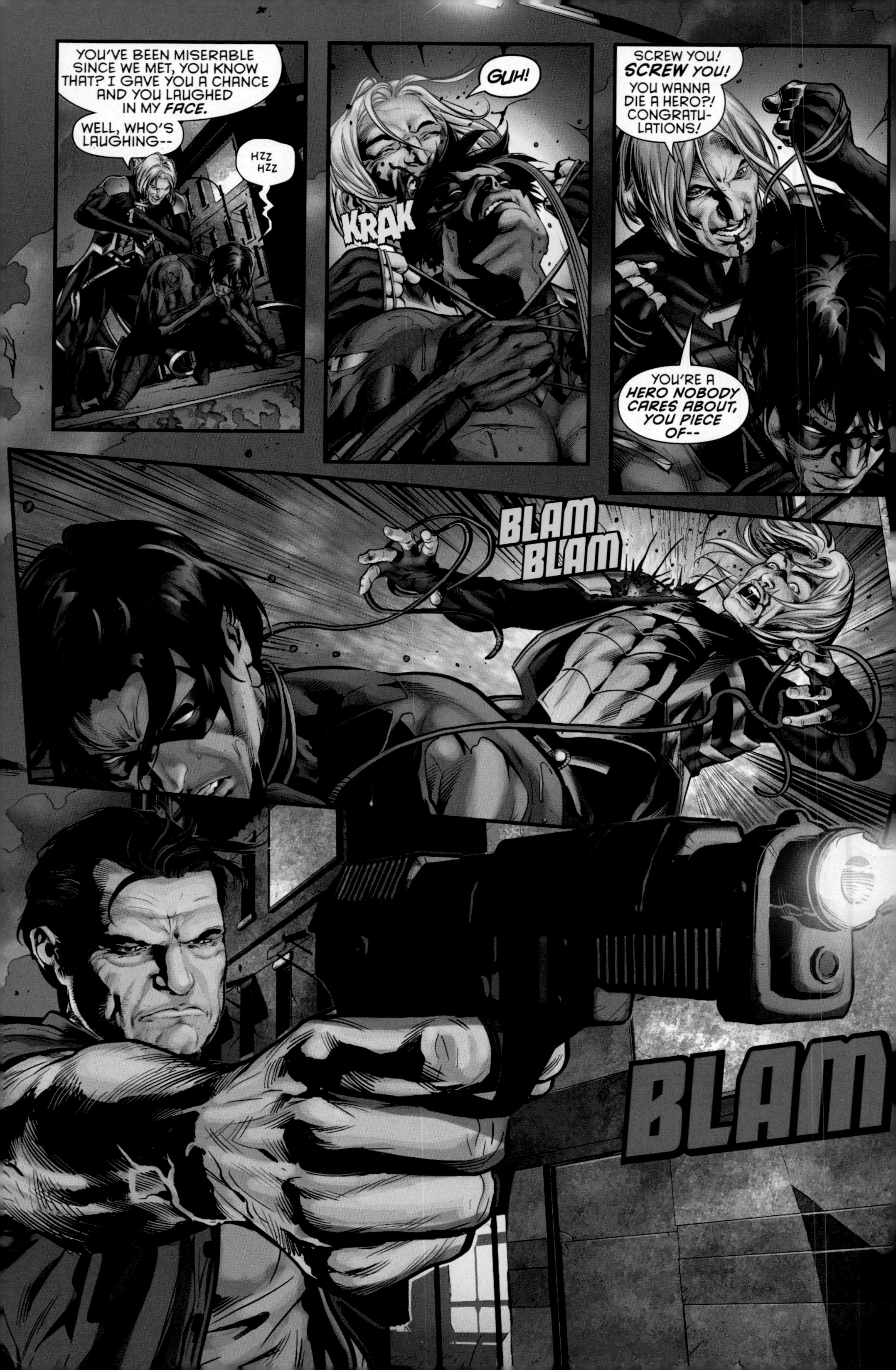

YOU'VE BEEN MISERABLE SINCE WE MET, YOU KNOW THAT? I GAVE YOU A CHANCE AND YOU LAUGHED IN MY *FACE*.
WELL, WHO'S LAUGHING--
HZZ HZZ
GUH!
KRAK
SCREW YOU! ***SCREW*** YOU!
YOU WANNA DIE A HERO?! CONGRATU-LATIONS!
YOU'RE A ***HERO NOBODY CARES ABOUT***, YOU PIECE OF--
BLAM BLAM
BLAM

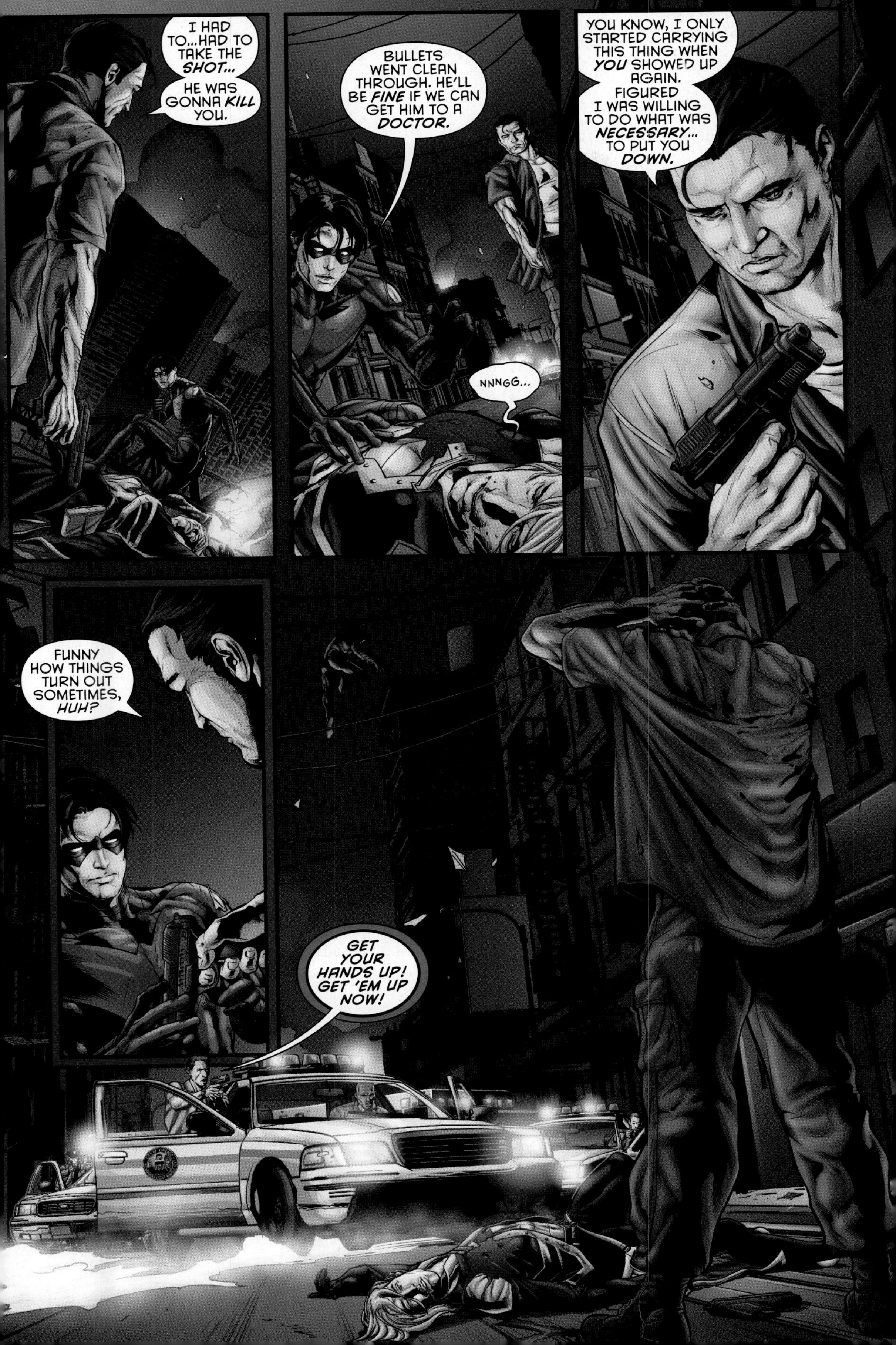
I HAD TO...HAD TO TAKE THE SHOT...
HE WAS GONNA KILL YOU.
BULLETS WENT CLEAN THROUGH. HE'LL BE FINE IF WE CAN GET HIM TO A DOCTOR.
NNNGG...
YOU KNOW, I ONLY STARTED CARRYING THIS THING WHEN YOU SHOWED UP AGAIN.
FIGURED I WAS WILLING TO DO WHAT WAS NECESSARY... TO PUT YOU DOWN.
FUNNY HOW THINGS TURN OUT SOMETIMES, HUH?
GET YOUR HANDS UP! GET 'EM UP NOW!

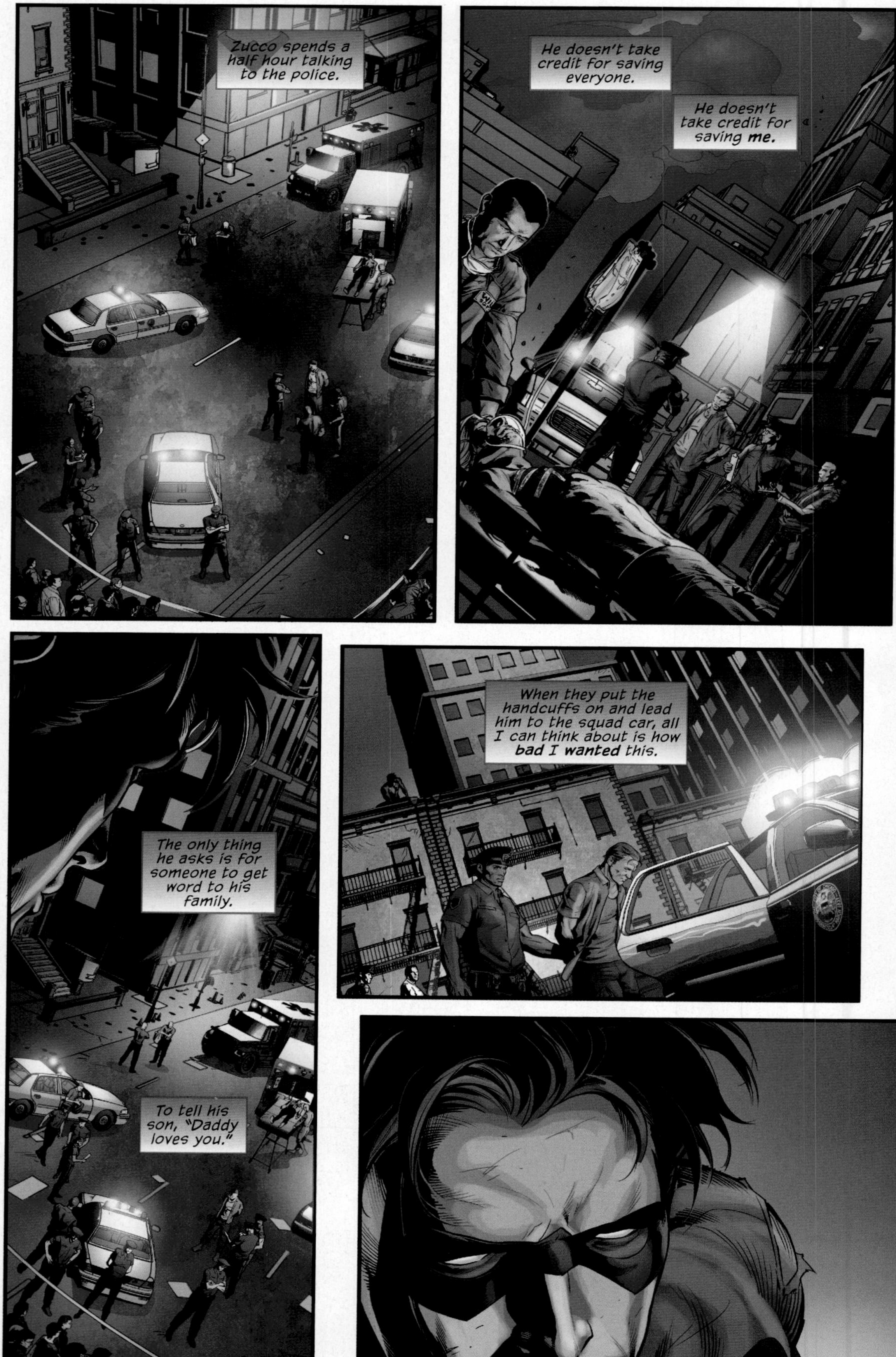
Zucco spends a half hour talking to the police.
He doesn't take credit for saving everyone.
He doesn't take credit for saving **me.**
The only thing he asks is for someone to get word to his family.
To tell his son, "Daddy loves you."
When they put the handcuffs on and lead him to the squad car, all I can think about is how **bad I wanted** this.

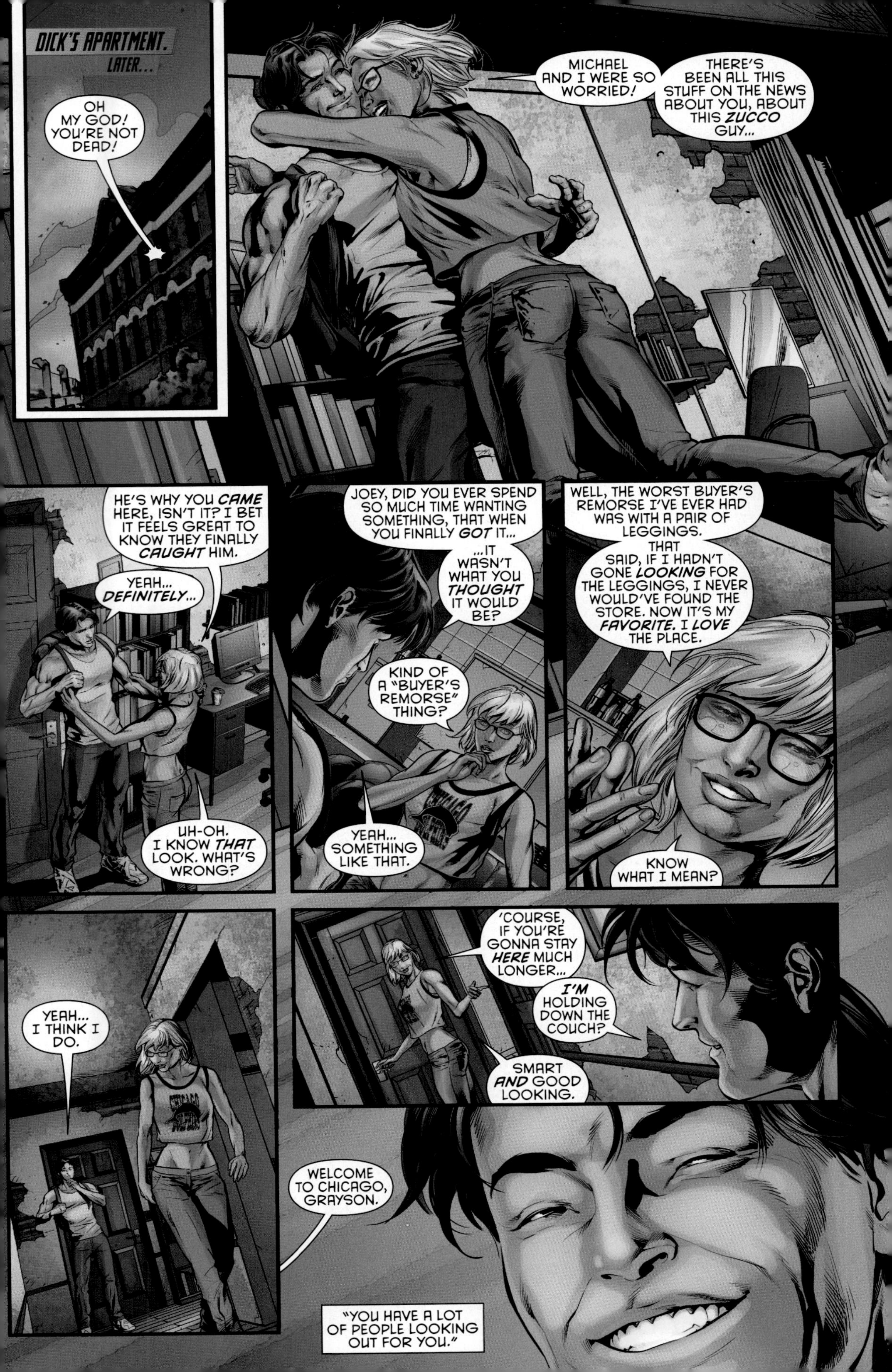

DICK'S APARTMENT. LATER...
OH MY GOD! YOU'RE NOT DEAD!
MICHAEL AND I WERE SO WORRIED!
THERE'S BEEN ALL THIS STUFF ON THE NEWS ABOUT YOU, ABOUT THIS ZUCCO GUY...
HE'S WHY YOU CAME HERE, ISN'T IT? I BET IT FEELS GREAT TO KNOW THEY FINALLY CAUGHT HIM.
YEAH... DEFINITELY...
UH-OH. I KNOW THAT LOOK. WHAT'S WRONG?
JOEY, DID YOU EVER SPEND SO MUCH TIME WANTING SOMETHING, THAT WHEN YOU FINALLY GOT IT...
...IT WASN'T WHAT YOU THOUGHT IT WOULD BE?
KIND OF A "BUYER'S REMORSE" THING?
YEAH... SOMETHING LIKE THAT.
WELL, THE WORST BUYER'S REMORSE I'VE EVER HAD WAS WITH A PAIR OF LEGGINGS.
THAT SAID, IF I HADN'T GONE LOOKING FOR THE LEGGINGS, I NEVER WOULD'VE FOUND THE STORE. NOW IT'S MY FAVORITE. I LOVE THE PLACE.
KNOW WHAT I MEAN?
YEAH... I THINK I DO.
'COURSE, IF YOU'RE GONNA STAY HERE MUCH LONGER...
I'M HOLDING DOWN THE COUCH?
SMART AND GOOD LOOKING.
WELCOME TO CHICAGO, GRAYSON.
"YOU HAVE A LOT OF PEOPLE LOOKING OUT FOR YOU."

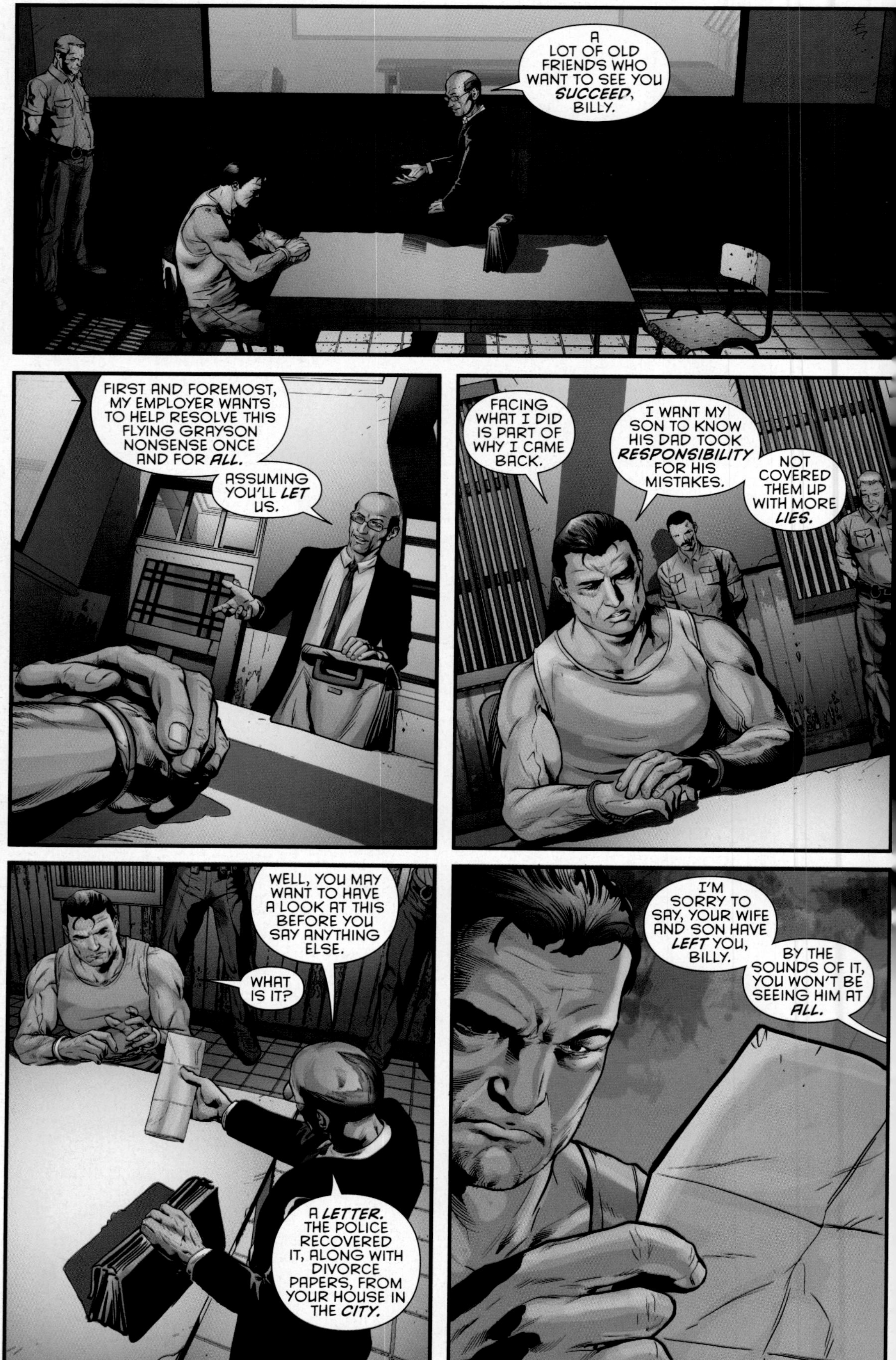
A LOT OF OLD FRIENDS WHO WANT TO SEE YOU SUCCEED, BILLY.
FIRST AND FOREMOST, MY EMPLOYER WANTS TO HELP RESOLVE THIS FLYING GRAYSON NONSENSE ONCE AND FOR ALL.
ASSUMING YOU'LL LET US.
FACING WHAT I DID IS PART OF WHY I CAME BACK.
I WANT MY SON TO KNOW HIS DAD TOOK RESPONSIBILITY FOR HIS MISTAKES.
NOT COVERED THEM UP WITH MORE LIES.
WELL, YOU MAY WANT TO HAVE A LOOK AT THIS BEFORE YOU SAY ANYTHING ELSE.
WHAT IS IT?
A LETTER. THE POLICE RECOVERED IT, ALONG WITH DIVORCE PAPERS, FROM YOUR HOUSE IN THE CITY.
I'M SORRY TO SAY, YOUR WIFE AND SON HAVE LEFT YOU, BILLY.
BY THE SOUNDS OF IT, YOU WON'T BE SEEING HIM AT ALL.

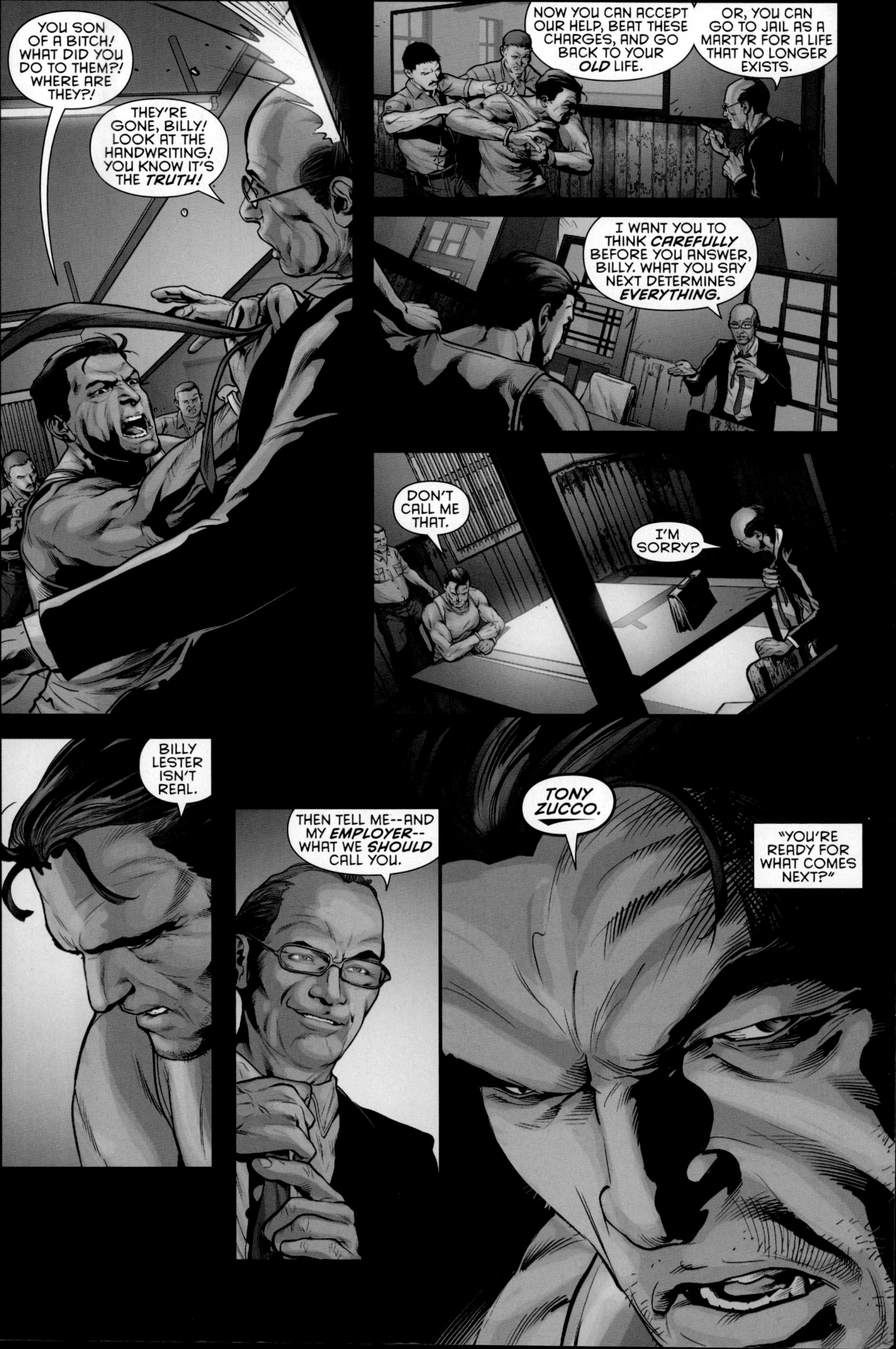
YOU SON OF A BITCH! WHAT DID YOU DO TO THEM?! WHERE ARE THEY?!
THEY'RE GONE, BILLY! LOOK AT THE HANDWRITING! YOU KNOW IT'S THE TRUTH!
NOW YOU CAN ACCEPT OUR HELP, BEAT THESE CHARGES, AND GO BACK TO YOUR OLD LIFE.
OR, YOU CAN GO TO JAIL AS A MARTYR FOR A LIFE THAT NO LONGER EXISTS.
I WANT YOU TO THINK CAREFULLY BEFORE YOU ANSWER, BILLY. WHAT YOU SAY NEXT DETERMINES EVERYTHING.
DON'T CALL ME THAT.
I'M SORRY?
BILLY LESTER ISN'T REAL.
THEN TELL ME--AND MY EMPLOYER--WHAT WE SHOULD CALL YOU.
TONY ZUCCO.
"YOU'RE READY FOR WHAT COMES NEXT?"

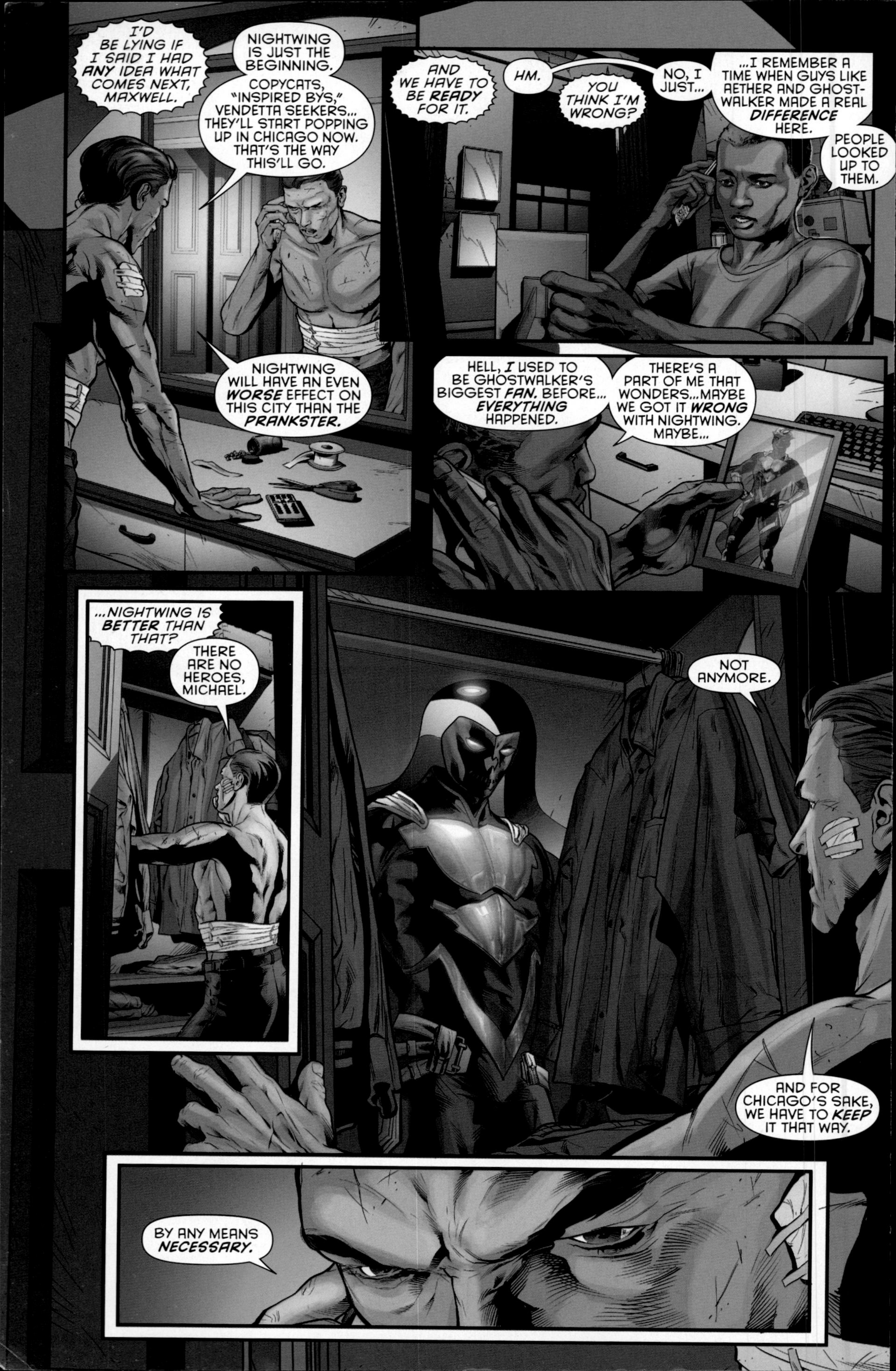
I'D BE LYING IF I SAID I HAD ANY IDEA WHAT COMES NEXT, MAXWELL.
NIGHTWING IS JUST THE BEGINNING.
COPYCATS, "INSPIRED BYS," VENDETTA SEEKERS... THEY'LL START POPPING UP IN CHICAGO NOW. THAT'S THE WAY THIS'LL GO.
AND WE HAVE TO BE READY FOR IT.
HM.
YOU THINK I'M WRONG?
NO, I JUST...
...I REMEMBER A TIME WHEN GUYS LIKE AETHER AND GHOST-WALKER MADE A REAL DIFFERENCE HERE.
PEOPLE LOOKED UP TO THEM.
NIGHTWING WILL HAVE AN EVEN WORSE EFFECT ON THIS CITY THAN THE PRANKSTER.
HELL, I USED TO BE GHOSTWALKER'S BIGGEST FAN. BEFORE... EVERYTHING HAPPENED.
THERE'S A PART OF ME THAT WONDERS...MAYBE WE GOT IT WRONG WITH NIGHTWING. MAYBE...
...NIGHTWING IS BETTER THAN THAT?
THERE ARE NO HEROES, MICHAEL.
NOT ANYMORE.
AND FOR CHICAGO'S SAKE, WE HAVE TO KEEP IT THAT WAY.
BY ANY MEANS NECESSARY.

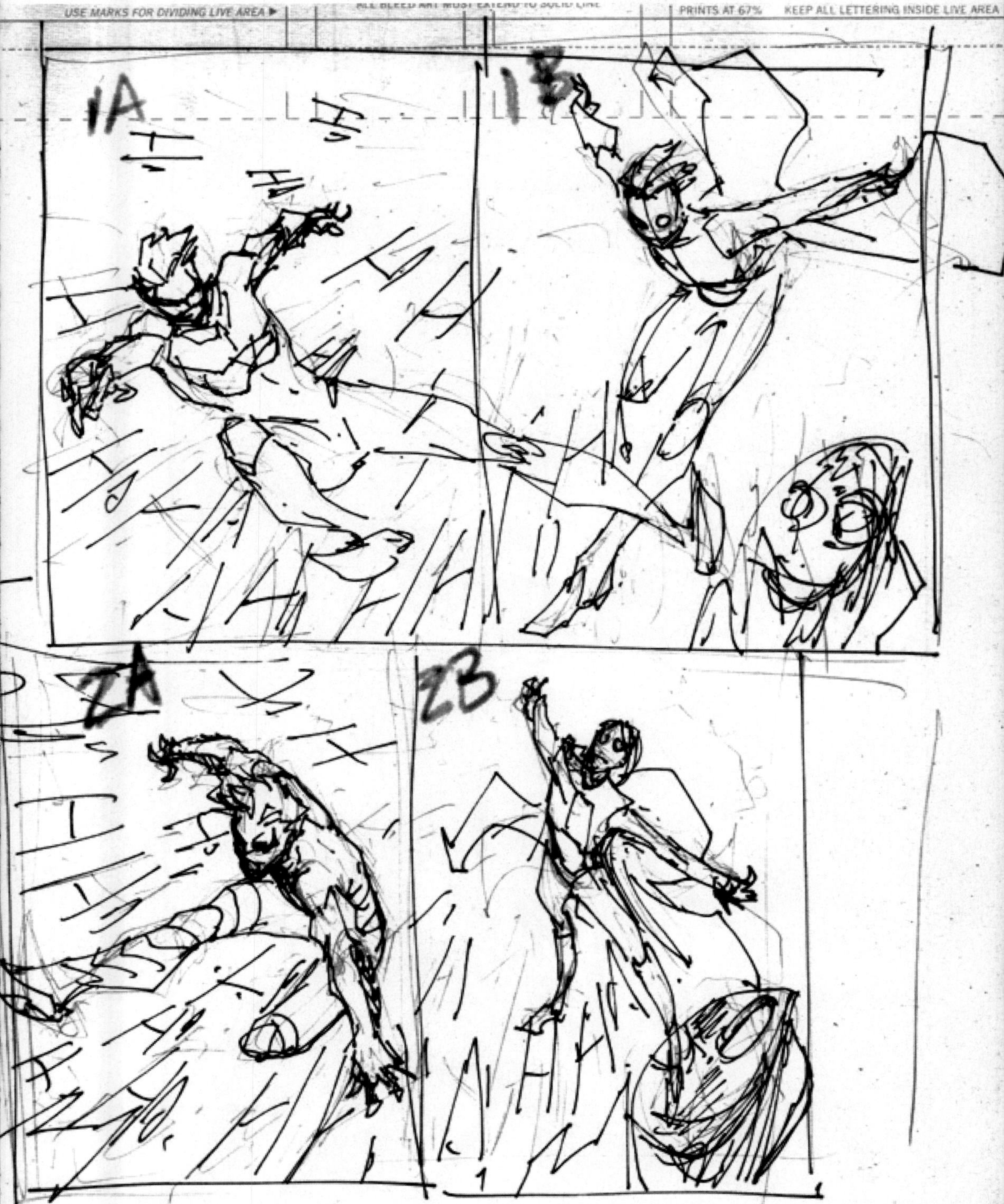
USE MARKS FOR DIVIDING LIVE AREA ▶
PRINTS AT 67%
KEEP ALL LETTERING INSIDE LIVE AREA
1A
1B
2A
2B

Issue #19 cover layouts

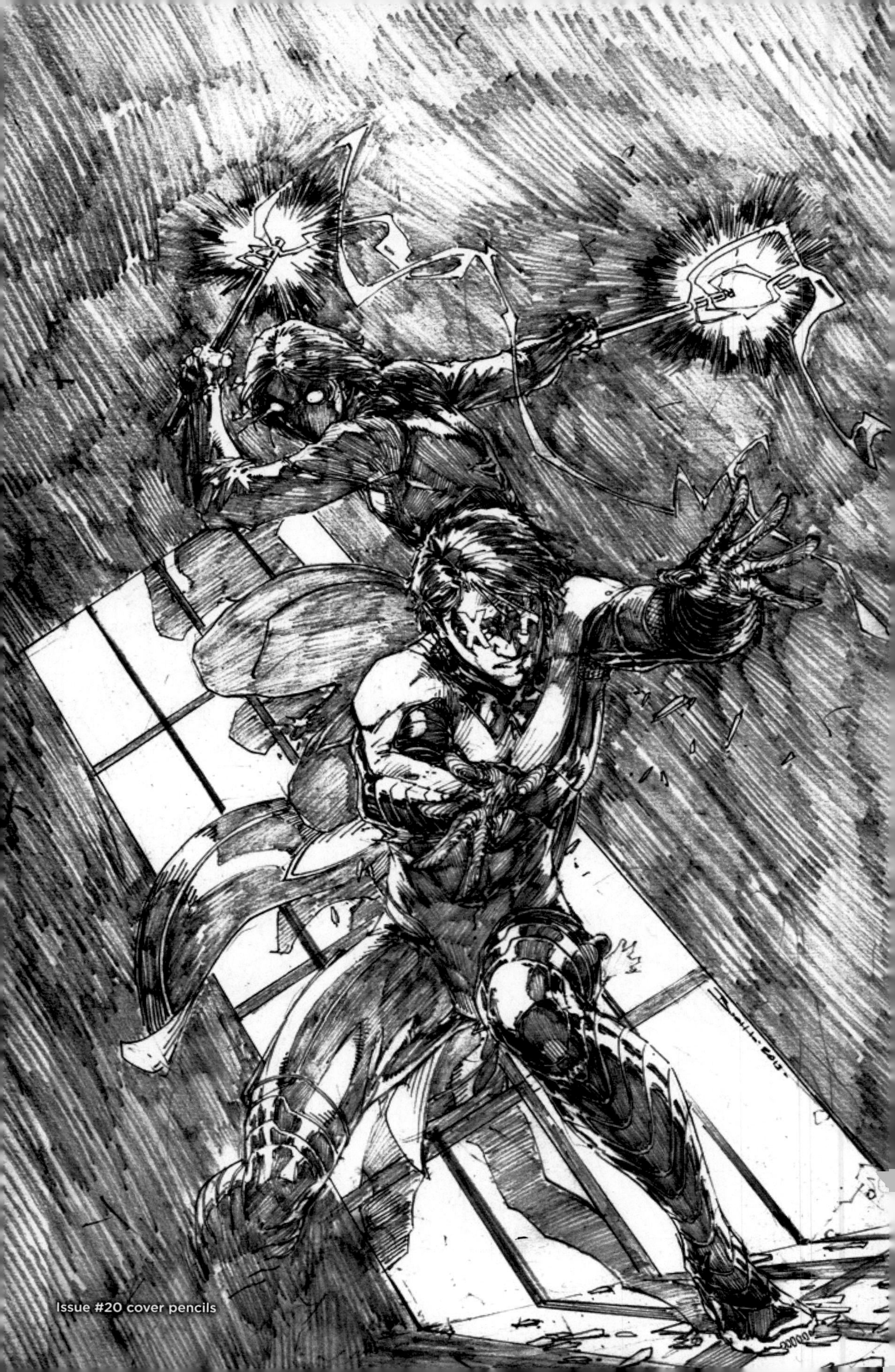

Issue #20 cover pencils

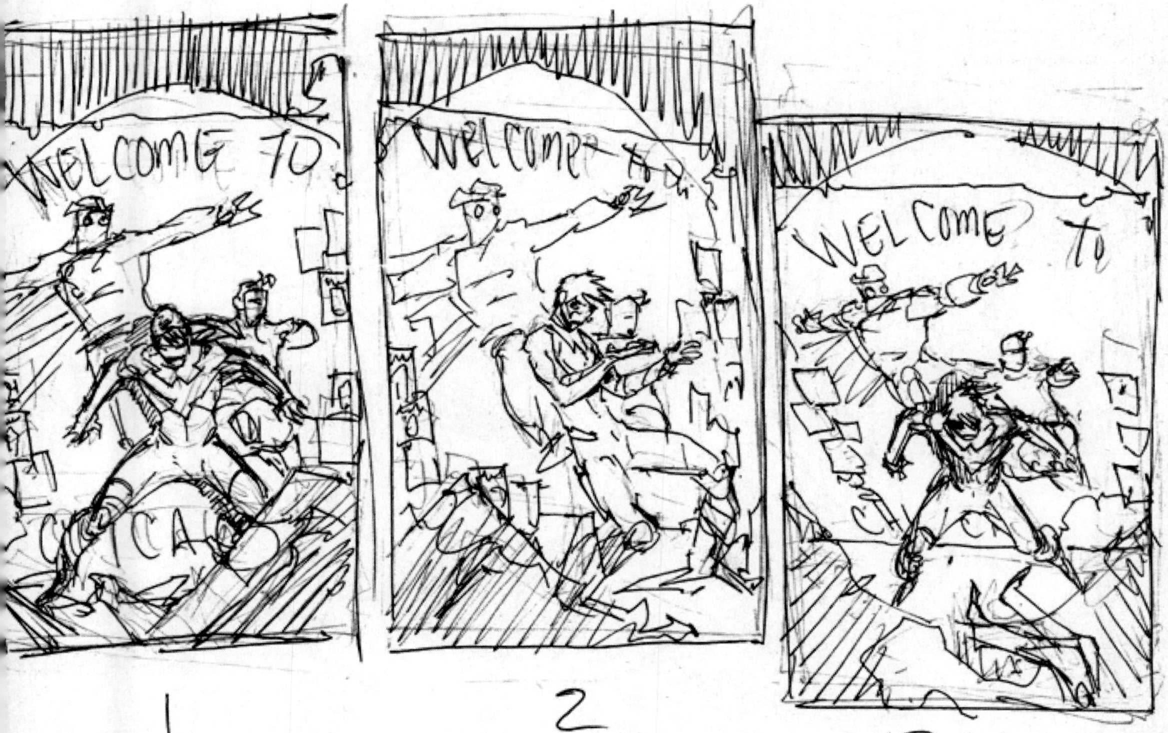
WELCOME TO
WELCOME TO
WELCOME TO

1 2 3

BLOOD ON HANDS

Issue #21 cover layouts

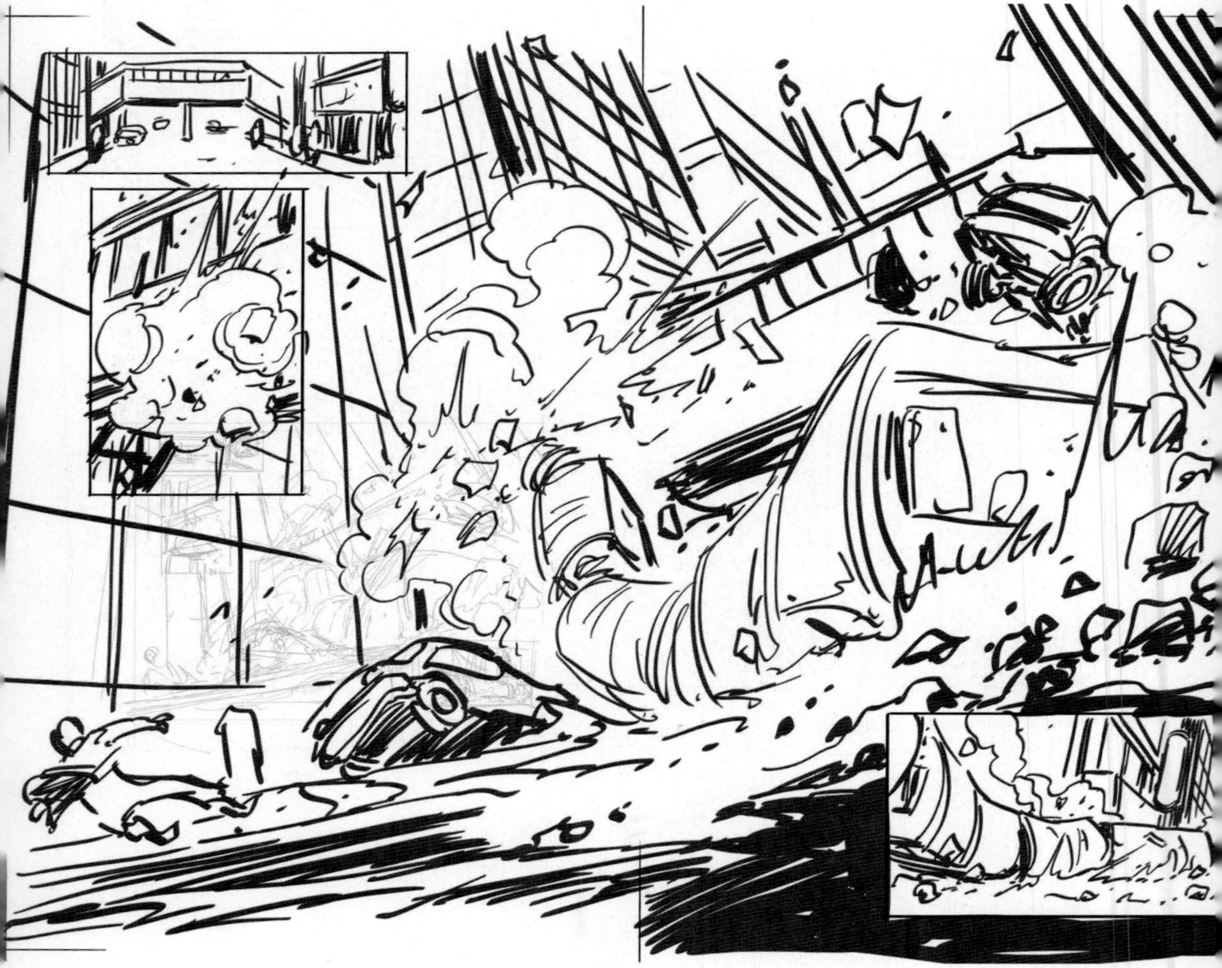

Issue #23

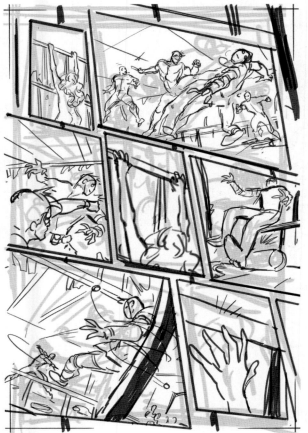

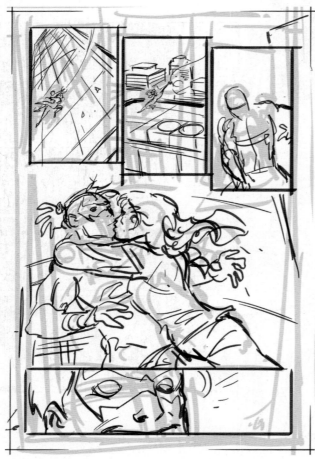

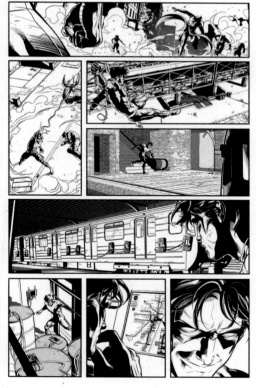